The Making of Modern German Christology

1750 – 1990

The Making of Modern German Christology

1750 – 1990

Second Edition

Alister E. McGrath

Wipf & Stock
PUBLISHERS
Eugene, Oregon

Wipf and Stock Publishers
199 W 8th Ave, Suite 3
Eugene, OR 97401

The Making of Modern German Christology, 1750-1990, Second Edition
By McGrath, Alister E.
Copyright©1994 Inter-Varsity Press, UK
ISBN: 1-59752-305-4
Publication date 8/26/2005
Previously published by Zondervan, 1994

Contents

Introduction

The German-speaking lands of Europe, above all Germany and northern Switzerland, have long been the source of a rich and fertile theological tradition. Two leading figures of the Reformation, the German Martin Luther and the Swiss Huldrych Zwingli, are witnesses to the importance of this tradition to the development of modern Western theology. Since the Enlightenment, the importance of the German-language tradition has become even more firmly established; a list of the leading theologians of the modern Western tradition – such as Karl Barth, Rudolf Bultmann, Jürgen Moltmann, Wolfhart Pannenberg and Paul Tillich – has an unquestionably Germanic ring to it.

Modern Western theology itself has been dominated by the agenda of the Enlightenment, which we shall explore in the present chapter. As the Enlightenment appears to have had its deepest theological impact in Germany, it is only to be expected that it is in the German theological tradition that we should find the most sustained and dedicated engagement with the issues raised by this major constituent element of modern Western culture. As will become clear, the Enlightenment was destined to have a major impact upon one specific area of Christian theology in particular: the doctrines of the person and work of Christ. The reasons for this are complex, and may be summarized as follows.

1. The Enlightenment emphasis upon the competence of reason raised questions concerning the necessity of divine revelation. If the unaided faculty of human reason was capable of discovering the nature and purposes of God, what continuing role was there for an historical

revelation of God in the person of Jesus Christ? Reason seemed to make revelation – and thus any idea of a 'revelational presence' in Christ – superfluous. The significance of Jesus Christ was thus stated by writers sympathetic to the Enlightenment in terms of his moral teaching and example. Far from being a supernatural redeemer of humanity, it was argued, Christ was actually the 'moral educator of humanity', offering the world a religious teaching which was consistent (although to what extent was a matter of debate) with the highest ideals of human reason. In his life, Jesus was an educator; in his death, he was an example of self-giving love for humanity.

2. The Enlightenment insisted that history was homogeneous. In other words, there was a consistency or uniformity within history; what happened in the past is analogous to what happens in the present. The idea of a past event being qualitatively distinct from present events is excluded, as a matter of principle. The past is to be regarded as a mirror of the present. This had two major consequences. In the first place, it led to a contraction of the ontological gap between Christ and other human beings. Christ was to be regarded as a human being like other human beings. If he differed from others, it was in the extent to which he possessed certain qualities. These considerations led to the development of what has become known as a 'degree Christology', in which the difference between Christ and others is understood to be one of degree, rather than kind. In the second, it led to growing historical scepticism concerning the resurrection. If history was continuous and homogeneous, the absence of resurrections in present-day human experience must, it was argued, cast serious doubt upon the New Testament reports of the resurrection. The Enlightenment thus tended to treat the resurrection as a non-event, at best a simple misunderstanding of a spiritual experience, and at worst a deliberate cover-up to hide the shameful end of Jesus's ministry on the cross.

3. The New Testament must therefore be regarded as having misrepresented the significance of Christ. Whereas Jesus of Nazareth was, in the view of most Enlightenment thinkers, actually little more than a thoroughly human itinerant rabbi, the New Testament writers presented him as a saviour and risen Lord. These beliefs were, it was argued, often little more than fanciful additions to or misunderstandings of the history of Jesus. By appropriate use of the latest historical methods, some writers of the Enlightenment period believed that it was possible to reconstruct Jesus 'as he actually was'. The origins of the

'quest of the historical Jesus' (as opposed to the 'mythical Christ of faith') lie in this period, based on such considerations.

It will thus be clear that the Enlightenment presented a major challenge to central aspects of Christian belief, felt with especial force in the field of Christology, in that the programme of religious criticism associated with the movement was concentrated and focused upon this particular area of theology. The present volume aims to document the nature of these challenges, and indicate the response to them within the German-speaking Protestant theological tradition. In many ways, this volume represents a complete story in itself. It is the opinion of many scholars, both in Germany and North America, that the German theological tradition is coming to a natural end, with a shift in theological emphasis away from Germany towards North America, with other issues (such as those associated with feminism, postliberalism and postmodernism) coming to the fore, and the issues traditionally associated with the Enlightenment becoming of considerably lesser importance. In effect, the German theological tradition has been seen to be linked to the agenda of the Enlightenment; as that agenda is seen to be of less and less importance, so the relevance of that tradition, and the seriousness with which it is taken in the post-Enlightenment Western world, have diminished accordingly. The present volume thus documents what is, in effect, a major single chapter in modern theology, which is now coming to its natural close.

It is, however, a fascinating study, of enormous interest to any concerned with Christian theology. Yet, in the past, students have been hindered from engaging with it, on account of the absence of a reliable and readable introduction to its central themes and personalities. This book is written for students beginning the study of this field. It assumes no knowledge of the German language. Important German-language terms are introduced and explained as necessary; a final glossary allows easy reference to all terms of major Christological importance. The book in its present form has arisen out of a decade of teaching experience in this field at Oxford University. I am indebted to my students over these years for their invaluable guidance concerning points of especial difficulty and interest. This book was originally published in 1987, as the text of an eight-lecture course given at Oxford University; it has been revised and expanded for the purposes of this new edition. The new material incorporated reflects recent developments in the field, major

9

new publications unavailable at the time of the earlier edition, and substantial new sections of explanatory material designed with the needs of students beginning the study of this field in mind. The extensive references to German-language sources in the notes of the original edition have been largely eliminated, with attention now being drawn primarily to readily accessible English-language studies.

Finally, I acknowledge with pleasure the assistance generously rendered by many academic colleagues. I owe a considerable debt to the generosity of Prof. Dr Gerhard Ebeling (Zürich), Prof. Dr Eberhard Jüngel (Tübingen), Prof. Dr Jürgen Moltmann (Tübingen), Prof. Dr Wolfhart Pannenberg (Munich), Prof. Dr Gerhard Sauter (Princeton), and Prof. Dr Reinhard Slenczka (Erlangen) for guidance in approaches to the theme of this study. Subsequently, I have been greatly assisted by Professor Richard Bauckham (St Andrews), Professor John Macquarrie (Oxford), and Professor Jonathan Webster (Toronto). I myself remain entirely responsible for errors of substance or interpretation, or for any failures to explain adequately the complex issues underlying the subject.

Alister E. McGrath
Oxford University

Note on Translations and Orthography

Wherever possible, I have used existing English translations of the central German texts. These have all been checked against the German originals, and corrected where necessary. The German term *Mensch* (which has the root meaning of 'a person' or 'a human being') has long been translated as 'man' in English. This non-inclusive translation is no longer regarded as acceptable, and is in any case a poor rendering of the German term. I have therefore adopted inclusive translations of this term as appropriate.

Major books are referred to as follows: the short *German* title of the original is given in italics, immediately followed by the title of the corresponding English translation in quotation marks. *Readers are warned that the English titles occasionally depart considerably from the German original.* Thus a seminal work by Wolfhart Pannenberg is referred to as follows: *Gründzuge der Christologie* ('Jesus – God and Man'). Thereafter, the English title of the work will be used within the text.

The orthography of older German works, such as the writings of Schleiermacher, has been modernized. The German character 'Esszett' (ß), unfamiliar to many readers, has been consistently represented as 'ss'. This practice has long been adopted within Swiss-German orthography. The practice, occasionally encountered in English-language works, of representing the Umlaut by placing the letter 'e' after the vowel in question (for example, 'Juengel' for 'Jüngel') has been consistently avoided.

The Enlightenment: A New Christological Style

During the sixteenth century, the German-speaking lands were dominated by the agenda of the Reformation. Martin Luther (1483–1546) and Huldrych Zwingli (1484–1531) established Germany and Switzerland respectively as centres of the new theological and religious trends which were sweeping through Western Europe. After the initial fervour of the Reformation had subsided, a period of system-building began. Lutheran and Reformed theologians concentrated upon developing systematic expositions of their respective positions, in order to give them increased credibility and intellectual weight in a period of considerable religious uncertainty. This period, which is often referred to as 'the period of Orthodoxy', can be argued to extend from the death of Calvin (1564) to the middle of the seventeenth century.

Christology was not a matter of major disagreement at the time of the Reformation, nor would it feature prominently in the theological debates of the period of Orthodoxy. The only major Christological debate of the period of any interest centres upon two groups of Lutheran theologians, who developed rival positions known as 'crypticism' and 'kenoticism' in relation to the nature of Christ's divine atttributes (see pp. 79–80). As a result, Protestant theology was perhaps ill-prepared to meet the new concentration upon the person and significance of Jesus Christ, which was the direct result of the rise of the Enlightenment in the early eighteenth century. It lacked the intellectual resources to meet the new challenge which was now developing in western culture.

With the benefit of hindsight, the Enlightenment can be said to have marked a decisive and irreversible change in the political, social and religious outlook of Western Europe and North America. The movement proved itself able to transcend national frontiers and cultural barriers. Although the movement is generally thought to have had its origins in English Deism of the seventeenth century, it achieved its maximum theological impact in Germany during the following century.[1] The German Enlightenment, often designated by the German term *Aufklär-ung*, opened the way to a new era of theological reflection, often, as we shall see, with very negative consequences for traditional Christian theology. Yet the term 'Enlightenment' is vague, and requires further consideration before we can consider its implications for Christian theology.

Defining the Enlightenment

The term 'Enlightenment' only came into general use in the closing decades of the nineteenth century. This is an important observation, as it suggests that the movement now known by this name had no recognized way of referring to itself at the time. The German term *Aufklärung*, which is probably best translated as 'a clearout', is encoun-tered in many writings of the period, such as those of Immanuel Kant (1724–1804). In his *Was ist Aufklärung?* ('What is Enlightenment?'), Kant offers the following definition of the term *Aufklärung*:

> *Aufklärung* is our release from our self-imposed tutelage – that is, a state of inability to make use of our own understanding without direction from someone else. This tutelage is self-imposed when its cause lies not in our own reason, but in a lack of courage to use it without direction from someone else . . . 'Have courage to use your own reason!' – that is the motto of *Aufklärung*.

Yet this term is not, however, especially helpful in trying to establish precisely what the agenda of the movement was. Any number of global definitions of the movement can be offered; these have all proved unsatisfactory, on account of their reductionist tendencies. 'Enlightenment' is a loose term, defying precise definition, embracing a cluster of ideas and attitudes characteristic of the period 1720–80,

14

especially the unrestricted use of pure human reason in an attempt to demolish old myths which were seen to have bound individuals and societies to the oppression of the past. If there is any common element underlying the movement, it perhaps lies more in *how* those who were sympathetic to its outlook thought than in *what* they thought.[2]

The term 'Age of Reason', often used as a synonym for the Enlightenment, is seductively misleading, in that it implies that reason had been hitherto ignored or marginalized in matters of philosophy or theology. In one sense, the Middle Ages was just as much an 'Age of Reason' as the Enlightenment; the crucial difference lay in the manner in which reason was used, and the limits which were understood to be imposed upon it. Most medieval theologians valued reason considerably, and had no hesitations in drawing upon its resources; Thomas Aquinas's (1225–74) 'Five Ways' (that is, arguments for the existence of God) are an excellent example of the constructive use of reason within this period. Nevertheless, reason was understood to have its limits as a theological resource. Most medieval theologians insisted that there was a set of revealed truths, to which access could not be gained by human reason.

Nor was the eighteenth century consistently rational in every aspect. In fact, the Enlightenment is now recognized to be intellectually heterogeneous, including a remarkable variety of anti-rational movements such as Mesmerism or Masonic rituals. Mesmerism is of particular interest. The movement takes its name from Franz Anton Mesmer (1734–1815), a German physician who achieved considerable success in Paris. Mesmerism was grounded in astrology and the occult, and laid particular emphasis upon the therapeutic powers of animal magnetism and the potential of hypnotic *séances*. The strongly irrational character of this movement, which gained a considerable following within the Paris social élite on the eve of the French Revolution, is a reminder that the 'Age of Reason' had its decidedly less reasonable aspects.

Despite these important qualifications, an emphasis upon the ability of human reason to penetrate the mysteries of the world is rightly regarded as a defining characteristic of the 'Enlightenment' outlook. However, the term 'rationalism' should also be used with caution when referring to the Enlightenment. The term is often used in an uncritical and inaccurate way, designating the general atmosphere of optimism, grounded in a belief in scientific and social progress, which pervades much of the writing of the period. This use of the term is confusing, and should probably be avoided. Rationalism, in its proper sense, is perhaps

15

best defined as the doctrine that the external world can be known by reason, and reason alone – in contrast to empiricism, which held that this world can only be known through experience. This rationalist doctrine, which is characteristic of earlier writers such as René Descartes (1596–1650), G. W. Leibnitz (1646–1716), Benedict Spinoza (1632–77) and Christian Wolff (1679–1754), was subjected to intense criticism during the later eighteenth century, as the influence of John Locke's (1632–1704) empiricist epistemology became widespread.

Kant, often portrayed as an exponent of the total sufficiency of pure reason, is in reality acutely aware of its limitations. The epistemology developed in his *Critique of Pure Reason* (1781) may be regarded as an attempt to synthesize the insights of rationalism and empiricism, in response to growing awareness of the limitations of pure reason in the face of the continuing successes of the natural sciences. This work may be regarded as bringing the early period of rationalism to a close. Despite according a particularly significant role to reason in his thought (as seen in *Religion within the Limits of Reason Alone*, published in 1793), Kant showed a keen appreciation of the implications of the empiricist emphasis upon sense experience. Nevertheless, rationalist attitudes persisted well into the nineteenth century, and constitute an important element of the general Enlightenment critique of Christianity.[3]

The Enlightenment ushered in a period of considerable uncertainty for Christianity in Western Europe and North America. The trauma of the Reformation and the resulting Wars of Religion had barely subsided on the continent of Europe, before a new and more radical challenge to Christianity arose. If the sixteenth-century Reformation challenged the church to rethink its external forms and the manner in which it expressed its beliefs, the Enlightenment saw the intellectual credentials of Christianity itself (rather than any one of its specific forms, such as Roman Catholicism) facing a major threat on a number of fronts. The origins of this challenge may be traced back to the seventeenth century, with the rise of Cartesianism on the continent of Europe, and the growing influence of Deism in England. The growing emphasis upon the need to uncover the rational roots of religion had considerable negative implications for Christianity, as subsequent events were to prove. Before considering these developments in any detail, however, it will be useful to consider the impact of the Enlightenment upon the German academic establishment, which, by the end of the eighteenth century, had become the centre of Protestant theological speculation.

Of all the Christian denominations, it was German Protestantism which was most deeply affected by the Enlightenment, making the study of German Protestant Christology an excellent case-study to examine the rise and fall of the influence of the Enlightenment over Christian theology. Whereas the French and English Enlightenments assumed quite definitely political programmes, the same freedom of action was largely denied to their German counterparts. The only area in which the new radical spirit of the age could find free expression was in the universities, which were relatively free of the restrictions which cramped the remainder of German society at the time. As a result, the universities of Germany became centres of radical thought, directed towards the undermining of the social and academic *ancien régime*. There would be no social upheaval in Germany to parallel the French Revolution; there was, however, a sustained critique of the underlying ideas of one of the major components of the existing social order – the Lutheran church. Theology came to be the object of particular criticism within the German Enlightenment, on account of the fact that it was an academic discipline within the university system, which was seen to be linked with the *status quo*.

Other reasons may be given for the seriousness with which the German Enlightenment took theology. Whereas the English and French Enlightenments tended to ignore theology, the German Enlightenment took it with considerable seriousness. Two additional reasons may be given for this. First, probably on account of the continuing influence of the Reformation heritage, Germany had developed a strong tradition of doctrinal reflection and development, quite absent in England or France. Theology was seen as an academically serious subject, worthy of attention. Second, the rise of Pietism had made religion relevant within German society, by exploring the relation of Christianity to religious feelings, and anchoring faith in the experiential world of ordinary people. Religion was thus taken with social seriousness in Germany, obliging the writers of the Enlightenment in that region to deal with it directly, instead of marginalizing it.

Pietism, perhaps best known in its English form of Methodism, placed considerable emphasis upon the experiential aspects of religion – for example, as in John Wesley's (1703–91) notion of 'experimental religion'. (The eighteenth-century term 'experimental', used in this religious context, is best rendered in modern English as 'experiential' or 'based upon experience'.) This concern for religious experience served

17

to make Christianity relevant and accessible to the ordinary life of the masses, contrasting sharply with the intellectualism of, for example, Lutheran Orthodoxy. Pietism forged a strong link between Christian faith and experience, thus making Christianity a matter of the heart, as well as of the mind.

Pietism was well established in Germany by the end of the seventeenth century, whereas the movement only developed in England during the eighteenth century, and in France not at all. The Enlightenment thus preceded the rise of Pietism in England, with the result that the great Evangelical revivals of the eighteenth century significantly blunted the influence of rationalism upon religion. In Germany, however, the Enlightenment followed after the rise of Pietism, and thus developed in a situation which had been significantly shaped by religious faith, even if it would pose a serious challenge to its received forms and ideas. (Interestingly, English Deism began to become influential in Germany at roughly the same time as German Pietism began to exert influence in England.) The most significant intellectual forces in the German Enlightenment were thus directed towards the reshaping (rather than the rejection or demolition) of the Christian faith. In France, however, Christianity was widely perceived as both oppressive and irrelevant, with the result that the *philosophes* were able to advocate the total rejection of Christianity as an archaic and discredited belief system. In his *Traité de la tolérance*, Denis Diderot (1713–84) argued that English Deism had compromised itself, permitting religion to survive where it ought to have been eradicated totally.

The Enlightenment and Protestantism

It was Protestant, rather than Roman Catholic or Eastern Orthodox, theology which was especially open to influence from the new currents of thought which arose from the Enlightenment and its aftermath. Four main factors have been noted which may explain this observation, at least in part.

1. *The relative weakness of Protestant ecclesiastical institutions*. The absence of an authoritarian centralized structure, such as the papacy, meant that national or regional Protestant churches were able to respond to local circumstances, intellectual and political, with a far greater freedom than Roman Catholicism. Similarly, until quite recently individual Protestant thinkers experienced a degree of academic freedom

denied to their Roman Catholic colleagues; the spirit of creative freedom which characterized Protestantism from its outset thus expressed itself in theological exploration and originality quite impossible for others.

2. *The nature of Protestantism itself.* While the 'essence of Protestantism' remains disputed within scholarly circles, there is agreement that a spirit of protest is part of the birthright of the movement. The Protestant predisposition to challenge religious authority, and the commitment to the principle *ecclesia reformata, ecclesia semper reformanda* ('the reformed church must always be the church which is reforming itself'), encouraged a spirit of critical inquiry concerning Christian dogma. This attitude resonated with the ideals of the Enlightenment, leading to an alignment of many Protestant writers with the movement, and a willingness to absorb its methods and outlooks. Thus G. E. Lessing (1729–81) argued that the leading characteristic of Luther's theology was his proclamation of the individual's total freedom in matters of religious opinion, unfettered by ecclesiastical interference, and contrasted this with the theological straitjacket imposed upon Roman Catholic writers by the *magisterium*. The German Enlightenment was thus portrayed as the natural successor to the German Reformation. (In fact, Luther was acutely aware of the dangers of unrestricted theological speculation, and did little to encourage it.)

3. *The relation of Protestantism and the universities.* From its inception, Protestantism recognized the importance of higher education in the training of its ministers. The foundation of the Genevan Academy and Harvard College are obvious illustrations of this point. During the late sixteenth and early seventeenth centuries, the Lutheran and Reformed churches in Germany established university faculties of theology as a means of ensuring a constant supply of well-educated clergy. As noted above, during the eighteenth century, political protest was stifled in Germany; the only means by which radicalism could express itself was intellectual. The German universities thus became centres of revolt against the *ancien régime*. As a result, German university theologians (who were virtually entirely Protestant) aligned themselves with the Enlightenment, whereas the more conservative church leadership tended to side with the *ancien régime*. Radicalism was thus able to express itself best theologically, at the level of religious ideas. Although apparently unable to achieve any significant social, political or ecclesiastical change, radicalism was able to mount a significant challenge to the ideas which undergirded the churches.

Protestant theology was thus significantly affected by the methods of the Enlightenment, whereas Roman Catholic theology was not.

4. *The varying local impact of the Enlightenment.* It must be stressed that the Enlightenment was not a chronologically uniform movement. Although well established in western central Europe by the eighteenth century, the Enlightenment cannot really be said to have taken hold in Russia or the countries of southern Europe (such as Spain, Italy or Greece) until the late nineteenth or early twentieth century.[4] Such countries were the strongholds of Roman Catholicism or Eastern Orthodoxy. In consequence, theologians of these churches did not feel under pressure to respond to the intellectual forces which were of such major significance in regions historically associated with Protestantism.

The Enlightenment Critique of Christianity

The Enlightenment criticism of traditional Christianity was based primarily upon the principle of the omnicompetence and universality of human reason. A number of stages in the development of this belief may be discerned. First, it was argued that the beliefs of Christianity were rational, and thus capable of standing up to critical examination. This type of approach may be found in John Locke's *Reasonableness of Christianity* (1695), and within the early Wolffian school in Germany. Christianity was a reasonable supplement to natural religion. The notion of divine revelation was thus maintained.

Second, it was argued that the basic ideas of Christianity, being rational, could be derived from reason itself. There was no need to invoke the idea of divine revelation. As this idea was developed within English Deist circles – such as by John Toland (1670–1722) in his *Christianity not Mysterious* (1696) and Matthew Tindal (1655–1733) in his *Christianity as Old as Creation* (1730) – Christianity was seen as essentially the republication of the religion of nature. It did not transcend natural religion, but was merely an example of it. All so-called 'revealed religion' is actually nothing other than the reconfirmation of what can be known through rational reflection on nature. In Germany, this view found support among the writers generally known as the *Neologen*, such as J. A. Ernesti (1707–81), J. D. Michaelis (1717–91), J. S. Semler (1725–91) and J. J. Spalding (1714–1804). 'Revelation' was simply a rational reaffirmation of moral truths already available to enlightened reason.

Third, reason came to be regarded as above revelation. The ability of reason to judge revelation was thus affirmed. As human reason was omnicompetent, it was argued that it was supremely qualified to judge Christian beliefs and practices, with a view to eliminating any irrational or superstitious elements. This view, associated with H. S. Reimarus (1694–1768) in Germany and the *philosophes* in France, placed reason firmly above revelation, and may be seen as symbolized in the enthronement of the Goddess of Reason in Notre Dame de Paris in 1793.

The Enlightenment was a Western European and North American phenomenon, and thus took place in cultures in which the most numerically significant form of religion was Christianity. This historical observation is of considerable importance: the Enlightenment critique of religion in general was often particularized as a criticism of Christianity in general. It was *Christian* doctrines which were subjected to a critical assessment of a vigour without any precedent. It was *Christian* sacred writings which were subjected to an unprecedented critical scrutiny, both literary and historical. In an influential article in *Essays and Reviews* (1860), Benjamin Jowett (1817–93) argued that the Bible 'should be treated like any other book'. It was the history of Jesus of Nazareth, rather than that of Moses or Mohammed, which was subjected to critical reconstruction. Christianity thus came to bear the brunt of a wide-ranging attack on religion in general.

While every generalization is dangerous, there are excellent reasons for suggesting that the Enlightenment witnessed growing sympathy for the notion of 'natural' or 'rational religion'. This approach is illustrated in the title of Matthew Tindal's highly influential work, *Christianity as Old as Creation, or, The Gospel a Republication of the Religion of Nature* (1730). On the basis of the foundational Enlightenment assumption of the rationality of reality, and the ability of human beings to uncover and apprehend this rationality, it was argued that whatever lay behind the various world religions was ultimately rational in character, and thus capable of being uncovered, described and analysed by human reason.

The idea of a universal rational religion was, however, at odds with the diversity of the world religions. As European knowledge of these religions deepened, through the growth of the genre of 'voyager literature', and through the increasing availability of Chinese, Indian, Persian and Vedic religious writings, it became increasingly clear that the notion of a universal religion of reason faced difficulties when con-

21

fronted with the evidence of the astonishing variety of human religious beliefs and practices. Many Enlightenment writers, perhaps more concerned with championing reason than with wrestling with the empirical evidence, developed a theory of religion which accounted for this diversity, at least in part.

In his *True Intellectual System of the Universe* (1678), Ralph Cudworth (1617–88) argued that all religions were ultimately based upon a common ethical monotheism – a simple religion of nature, basically ethical in character, and devoid of all the arbitrary doctrines and religious rites of Christianity or Judaism. The primordial rational religion of nature had become corrupted through its early interpreters. One theory which gained an especially wide hearing was that the religions were essentially the inventions of cultic leaders or priests, whose main motivation was the preservation of their own interests and status. The Roman historian Tacitus (*c.* 55–120) had suggested (*Histories*, Book 5) that Moses invented the Jewish religious rites as a means of ensuring religious cohesion after the expulsion from Egypt; many writers of the early Enlightenment developed this notion, arguing that the variety of human religious rites and practices were simply human inventions in response to specific historical situations, now firmly in the past. The way was open to the recovery of the universal primordial religion of nature, which would put an end to the religious squabbles of humanity.

The Enlightenment also witnessed the development of a rudimentary psychology of religion, as seen in a more developed form in David Hume's (1711–76) *Natural History of Religion* (1757).[5] (Although the term 'psychology' was introduced in the sixteenth century, it failed to achieve general acceptance until the eighteenth.) In his *Natural History of Superstition* (1709), John Trenchard developed the idea of the inherent credulity of humanity, which permitted natural monotheism to degenerate into the various religious traditions of humanity. The enthusiasm with which this idea was received can be judged from the comments of the *Independent Whig* (31 December 1720), to the effect that 'the peculiar Foible of Mankind is Superstition, or an intrinsick and pannick Fear of invisible and unknown Beings'. For Trenchard, the religions represented the triumph of superstition over reason. By eliminating such superstitious beliefs and rites, a return to the universal and simple religion of nature could be achieved. A similar idea was developed during the French Enlightenment by Paul Henri Thiry, Baron d'Holbach (1723–89), who argued (for example, in his *La contagion*

22

sacrée, ou, Histoire naturelle de la superstition, 1768) that religion was a form of pathological disorder. G. E. Lessing emphasized the universalizability of religion, a point developed with some force in his play 'Nathan the Wise'.

The Enlightenment Critique of Traditional Christologies

Having outlined the general principles of the Enlightenment challenge to traditional Christian thought, it is now appropriate to explore how these impacted on specific areas of traditional Christian theology with a direct bearing upon Christology.

Miracles

Much traditional Christian apologetic concerning the identity and significance of Jesus Christ was based upon the 'miraculous evidences' of the New Testament, culminating in the resurrection. The new emphasis upon the mechanical regularity and orderliness of the universe, perhaps the most significant intellectual aspect of the legacy of Newtonianism, raised doubts concerning the New Testament accounts of miraculous happenings. Hume's *Essay on Miracles* (1748) was widely regarded as demonstrating the evidential impossibility of miracles. Hume emphasized that there were no contemporary analogues of New Testament miracles, such as the resurrection, thus forcing the reader of the New Testament to rely totally upon human testimony to such miracles. For Hume, it was axiomatic that no human testimony was adequate to establish the occurrence of a miracle, in the absence of a present-day analogue. There were no resurrections today (or, at least, none that Hume knew about personally); could anyone therefore believe that they really happened in the past? Reimarus and G. E. Lessing denied that human testimony to a past event (such as the resurrection) was sufficient to make it credible if it appeared to be contradicted by present-day direct experience, no matter how well documented the original event may have been. Related arguments based upon the 'principle of analogy' or the 'homogeneity' of history, would be developed by later writers, such as Ernst Troeltsch (1865–1923; see pp. 115–22).

Similarly, Diderot declared that if the entire population of Paris were to assure him that a dead man had just been raised from the dead, he would not believe it. This growing scepticism over the 'miraculous evidences' of the New Testament forced traditional Christianity to defend the doctrine of the divinity of Christ on grounds other than miracles – which, at the time, it proved singularly incapable of doing. Of course, it must be noted that other religions claiming miraculous evidences were subjected to equally great sceptical criticism by the Enlightenment: Christianity was singled out on account of its religious domination of the cultural milieu in which the Enlightenment developed.

Divine Revelation

The concept of revelation was of central importance to traditional Christian theology. While many Christian theologians (such as Thomas Aquinas and John Calvin) recognized the possibility of a natural knowledge of God, they insisted that this required supplementation by supernatural divine revelation, such as that witnessed to in Scripture. The Enlightenment witnessed the development of an increasingly critical attitude to the very idea of supernatural revelation, a trend which culminated in works such as J. G. Fichte's (1762–1814) *Versuch einer Kritik aller Offenbarung* ('Essay on the Criticism of all Revelation', 1792). In part, this new critical attitude was also due to the Enlightenment depreciation of history. For Lessing, there was an 'ugly broad ditch' between history and reason (see pp. 28–33). Revelation took place in history – but of what value were the contingent truths of history in comparison with the necessary truths of reason? The *philosophes* in particular asserted that history could at best confirm the truths of reason, but was incapable of establishing those truths in the first place. Truths about God were timeless, open to investigation by human reason but not capable of being disclosed in 'events' such as the history of Jesus of Nazareth.

Original Sin

The idea that human nature is in some sense flawed or corrupted, expressed in the orthodox doctrine of original sin, was vigorously opposed by Enlightenment writers. Voltaire (1694–1778) and Jean-Jacques Rousseau (1712–78) criticized the doctrine as encouraging pessimism in regard to human abilities, thus impeding human social and political development and promoting *laissez-faire* attitudes. German Enlightenment thinkers tended to criticize the doctrine on account of its historical origins in the thought of Augustine of Hippo (354–430), which they regarded as invalidating its permanent validity and relevance. The rejection of original sin was of considerable importance, as the Christian doctrine of redemption rested upon the assumption that humanity required to be liberated from bondage to it. For the Enlightenment, it was the *idea* of original sin itself which was oppressive, and from which humanity required liberation. This intellectual liberation was provided by the Enlightenment critique of the doctrine.

The Development of Doctrinal Criticism

Where French writers dismissed the notion of original sin on account of its pessimistic view of human nature, writers of the German Enlightenment adopted a considerably more sophisticated approach. The Enlightenment witnessed the origin of the discipline of doctrinal criticism, in which the received teachings of the Christian church were subjected to a penetrating analysis concerning their historical origins and foundations.

The origins of the 'history of dogma' (to use the traditional English rendering of the German term *Dogmengeschichte*) date from the period of the Enlightenment. The consolidation of the discipline dates from later: more specifically, the period of liberal Protestantism, especially during the second half of the nineteenth century. The discipline is generally regarded as having been initiated in the eighteenth century by Johann Friedrich Wilhelm Jerusalem (1709–89), who argued that dogmas such as the doctrine of the two natures of Christ and the Trinity were not to be found in the New Testament. These, he argued, arose through confusion of the Platonic Logos-concept with that found in the Fourth Gospel, and the mistaken apprehension that Jesus personified, rather than exemplified, this Logos. The history of dogma was thus a history of mistakes – mistakes, however, which were in principle reversible, were it not for the monolithic hostility of the institutional churches to any such reconstruction.

One of the most significant works dating from this period argued that a series of assumptions, each of central importance to the Anselmian doctrine of penal substitution, had become incorporated into Christian theology by what were little more than historical accidents. In his *System der reinen Philosophie* (1778), G. S. Steinbart argued that historical investigation disclosed the intrusion of three 'arbitrary assumptions' into Christian reflection on salvation:

1. the Augustinian doctrine of original sin;
2. the concept of satisfaction (a central theme of medieval and Reformation theories of the atonement); and
3. the doctrine of the imputation of the righteousness of Christ (a major element of Reformation doctrines of justification).

For such reasons, Steinbart felt able to declare the substructure of orthodox Protestant thinking on the person and work of Christ to be little more than a relic of a bygone era.

Initial attempts at writing histories of dogma were somewhat unpromising, often being little more than disorganized lists of quotations and pieces of information which appealed to their writers. The first serious attempt to give structure to this enterprise, and discern general principles of development within the history of dogma, is due to Ferdinand Christian Baur (see pp. 63–7). While the nature and extent of Hegelian influence upon Baur's understanding of history remain contested, it is clear that he views the development of doctrine through an idealist prism. Baur evidently regards the development of doctrine as a unity, rather than a series of unrelated episodes. The histories of dogma influenced by Enlightenment rationalism tended to treat history as a web of irrationalities, interspersed with depressingly few rays of light.

The Enlightenment historians of dogma tended to regard themselves as rational individuals studying a thoroughly irrational subject. Baur's studies – such as *Die christliche Lehre von der Versöhnung* ('The Christian Doctrine of Reconciliation', 1838) and *Die christliche Lehre von der Dreieinigkeit und Menschwerdung Gottes* ('The Christian Doctrines of the Trinity and the Incarnation of God', 1841–3) – were, however, able to draw upon Hegel's philosophy of history in an attempt to discern continuity and development within history, rather than perpetuate a wooden tradition of monolithic hostility towards the rationality of the past. History was going somewhere, and the discerning historian could grasp its unity and dynamism, while at the same time attempt to comprehend its meaning and thus illuminate his own present situation. Retaining the Enlightenment view that the doctrinal legacy of the past was unusable in the modern period, Baur held that the development of doctrine nevertheless afforded insights into the manner in which modern views developed.

The Quest of the Historical Jesus

A final area in which the Enlightenment made a significant challenge to orthodox Christian belief concerns the person of Jesus of Nazareth. One particularly important development may be noted: the development of the 'quest of the historical Jesus'.

Both Deism and the German Enlightenment developed the thesis that there was a serious discrepancy between the real Jesus of history and the New Testament interpretation of his significance. Underlying the New Testament portrait of the supernatural redeemer of humanity lurked a simple human figure, a glorified teacher of common sense. While a supernatural redeemer was unacceptable to Enlightenment rationalism, the idea of an enlightened moral teacher was not. This idea, developed with particular rigour by H. S. Reimarus (see pp. 33–5), suggested that it was possible to go behind the New Testament accounts of Christ as saviour, and uncover a simpler, more human Jesus, who would be acceptable to the new spirit of the age. And so the quest for the real and more credible 'Jesus of history' began. Although this quest would ultimately end in failure, the later Enlightenment regarded this 'quest' as holding the key to the credibility of Jesus within the context of a rational natural religion. Jesus' moral authority resided in the quality of his teaching and religious personality, rather than in the unacceptable orthodox suggestion that he was God incarnate.

This point is made forcefully by Immanuel Kant, both in his *Religion within the Limits of Reason Alone,* and his celebrated work on the basis of human morality, *Grundlegung zur Metaphysik der Sitten* ('Fundamental Principles of the Metaphysics of Morals'). It is reason and its associated ideas of moral perfection which are authoritative in matters of religion. Christ cannot be allowed to establish ideas of morality (which would compromise the autonomy of human reason, in that it would amount to the imposition of standards of morality upon it). Rather, he has authority only to the extent that he reflects those moral ideals which are themselves grounded in human reason. 'Even the Holy One of the gospel must first be compared with our ideal of moral perfection before we can recognize him as such.'[6] This outlook has been the subject of considerable criticism, not least on account of its radical individualism, which elevates the subjective consciousness of the individual to the heights of moral judgment. The twentieth-century British novelist Iris Murdoch identifies this radical individualism and hints at its cultural arrogance when she writes:

> How recognizable, how familiar to us, is the man so beautifully portrayed in the *Grundlegung*, who confronted even with Christ turns away to consider the judgment of his own conscience and to hear the voice of his own reason. Stripped of the exiguous metaphysical background which Kant was prepared to allow him, this man is still with us, free, independent, lonely, powerful, rational, responsible, brave, the hero of so many novels and books of moral philosophy.[7]

A second area of importance in which orthodox doctrines concerning Jesus were challenged related to the significance of his death. The orthodox approach to Jesus' death on the cross was to interpret it from the standpoint of the resurrection (which the Enlightenment was not prepared to accept as an historical event) as a way in which God was able to forgive the sins of humanity. The Enlightenment subjected this 'theory of the atonement' to increasing criticism, as involving arbitrary and unacceptable hypotheses such as original sin. Jesus' death on the cross was reinterpreted in terms of a supreme moral example of self-giving and dedication, intended to inspire similar dedication and self-giving on the part of his followers. Where orthodox Christianity tended to treat Jesus' death (and resurrection) as possessing greater inherent importance than his religious teaching, the Enlightenment marginalized his death and denied his resurrection, in order to emphasize the quality of his moral teaching.[8]

To explore the full impact of such Enlightenment ideas upon traditional Christologies, we may explore the writings of two leading figures of the period: G. E. Lessing (1729–81) and H. S. Reimarus (1694–1768).

Faith and History: G. E. Lessing

If one pole of the Enlightenment critique of traditional Christianity was a belief in the omnicompetence of reason, a second pole was a growing scepticism concerning the epistemic value of history. There was a growing belief that history – including both historical figures and events – could not give access to the kind of knowledge that was necessary for a rational religious or philosophical system.[9] How can the move from history (which is a collection of accidental and contingent truths) to reason (which is concerned with necessary and universal truths) take place? G. E. Lessing argued that historical and rational truth were incommensurable; there was a gap between them which could not be bridged:

> If no historical truth can be demonstrated, then nothing can be demonstrated by means of historical truths. That is: accidental truths of history can never become the proof of necessary truths of reason . . . That, then, is the ugly broad ditch which I cannot get across, however often and however earnestly I have tried to make the leap.[10]

Lessing's phrase 'an ugly broad ditch (*garstiger breiter Graben*)' between faith and history has been seen as summing up the gulf fixed between historical and rational approaches to Christian theology. So what are the main elements of this ditch?

Broadly speaking, three elements can be discerned within Lessing's account of the problem of faith and history:

1. a *chronological* ditch, which separates the past from the present;
2. a *metaphysical* ditch, which separates accidental historical truths from universal and necessary rational truths; and
3. an *existential* ditch, which separates modern human existence from the religious message of a distant past.

It will be clear that these three elements are not absolutely distinct. There is a significant degree of interaction between them. However, together they build up to form the overall problem of 'faith and history', which will be of such importance in relation to modern German Christology. We shall consider each of these elements in turn.

The Chronological Ditch

The gospel accounts of Jesus Christ place him firmly in the past. We are unable to verify those accounts, but are obliged to rely upon the eyewitness reports which underlie the gospels for our knowledge of Jesus. But, Lessing asked, how reliable are those accounts? Did the events which the gospels relate actually take place? Lessing notes that he does not have personal firsthand experience of the resurrection of Jesus Christ; so why, he asks, should he be asked to believe in something which he has not seen? The problem of chronological distance, according to Lessing, is made all the more acute on account of his doubts (which he evidently assumes others will share) concerning the reliability of the eyewitness reports. Our faith eventually rests upon the authority of others, rather than the authority of our own experience and rational reflection upon it:

> But since the truths of these miracles has completely ceased to be demonstrable by miracles happening now, since they are no more than reports of miracles . . . I deny that they can and should bind me to the very least faith in the other teachings of Jesus.[11]

At issue here is a central theme of the Enlightenment: human autonomy. Reality is rational, and human beings have the necessary epistemological capacities to uncover this rational ordering of the world. Truth is not something which demands to be accepted upon the basis of an external authority; it is to be recognized and accepted by the autonomous thinking person, on the basis of the perception of congruence between what that individual knows to be true, and the alleged 'truth' which presents itself for verification. Truth is something which is discerned, not something which is imposed. For Lessing, being obligated to accept the testimony of others is tantamount to the compromising of human intellectual autonomy.

It is clear that Lessing has in mind the reported miracles of Jesus, above all his resurrection from the dead, upon which such doctrines as the divinity of Christ ultimately rest. These might indeed have constituted 'the strongest inducement' to those who were fortunate enough to have experienced them at first hand; but what about someone like Lessing himself, who is forced to rely upon the significantly weaker evidence of human testimony? Declaring this to be 'an inconceivable truth', Lessing argues that an exceptionally difficult and significant claim to truth is being made, which ultimately rests upon unverifiable grounds:

> How is it to be expected of me that the same inconceivable truths which sixteen to eighteen hundred years ago people

believed on the strongest inducement should be believed by me on an infinitely less inducement? Or is it invariably the case, that what I read in reputable historians is just as certain for me as what I myself experience? I do not know that anyone has ever asserted this.[12]

But suppose that the resurrection of Christ had taken place in Lessing's back yard. Would he then believe in the divinity of Christ? No – on account of the second ditch, to which we may now turn.

The Metaphysical Ditch

'If on historical grounds I have no objection to the statement that this Christ himself rose from the dead, must I therefore accept that this risen Christ was the Son of God?'[13] In answering this question in the negative, Lessing draws a distinction between two different classes of truth. If the chronological ditch concerned a dispute about historical facts (what actually happened in the past), the second ditch concerns the interpretation of those events. How can the transition from the 'accidental truths of history' to the 'necessary truths of reason' be made? Lessing argues that these are two radically different and totally incommensurable classes of truth.

Rational truth was regarded as possessing the qualities of necessity, eternity and universality. It was the same at all times and all places. Human reason was capable of penetrating to this universal static realm of truth, which could act as the foundation of all human knowledge. This notion of truth can be found in a definitive form in the writings of Benedict Spinoza, who argued that human reason is capable of basing itself upon self-evident first principles, and, by following these through logically, deducing a complete moral system. Just about everyone who favours this approach makes some sort of appeal to Euclid's five principles of geometry. On the basis of his five principles, he was able to construct his entire geometrical system. Many of the more rationalist philosophers, such as Leibnitz and Spinoza, were deeply attracted to this, believing that they could use the same method in philosophy. From a set of certain assumptions, a great secure edifice of philosophy and ethics could be erected. Of course, the dream later turned sour. The discovery of non-Euclidian geometry during the nineteenth century destroyed the appeal of this analogy. It turned out that there were other ways of doing

31

geometry, each just as internally consistent as Euclid's. But this development was not known to writers such as Spinoza or Lessing, who believed that reason was capable of erecting a self-sufficient and universally valid system on the basis of the necessary truths of reason.

Part of Lessing's case against Orthodoxy here concerns the 'scandal of particularity'. Why should one specific historical event have such momentous significance? Why should the history of Jesus of Nazareth – even assuming that it could be known with a degree of certainty that Lessing personally believed to be impossible – be elevated to such epistemological heights? Lessing argued that the universal human faculty of reason, available at all times and in all places to all people, avoided this scandal. Rationalism thus possessed both a moral and intellectual superiority to the particularist Christology associated with traditional Christianity.

Lessing's assumption about the existence of a universal rationality has, however, been subject to considerable criticism in modern times. The sociology of knowledge has demonstrated that, for example, 'Enlightenment rationalism' is far from being universal, but is merely one of a number of intellectual options. The suggestion that historicity limits intellectual options raises a number of difficulties for Enlightenment rationalism. For our purposes, it is particularly important to stress that individuals (whether theologians, philosophers or natural scientists) do not begin their quest for knowledge *de novo*, as if they were isolated from society and history. The Enlightenment emphasis upon knowledge gained through individual critical reflection, deriving from Descartes, has been the subject of considerable criticism in recent years on account of its uncritical rejection of the corporate foundations of knowledge.

The Existential Ditch

Finally, Lessing poses a series of questions which are existential in their orientation. What, he asks, is the *relevance* of such an outdated and archaic message for the modern world? The original Christian message is implausible for the modern reader. There is an insuperable credibility gap between a first-century and eighteenth-century worldview. How can learned and culturally sensitive Europeans enter into the backward world of the New Testament and appropriate its outdated religious message?

It is difficult to analyse this aspect of Lessing's discussion of the problem of faith and history, simply because he himself appears to have some difficulty in conceptualizing the point at issue. Nevertheless, the point is important, and will be a recurring feature of our study of modern German Christology. Perhaps it could be said that it is only with the rise of existentially orientated Christologies in the twentieth century (see pp. 162–8) that Lessing's point has been fully addressed, and answered.

Lessing's name is also connected with that of Hermann Samuel Reimarus, to whom we may now turn.

The Wolfenbüttel Fragments: H. S. Reimarus

H. S. Reimarus, professor of Oriental Languages (*i.e.*, Semitic languages, especially Hebrew) at Hamburg, had been strongly influenced by the rationalist philosophy associated with Christian Wolff, which he developed in a more radical direction. For example, Reimarus held that miracles were impossible; therefore, those portions of Scripture in both the Old and New Testaments which made reference to miracles must be regarded as incredible. Equally, if Jesus or his disciples claimed authority on the basis of alleged miracles, they were to be regarded as fraudulent. During his lifetime, he became increasingly convinced that both Judaism and Christianity rested upon fraudulent foundations, and conceived the idea of writing a major work which would bring this to public attention. The resulting work laboured under the somewhat clumsy title of *An Apology for the Rational Worshipper of God*. The volume subjected the entire biblical canon to the standards of rationalist criticism. However, reluctant to cause any controversy, he did not publish the work. It remained in manuscript form until his death.

At some point afterwards, the manuscript fell into the hands of Lessing, who argued that it ought to be published. However, Reimarus' family were hostile to any attempt to publish the work. At this time, Lessing was librarian at Wolfenbüttel, and conceived the idea of publishing the more controversial sections of the book as part of a programme of making more generally available some of the treasures of the Wolfenbüttel library collection. The first two such publications dealt with safe subjects; the next (1774) reproduced some extracts from Reimarus' work. It was the fourth selection of extracts from the work, published in 1778, which caused a sensation. The volume contained five 'fragments of an unknown writer (*Fragmenten eines Ungekannten*)', including a sustained attack on the historicity of the resurrection. Lessing allowed it to be understood that the 'unknown writer' was, in fact, Johann Lorenz Schmidt who, having died in 1749, would not be disadvantaged by the resulting controversy.

In these fragments, Reimarus applied the rationalist insights of the Enlightenment with an unprecedented vigour and enthusiasm. The concept of revelation was declared to be intellectually and morally untenable, in that the historical character of revelation is inconsistent with the universal and necessary character of rational truth (a point which Lessing himself made forcefully). In any case, if revelation did take place in history, our knowledge of it would be dependent upon eyewitness reports of that revelation, thus making divine revelation dependent upon the reliability of human beings. Furthermore, if salvation was made to depend upon acceptance of a truth which was available only at, or after, a certain point in history, it necessarily followed that knowledge of these truths, and hence salvation, were an impossibility for those who lived before this point. It is in this work that the 'scandal of particularity' is first stated with its full force in the modern period.

But perhaps the most radical suggestion Reimarus made is found in the final fragment, entitled 'On the aims of Jesus and his disciples'. This concerned the nature of our knowledge of Jesus Christ, and raised the questions of whether the gospel accounts of Jesus had been tampered with by the early Christians. Reimarus argued that a radical dichotomy exists between the beliefs and intentions of Jesus himself, and those of the apostolic church. Jesus' language and images of God were, according to Reimarus, those of a Jewish apocalyptic visionary, with a radically limited chronological and political reference and relevance. Jesus accepted the late Jewish expectation of a Messiah who would deliver his people from Roman occupation, and believed that God would assist him in this task. His cry of dereliction on the cross represented his final realization that he had been deluded and mistaken.

However, according to Reimarus, the disciples were not prepared to leave things like this. They invented the idea of a 'spiritual redemption', in the place of Jesus' concrete political vision of an Israel liberated from foreign occupation. They invented the idea of the resurrection of Jesus, in order to cover up the embarrassment caused by the death of Jesus. As a result, the disciples invented doctrines quite unknown to Jesus, such as his death being an atonement for human sin, adding such ideas to the biblical text to make it harmonize with their beliefs. As a result, the New

Testament as we now have it is riddled with fraudulent interpolations. The real Jesus of history has thus been concealed by the apostolic church, which has substituted a fictitious Christ of faith, the redeemer of humanity from sin, in the place of a thoroughly human figure, whose failure to live up to his followers' expectations led to their preferring a glorious invention to a failed reality.

Albert Schweitzer summarizes the importance of Reimarus' radical suggestions as follows: according to Reimarus, if

> . . . we desire to gain an historical understanding of Jesus' teaching, we must leave behind what we learned in the catechism regarding the metaphysical divine sonship, the Trinity, and similar dogmatic conceptions, and go out into a wholly Jewish world of thought. Only those who carry the teachings of the catechism back into the preaching of the Jewish Messiah will arrive at the idea that he was the founder of a new religion. To all unprejudiced persons it is manifest that 'Jesus has not the slightest intention of doing away with the Jewish religion and putting another in its place.'[14]

Jesus was simply a Jewish political figure, who confidently expected to cause a decisive and victorious popular rising against Rome, and was shattered by his failure.

Although Reimarus found few, if any, followers at the time, he raised questions which would become of fundamental importance in subsequent years. In particular, his explicit distinction between the legitimate historical Jesus and the fictitious Christ of faith proved to be of enormous significance. The resulting 'quest of the historical Jesus' arose as a direct result of the growing rationalist suspicion that the New Testament 'portrayal of Christ (*Christusbild*)' was a dogmatic invention. It was possible to reconstruct the real historical figure of Jesus, and disentangle him from the dogmatic ideas in which the apostles had clothed him.

By 1790, the Enlightenment appeared to be at its zenith in Germany. Yet developments were taking place which would redirect the movement, and open a new chapter in the making of modern German Christology. It is to those developments that we must turn.

2

F. D. E. Schleiermacher

Pure rationalism became increasingly unpopular as the eighteenth century drew to its close. In part, this was due to a degree of popular revulsion against the excesses of the French Revolution, especially the Reign of Terror; this suggested to many that the new Age of Reason had perhaps less to offer humanity than they had hoped for. But other developments were taking place, reducing the credibility and appeal of rationalism. Two such developments are of particular importance: empiricism and romanticism. We have already touched upon the importance of the former to the ending of the 'Age of Pure Reason' (see pp. 16–17); the story now needs to be told in greater detail.

The Revolt against Reason: Empiricism and Romanticism

Under the influence of the type of empiricism associated with John Locke, many German writers of the 1780s and 1790s began to have doubts about the pure rationalism of the early Enlightenment. The seminal doctrines of rationalism, as found in the writings of Descartes, Spinoza, Leibnitz and Christian Wolff, can be summarized in three propositions:

1. the external world can be known by reason alone.
2. knowledge constitutes a system.
3. the proper method of inquiry is deductive.

We have already noted the impact of such rationalist presuppositions upon G. E. Lessing, and especially in relation to his hesitations concerning the relation of historical and rational knowledge.

British empiricism raised a series of difficulties for this standpoint. John Locke (1632–1704) rejected the notion of *a priori* knowledge, insisting upon the priority of experience over knowledge. Locke himself distinguished two types of experience: external sensation and internal reflection. However, the popularization of Locke's ideas by Etienne Bonnot de Condillac (1714–80) led to the aspects of Locke's epistemology relating to the role of external sensation being emphasized, with a corresponding neglect of his theories concerning internal reflection.[1] In his three-volume *Treatise of Human Nature* (1739–40), David Hume argued that the human knowledge of the world was limited to a series of perceptions (that is, ideas and impressions) gained from observation and introspection. All concepts and terms which were not derived from experience and observation (such as innate ideas) were to be rejected.[2]

As we noted earlier (pp. 16–17), the growing impact of British empiricism can be seen in the writings of Immanuel Kant (1724–1804), especially his *Critique of Pure Reason*. Kant agreed with empiricists such as Locke in denying the existence of innate ideas. No ideas could be held to be known prior to sense experience. However, David Hume had pointed out the sceptical aspects of empiricism, and demonstrated that the most fundamental human beliefs and values could not be validated by an appeal to sensory experience. (According to Hume, these beliefs are best explained as the result of an ultimately inexplicable natural human inclination to hold them.) Detecting a fatal weakness at this point, Kant argued for the need to integrate rationalism and empiricism within a single theory.

Kant's approach, as developed in the *Critique of Pure Reason*, can be summarized as follows. Experience is a complex activity, embracing a number of different categories (such as time and space). Reason acts as a grid or framework, by which our sense experience is organized and interpreted – for example, into the 'categories' of space or time. Experience is thus seen as more than mere sensation; it is an active phenomenon, in which the mind is active. In this manner, Kant was able

37

to achieve at least a partial synthesis of rationalism and empiricism. The idea of 'pure reason' is thus seen to be something of a fiction; reason required to be supplemented with experience, as much as experience needs to be actively interpreted by reason.

With this criticism of the omnicompetence of reason, the credibility of the earlier Enlightenment attitude to the religious role of reason became undermined. For Lessing, there was an unbridgeable gap between the realms of the truths of reason and experience; Kant's analysis suggested that this gap could, in fact, be bridged. The force of Lessing's metaphysical argument against traditional Christologies was thus significantly blunted as the eighteenth century came to a close. Attention would now turn decisively towards the exploration of the chronological and existential aspects of the 'faith and history' debate. Lessing's arguments had indicated that there was nothing to be gained by the investigation of the history of Jesus of Nazareth; on the basis of Lessing's rationalist presuppositions, no historical event or historical figure could give access to the kind of truth necessary for the construction of a religious or moral system. With the demise of the credibility of pure rationalism, a new interest in history developed.

The second development which eroded the credibility and appeal of rationalism was the rise of German Romanticism. In the closing decade of the eighteenth century, increasing misgivings came to be expressed concerning the arid quality and severe spiritual limtations of rationalism. Reason, once seen as a liberator, came increasingly to be regarded as spiritually enslaving. These anxieties were not expressed so much within university faculties of philosophy as within literary and artistic circles, particularly in the Prussian capital, Berlin, where the Schlegel brothers – August Wilhelm (1767–1845) and Friedrich (1772–1829) – became particularly influential.

'Romanticism' is notoriously difficult to define.[3] The movement is perhaps best seen as a reaction against certain of the central themes of the Enlightenment, most notably the claim that reality can be known to the human reason. This reduction of reality to a series of rationalized simplicities seemed, to the Romantics, to be a culpable and crude misrepresentation. Where the Enlightenment appealed to the human reason, Romanticism made an appeal to the human imagination, which was capable of recognizing the profound sense of mystery which arises from realizing that the human mind cannot comprehend even the finite world, let alone the infinity beyond this. A strong sense of standing upon the borderlands of some greater reality, which the Romantics held to be both unknown and unknowable to pure reason, pervades the movement, and proved to be enormously attractive to an age which had become increasingly bored with the banalities of rationalism.

The ethos of the movement, like that of Enlightenment rationalism, proved capable of crossing national frontiers, with the result that German Romanticism soon made its presence felt in England. The basic ethos of the movement is expressed particularly well in the writings of the English poet William Wordsworth (1770–1850), who spoke of the human imagination in terms of transcending the limitations of human reason, and reaching beyond its bounds to sample the infinite through the finite. Imagination

Is but another name for absolute power
And clearest insight, amplitude of mind,
And Reason in her most exalted mood.

Romanticism thus found itself equally unhappy with traditional Christian doctrines and the rationalist moral platitudes of the Enlightenment. They both failed to do justice to the complexity of the world in an attempt to reduce the 'mystery of the universe' – to use a phrase found in the writings of August Wilhelm Schlegel – to neat formulae.

A marked limitation of the competence of reason may be discerned in such sentiments. Reason threatens to limit the human mind to what may be deduced; the imagination is able to liberate the human spirit from this self-imposed bondage, and allow it to discover new depths of reality – a vague and tantalizing 'something', which can be discerned in the world of everyday realities. The infinite is somehow present in the finite, and may be known through feeling and the imagination. As John Keats (1795–1821) put it, 'I am certain of nothing except the holiness of the heart's affections, and the truth of the imagination.'

The reaction against the aridity of reason was thus complemented by emphasis upon the epistemological significance of human feelings and emotions. Under the influence of Novalis (Friedrich von Hardenberg, 1772–1801), German Romanticism came to develop two axioms concerning *das Gefühl* (a German term perhaps best translated as 'feeling' or 'sentiment', though neither conveys the full range of meanings associated with the original).

First, *das Gefühl* concerns the individual thinker, who becomes

39

aware of his or her subjectivity and inward individuality. Although there are clear connections between this idea and the later Enlightenment notion of the *Selbstdenker* – the individual who is aware of his or her subjectivity – there is nevertheless an emphasis here upon a yearning for solitude and the enhancement of individual emotions which is not characteristic of the Enlightenment. Rationalism may have made its appeal to individual reason; Romanticism retained the emphasis upon the individual, but supplanted a concern with reason by an new interest in the imagination and personal feeling. The Enlightenment looked inward to human reason; Romanticism looked inward to human feelings, seeing in these 'the way to all mysteries' (Novalis).

Second, *das Gefühl* is orientated towards the infinite and eternal, and provides the key to these higher realms. It is for this reason, Novalis declares, that the Enlightenment proscribed the imagination and feeling as 'heretical', in that they offered access to the 'magical idealism' of the infinite; by its wooden appeal to reason alone, the Enlightenment attempted to suppress knowledge of these higher worlds through an appeal to the aridities of philosophy. Human subjectivity and inwardness were now seen as a mirror of the infinite. A new emphasis came to be placed upon music as a 'revelation of a higher order than any morality or philosophy' (Bettina von Arnim, 1785–1859).

The development of Romanticism had considerable implications for Christianity in Europe. Those aspects of Christianity (especially Roman Catholicism) which rationalism found distasteful came to captivate the imaginations of the Romantics. Rationalism was seen to be experientially and emotionally deficient, incapable of meeting real human needs, traditionally addressed and satisfied by Christian faith. As F. R. de Chateaubriand (1768–1848) remarked of the situation in France in the first decade of the nineteenth century, 'there was a need for faith, a desire for religious consolation, which came from the very lack of that consolation for so long'. Similar sentiments can be instanced from the German context in the closing years of the eighteenth century.

That rationalism had failed to neutralize or destroy the appeal of religion is evident from developments in England, Germany and North America. The new strength evident in German Pietism and English evangelicalism in the eighteenth century is evidence of the failure of rationalism to provide a cogent alternative to the prevailing human sense of personal need and meaning. Philosophy came to be seen as sterile, academic in the worst sense of the word, in that it was detached from the outer realities of life and the inner life of the human consciousness.

It was in the context of these developments that the ideas of perhaps the most important German theologian of the nineteenth century developed. We may therefore turn to the religious ideas of Friedrich Daniel Ernst Schleiermacher (1768–1834), to explore the implications of these ideas for Christology.

The Dignity and Effect of Christ

Schleiermacher's background was that of Moravian Pietism, which placed considerable emphasis upon personal devotion to Christ. In 1796, Schleiermacher moved to Berlin to take up his new duties as a hospital chaplain. Within a year of his arrival, he had attached himself to 'The Athenaeum', a group of thinkers and writers who were hostile to the spirit of the Enlightenment. He mixed with leading figures of the Romantic movement, such as Novalis and Friedrich Schlegel. The outcome of this interaction was a theology deeply grounded in the outlook of Romanticism, with a new emphasis upon the role of the individual's religious consciousness and feeling.[4]

The first expression of Schleiermacher's theological method can be found in his *On Religion: Speeches to its Cultured Despisers*, published anonymously in 1799. (Although entitled 'Speeches (*Reden*)', the book did not actually have its origins in a series of lectures or addresses.) The work develops a defence of Christianity, based partly on the argument that religion is a vivid sense or consciousness of a greater whole, of which the individual is but part and upon which he or she is totally dependent. The essence of religion is declared to lie in a 'fundamental, distinct and integrative element of human life and culture'. This Schleiermacher identifies as a feeling of being totally and utterly dependent upon something infinite, which is nevertheless made known in and through finite things. Religion in general (rather than Christianity in particular) is commended as the necessary context of science and art, without which human culture is needlessly impoverished. There is relatively little of specifically Christological importance within the work; nevertheless, it set the scene for his *magnum opus* which, in its second edition (1834), established itself as the most important work of Protestant theology since Calvin's *Institutes* of 1559 – *The Christian Faith*.

In this work, which he often refers to affectionately as his *Glaubens-*

41

lehre ('Doctrine of Faith'), Schleiermacher emphasizes that the Christian faith is not primarily conceptual; rather, doctrines are to be seen as second-order expressions of its primary religious truth, the experience of redemption. Christian piety (*Frömmigkeit*) may be regarded as the fundamental basis of Christian theology; however, this should not be understood to mean the piety of the individual, but the corporate piety of the church. The essence of this piety is not some rational or moral principle, but *das Gefühl*, the immediate self-consciousness. The general human consciousness of being dependent is, according to Schleiermacher, recognized and interpreted within the context of the Christian faith as a sense of total dependence upon God. This 'feeling of absolute dependence (*das Gefühl schlechthinniger Abhängigkeit*)' constitutes the starting point for Christian theology. As A. E. Biedermann (see pp. 78–9) later commented, Schleiermacher's theology may be regarded as the subjection of the deep inner feelings of humanity to critical inquiry. The human intellect (*das Verstand*) reflects upon human feeling, and by doing so, interprets it. Critical introspection reveals that human subjectivity is dipolar, centring around consciousness of oneself, and consciousness of another, coexisting. There is an important connection with a Kantian epistemology here, in which experience – understood, however, as *das Gefühl* rather than sensations of the outside world – requires to be interpreted by a cognitive framework. Whereas Kant argued that this grid was provided by human reason, Schleiermacher argues that it is provided by Christian doctrine.[5]

So how does this feeling relate to Christology? Schleiermacher argues that its origins require to be explained. How do individuals come to develop this feeling of absolute dependence upon God? Schleiermacher answers this question in an early programmatic statement in *The Christian Faith*:

> Christianity is a monotheistic faith, belonging to the teleological
> type of religion, and is essentially distinguished from other such
> faiths by the fact that in it everything is related to the redemp-
> tion accomplished by Jesus of Nazareth.[6]

Schleiermacher argues that the origins of this feeling are to be located in the impact of Jesus of Nazareth upon the collective consciousness of the Christian community. (Note, incidentally, that Schleiermacher avoids a purely individualistic approach to such feelings; the feelings in question are the common property and heritage of the Christian church.) Schleiermacher thus argues that a Christology is to be inferred from the present impact of Jesus of Nazareth upon believers within the church, arguing back from the observed effect to its sufficient cause.

The question of the identity of Jesus comes to be inextricably linked with that of his function. The person of Jesus (which Schleiermacher expresses in terms of his *dignity*), must be commensurate with and grounded in his work (or *activity*), and vice versa, in that they are

> . . . most intimately related and mutually determined. So that it is vain to attribute to the Redeemer a higher dignity than the activity at the same time ascribed to him demands, since nothing is explained by this surplus of dignity. It is equally vain to attribute to him a greater activity than follows naturally from the dignity which one is ready to allow him . . . Therefore every doctrine of Christ is inconsistent, in which this equality (of dignity and activity) is not essential, whether it seeks to disguise the detraction from the dignity by praising him in great but really alien activities, or, conversely, seeks to compensate for the lesser influence which it allows him by highly exalting him, yet in a fashion which leads to no result.[7]

The doctrines of the person and work of Christ are so intimately connected that it is impossible to isolate them; a statement about the identity or dignity of Jesus is simultaneously a statement about his function or activity.

Schleiermacher argues that redemption consists in the stimulation and elevation of the natural human God-consciousness (*Gottesbewusstsein*) through the 'entrance of the living influence of Christ'. He attributes to Christ 'an absolutely powerful God-consciousness', which is impregnated with an assimilative power of such intensity that it is able to effect the redemption of humanity. Schleiermacher is perhaps less specific about the nature and manner of conception of this assimilative power than we might like. However, he seems to have in mind a model along the lines of a charismatic leader, who is able to communicate his socio-political vision with such clarity and power that it is both understood by his audience, yet captivates them in such a way that they are transformed by it and come to be caught up in it. Yet it remains his idea; he has assumed others into it, without compromisng his personal

43

uniqueness, in that it is and remains *his* vision:

> Let us now suppose that some person for the first time com-
> bines a naturally cohesive group into a civil community (legend
> tells of such cases in plenty); what happens is that the idea of
> the state first comes to consciousness in him, and takes pos-
> session of his personality as its immediate dwelling-place. Then
> he assumes the rest into the living fellowship of the idea. He
> does so by making them clearly conscious of the unsatisfactori-
> ness of their present condition by effective speech. The power
> remains with the founder of forming in them the idea which is
> the innermost principle of his own life, and of assuming them
> into the fellowship of that life.[8]

So who must Jesus of Nazareth be if he is able to have this effect?

Two central German terms – *Urbildlichkeit* and *Vorbildlichkeit* – are
employed by Schleiermacher in exploring this question, both of which
are difficult to translate adequately into English. In what follows, we
have used rather free paraphrases of the ideas, aiming to do justice to
Schleiermacher's theological understanding of these two terms, rather
than their literal meanings.

1. *Urbildlichkeit*, 'the quality of being an ideal'. For Schleiermacher,
Jesus of Nazareth is the ideal of human God-consciousness, and the
ultimate in human 'piety' (*Frömmigkeit*). Taken on its own, this notion
might seen to come close to the rationalist notion of Jesus as a human
moral example. Schleiermacher is able to evade this, in two ways. First,
he stresses that Jesus of Nazareth is not simply a moral example,
someone who illustrates permanent moral truths. He is the one ideal
example of a perfect human consciousness of God – a *religious*, rather
than a purely moral or rational, idea. Second, Christ possesses the
ability to communicate this God-consciousness to others, as noted above
– a quality which Schleiermacher discusses in terms of *Vorbildlichkeit*,
to which we may now turn.

2. *Vorbildlichkeit*, 'the quality of being able to evoke an ideal in
others'. Jesus of Nazareth is not simply the instantiation of an ideal, but
one who possesses an ability to evoke or arouse this quality in others.
On the basis of this approach, Schleiermacher criticizes existing manners
of conceiving the person of Christ. For Enlightenment writers, Jesus of
Nazareth was merely a religious teacher of humanity, or perhaps the

exemplar of a religious or moral principle. As noted earlier, this does not mean that Jesus established such principles or teachings; their authority lies in their being recognized to be consonant with rational ideas and values. The authority of Jesus is thus derivative and secondary, while that of reason is immediate and primary. Schleiermacher designates this as an 'empirical' understanding of the work of Christ, which 'attributes a redemptive activity on the part of Christ, but one which is held to consist only in bringing about an increasing perfection in us, and which cannot take place other than by teaching and example'.[9]

The understanding of the work of Christ associated with Protestant Orthodoxy receives equally blunt treatment. Dismissing this approach as 'magical', Schleiermacher insists that it improperly attributes to Christ a purely objective transaction (such as the forgiveness of sins or the imputation of righteousness) which 'is not mediated by anything natural, yet is attributed to a person'. By insisting that redemption comes by natural channels and eliminating the necessity for the category of the 'supernatural' in any discussion of Christology or soteriology, Schleiermacher believed he had removed a fundamental obstacle to Christian faith in an intellectual situation dominated by Enlightenment naturalism.

The approach that Schleiermacher adopts meets the Enlightenment critique of traditional Christologies in three respects:
1. He is able to avoid the difficulties raised by an ontological approach to the doctrine of the two natures of Christ by insisting that the doctrine refers to an immediate existential relationship. The relation between Christ's dignity and activity is such that he is to be treated as both divine and human, on account of his redemptive activity within the world. We shall explore this point further in the following section.
2. He is able to distance himself from the reductionist degree-Christology of the Enlightenment, which treated Jesus of Nazareth as an itinerant moral teacher. Christ is unique, Schleiermacher insists, precisely on account of the irreducible character of his God-consciousness.
3. He is able to meet growing historical scepticism concerning the gospels by arguing that these historical accounts merely substantiate and verify what may be had directly through critical introspection.

The Christological Heresies

In an earlier section, we noted how Schleiermacher insisted that dogmatics must attribute to Jesus the 'dignity' which his 'activity' demands. So what happens if this criterion is not met? The answer may be stated in a word: heresy. Not unbelief (which, in Schleiermacher's terms is something quite distinct), but *a deficient or truncated form of belief*, which ends up calling into question the foundations of the Christian faith itself. Schleiermacher argues that heresy is a deficient form of Christian belief which preserves the *appearance* of Christianity, yet contradicts its *essence*:

> If the distinctive essence of Christianity consists in the fact that in it all religious emotions are related to the redemption wrought by Jesus Christ, there will be two ways in which heresy can arise. That is to say: this fundamental formula will be retained in general . . . but *either* human nature will be so defined that a redemption in the strict case cannot be accomplished, *or* the Redeemer will be defined in such a way that he cannot accomplish redemption.[10]

Schleiermacher's discussion of heresy is of such interest that we shall consider it in detail, partly because it illuminates the distinction between heresy and unbelief, and partly because it shows the continuing need for the notion of 'heresy' in Christology, even if the word itself has become discredited in certain circles through overuse.[11]

If, as Schleiermacher suggests, the distinctive essence of Christianity consists in the fact that God has redeemed us through Jesus Christ, and in no-one else and in no other way, it must follow that the Christian understanding of God, Jesus Christ and human nature should be consistent with this understanding of redemption. Thus the Christian understanding of God must be such that he can effect the redemption of humanity through Christ; the Christian understanding of Christ must be such that God may effect our redemption through him; the Christian understanding of humanity must be such that redemption is both possible and genuine. In other words, it is essential that the Christian understanding of God, Christ, and humanity is *consistent with* the principle of redemption through Christ alone.

According to Schleiermacher, the rejection or denial of the principle that God has redeemed us through Jesus Christ is nothing less than the rejection of Christianity itself. In other words, to deny that God has redeemed us through Jesus Christ is to deny the most fundamental truth claim which the Christian faith dares to make. The distinction between what is *Christian* and what is not lies in whether this principle is accepted: the distinction between what is *orthodox* and what is *heretical*, however, lies in how this principle, once conceded and accepted, is understood. In other words, heresy is not a form of unbelief; it is something that arises within the context of faith itself. For Schleiermacher, heresy is fundamentally *an inadequate or inauthentic form of Christian faith*.

Heresy arises through accepting the basic principle, but interpreting its terms in such a way that internal inconsistency results. In other words, the principle is granted, but it is inadequately understood. The principle may be accepted, and yet:

1. it is interpreted in such a way that Christ cannot effect the redemption of humanity; *or*

2. it is interpreted in such a way that humanity – the object of redemption – cannot, in the proper sense of the term, be redeemed.

Let us examine each of these possibilities.

Who is the Redeemer? The answer given to this question must be able to account for the uniqueness of his office and for his ability to mediate between God and humanity. There must therefore be an essential similarity between Christ and humanity, if he is able to mediate between them and God, and yet at the same time there must be something fundamentally different about him. After all, not every human being *is* a redeemer, whereas all require *to be* redeemed. Heresy can arise simply by failing to uphold these two points simultaneously, so that the affirmation of one amounts to the denial of the other.

If the superiority of Jesus Christ over humanity is emphasized, without maintaining his essential similarity to them, his ability to reconcile humanity to God is lost, in that he no longer has a point of contact with those whom he is supposed to redeem. On the other hand, if his similarity to humanity is emphasized, without acknowledging that in at least one respect he is fundamentally different, then the Redeemer himself requires redemption. If the Redeemer is treated as being similar in every respect to humanity, he must be acknowledged to share the human need for redemption. Therefore *either* every human being must be thought of as a potential or actual redeemer, to a greater or lesser extent, *or else* the Redeemer cannot himself redeem.

It will be obvious that the doctrine of redemption through Christ requires that he should share the basics of the common human condition, *except* its need for redemption. According to Schleiermacher, orthodox

47

Christianity has upheld this crucial insight by insisting that Jesus Christ is at one and the same time both God and human. It would be much simpler to suggest that Jesus was just God, or just human; but to uphold the possibility and actuality of our redemption, it is necessary to insist that they are both true.

From the above discussion, it will be obvious that two heresies may arise through upholding the principle of redemption through Christ, but interpreting the person of Christ in such a way that this redemption becomes impossible. On the one hand, Jesus Christ loses his point of contact with those he is meant to redeem – thus giving rise to the heresy generally known as *Docetism*. On the other, he loses his essential dissimilarity from those whom he came to redeem, and comes to be treated simply as a particularly enlightened human being – thus giving rise to the heresy which Schleiermacher styles *Ebionitism*.

In a similar manner, Schleiermacher explores the question: who are the redeemed? The answer to this question must be capable of explaining why redemption is necessary from outside humanity itself – in other words, why we cannot redeem ourselves. The object of redemption must both require redemption in the first place, and be capable of accepting that redemption when it is offered. These two aspects of the question must be maintained at one and the same time, just like the humanity and divinity of Christ.

If the human need for redemption is granted, yet our powerlessness to redeem ourselves is denied, the conclusion follows that we could be the agents of our own redemption. Reconciliation could then be effected by at least some individuals, if not by all, to varying degrees – which immediately contradicts the principle of redemption through Jesus Christ alone. And if our impotence to accept redemption, once it is offered to us, is denied, that redemption again becomes an impossibility. Broadly speaking, these two positions correspond to the Pelagian and the Manichaean heresies.

The four heresies described above may, according to Schleiermacher, be regarded as the four natural heresies of the Christian faith, each of which arises through an inadequate interpretation of the person and work of Christ. For Schleiermacher, it is no accident that these were by far the most important heresies to be debated in the early church. Christological considerations are thus shown to lie at the heart of the Christian faith. A defective Christology thus turns out to be tantamount to a deficient and inadequate conception of Christianity itself. Within the context of

Schleiermacher's conception of theology, Christology can thus be seen to be of central and defining importance both to the Christian faith and to its resulting theology. Although his theology is experience-orientated, it also proves to be Christ-centred.

Although Schleiermacher cannot really be said to have had followers, in the strict sense of the term, his influence transcended that of a mere school of thought. His critique of the rationalism of the Enlightenment opened the door for new styles of Christology in the later nineteenth and twentieth centuries. Yet to the religiously restless and politically alienated generation which immediately succeeded him, it seemed that his ideas were fatally flawed. Such was the ferocity of the left-wing Hegelian attack upon his ideas that Karl Marx, surveying the condition of German culture in 1844, concluded that the criticism of religion was essentially complete. It is to this criticism, and its Christological implications, that we now turn.

3

The Hegelian School: from Strauss to Feuerbach

If Schleiermacher was one of the major luminaries in the cultural firmament at Berlin in the early nineteenth century. the other was the great philosopher Georg Wilhelm Friedrich Hegel (1770–1831). It is beyond doubt that Hegel is the most significant German philosopher of the nineteenth century, exercising a major influence over the development of philosophy, theology and political thought which has extended to our own day. Hegel's philosophy of history has had a decisive impact upon the development of Marxism, with the result that the Marxist heritage of the West, until so recently a major force in world politics and culture, can be argued to owe its intellectual foundations and resilience to its Hegelian foundations. Indeed, on a more theological note, the Christology of Wolfhart Pannenberg (see pp. 187–98), which rests on an appeal to universal history, can be argued to illustrate the substantial and continuing impact of Hegelian ideas upon the themes of the present work.

It is therefore inevitable that this volume must engage with the Hegelian heritage in German-language Christology. Not only is an apparently Christological idea (incarnation – *Menschwerdung*) at the heart of Hegel's all-embracing philosophical system; that system itself is quasi-religious in its nature. Readers are warned that the present chapter of this book is its most difficult, on account of both the inherent complexity and wide scope of Hegel's ideas. Attempts to simplify those ideas, such as those to be offered here, will inevitably fall far short of

50

the reality. In view of the difficulties that Hegel's system offers to those who have not the time to engage with it fully, it is proposed to offer a brief overview of his system, before exploring its more specifically Christological aspects later.

G. W. F. Hegel

Hegel's general theory of religion could be summarized along the following lines. The goal of both religion and philosophy is to bring about the reconciliation (*Versöhnung*) between humanity and divinity by which human destiny can be achieved. This reconciliation is thwarted by human alienation, which has as its inevitable consequences separation and estrangement from God. In the incarnation, the possibility of reconciliation (in Hegel's sense of the word) is proclaimed and embodied in an historical form.

God is to be regarded as 'Spirit (*Geist*)', a term which here conveys the two ideas of rationality and the supernatural. He (or she, or it: Hegel is slightly vague here) has appeared in and is made known through history. Every religion, in its own different and distinctive manner, is to be regarded as an expression of the same basic thing – namely, the 'nature of Spirit which has entered the world to bring itself to consciousness'. All these expressions of the nature of Spirit are fragmentary and imperfect; each contains elements of the truth, but is unable either to perceive the whole truth or to recognize or account for the existence of truth in others.

Christianity is different, according to Hegel. Christianity alone 'represents the being of Spirit in realized form'. Christianity is the supreme religious representation of the great philosophical truth of incarnation – that is, the union of God with humanity. The coming of Christ is the 'axis upon which the history of the world turns', in that the essential unity of divinity and humanity is made known and historically incarnated at a specific moment in history. For the thinkers of the Enlightenment, this represented a 'scandal of particularity'; for Hegel, it is seen in a very different light. On the basis of his axiom that the universal must pass through the particular, Hegel declares that it is entirely proper that a universal truth should appear in a specific form in this way.

Hegel himself indicates the potentially high importance of Christology in this respect. Having defined incarnation as the 'speculative mid-point (*Mittelpunkt*) of philosophy', and having emphasized the supremacy of Christianity as a means of representing such philosophical truths at the religious level, the importance of Christology within Hegel's system can easily be ascertained (although it must be emphasized that he did not employ the language of classical Christology in its exposition.) Hegel appears to establish the necessity, possibility and actuality of the 'incarnation' of God in a single individual on the basis of the anthropology of the divine-human union. The ideal unity of God and humanity is demonstrated through the appearance (*Erscheinung*) of God in the world in the flesh. Hegel's distinction between *Vorstellung* ('representation') and *Begriff* ('concept') permitted the criticism of specific forms of religious expressions without undermining their philosophical content.

On the basis of this mediating approach, it was possible to assert that the eternal divine 'Idea' or 'Archetype' found full realization in the specific concrete instance of the historic human figure of Jesus of Nazareth, an idea developed with particular clarity by the right-wing Hegelian Philipp Konrad Marheineke (1780–1846). Although the followers of Hegel and Schleiermacher might have very different reasons for making this assertion, both grounded the doctrines of particular incarnation, historical revelation and positive religion upon it.

Hegel's Christology has been the subject of considerable attention recently, reflecting the renaissance in Hegel studies in general.[1] In his earlier period, Hegel's Christology was remarkably similar to that of the Enlightenment, Jesus being represented as an intinerant Kantian. In his later writings, however, Hegel moved away from this position to his mature discussion of the *Vorstellung* of the incarnation. The Hegelian analysis of sensuous experience in general is characterized by the transition from 'representation' (*Vorstellung*) to 'concept' (*Begriff*). Hegel understands *Vorstellung* to be the product of the analytical faculty of reason (*Verstand*) and the imaginative faculty of *Phantasie* to yield a perceptual image of experience. As such, *Vorstellung* is the mediating principle between *Anschauung* and *Denken*, between mere subjectivity and rational, or pure, objectivity. The philosophical mediation of truth is characterized by the constant oscillation between *Vorstellung* and *Begriff*, as one is compared with the other and refined accordingly. Hegel argues that such religious *Vorstellungen* are the first cognitive representations of the concept (*Begriff*) of God (that is, the Infinite).

Religion initially comprises *Vorstellungen* of God which, although speculatively deficient, in that they combine 'finite' and 'infinite' elements, are capable of being resolved into the *Begriff* of God. It is therefore necessary to progress from the sensuously mediated images and experiences of *Vorstellung* to the *Begriff* of God. Hegel's *ordo cognoscendi* – that is, the order in which things are known – is thus:

1. *Anschauung* – a general perception or experience;
2. *Vorstellung* – a way of representing that experience, and making some preliminary judgments concerning its importance;
3. *Gedank* – the idea which arises in response to these representations;
4. *Begriff* – the reality which lies behind both experience and the human attempts to comprehend it.

The two most important notions here are those of *Vorstellung* and *Begriff*. In effect, Hegel is able to argue along the following lines. All human religions attempt to represent the pure concept of God; the fact that they employ different representations does not detract from the fact that they are all representations of the same concept. Hegel emphasizes that in the *ordo essendi* (that is, the way in which things are in reality), the *Begriff* is prior to the *Vorstellungen* which embody it. For Hegel, the incarnation is the supreme religious *Vorstellung* from which theological and philosophical speculation may begin.[2]

This *Vorstellung*, according to Hegel, is empirically and objectively grounded in the history of Jesus of Nazareth. Hegel assumes that the idea (*Gedank*) of incarnation is common to all religions, although the Christian representation (*Vorstellung*) of this idea alone is absolutely adequate (*schlechthin gemäss*). Although *Vorstellungen* in all religions implicitly, and with varying degrees of adequacy, bear witness to the incarnational truth of the human and divine natures and to the reconciling action of God in the midst of human alienation, it is the Christian *Vorstellung* of this idea which is supreme. Christianity renders explicit what is only implicit in other religions. Thus the principle which Hegel understands the *Gedank* of incarnation to express is that the infinite Spirit (God) and the finite spirit (humanity) are neither radically different nor mutually incompatible.

The *Begriff* of God as the subsistent cause of all reality is revealed in the history of Jesus of Nazareth. The *Vorstellung* of the incarnation is thus inextricably linked with the external empirical event of the life of Jesus, although the process of reflection upon this event, by which the *Vorstellung* is transformed to the *Gedank* and finally to the *Begriff*, necessarily entails increasing the epistemic distance or knowledge-gap between this history and the concept underlying it.

It will, however, be clear that there are certain questions raised by Hegel's discussion of the *Vorstellung* of the incarnation which require further consideration. Upon what grounds can the identification of the historical individual Jesus of Nazareth with the speculative principle of the incarnation be justified? It will be evident that others in the course of history made similar claims. How may Jesus be distinguished from them? Hegel's philosophy stresses what we might call an 'incarnational principle': that is to say, that it is in the nature of God to reveal himself in and through human nature. God and human nature do not represent two mutually exclusive entities; rather, they are capable of real intercommunion. For Hegel, this principle reaches its climax (at least, in terms of its public representation) in the incarnation of Jesus Christ, which he held to be a perfect instantiation of the unity of divinity and humanity.

But why Jesus? Hegel's philosophical principle of incarnation is rationally justified within the context of his system; but what of its specific connection with an historical event, in the life of Jesus of Nazareth? While Hegel concedes that others made similar claims, or that such claims were made on their behalf, he insists that these were but imperfect manifestations of the infinite Spirit:

> The Idea . . . when it was ripe and the time was fulfilled, was able to attach itself only to Christ, and to realize itself only in him. The nature of Spirit is still imperfectly realized in the heroic deeds of Hercules. The history of Christ, however, belongs to the community, since it is absolutely adequate in relation to the Idea . . . It is the Spirit, the indwelling idea, which has witnessed to Christ's mission, and this is the verification for those who have believed and for us who possess the developed concept (*Begriff*).[3]

The weakness of this argument will be evident. Hegel actually employs an argument similar to Calvin's *testimonium internum Spiritus Sancti* to justify his Christological commitment. By doing so, he effectively weakens the link between the *Vorstellung* and the *Begriff* of incarnation, so that it was possible for his successors to divorce what he had held together. If the grounds for holding together the history of Jesus of

Nazareth and the concept of incarnation (understood in the Hegelian sense of the term) were defined solely in terms of a direct, immediate, inward certainty given by the Spirit, it would not prove difficult for a critic to challenge this somewhat weak Christological principle.

The breakdown of this mediating *modus vivendi* between philosophy and theology may be regarded as having taken place in the fourth and fifth decades of the century. Although there were Hegelians – such as Marheineke, Karl Daub (1765–1836) and Karl Friederich Göschel (1784–1861) – upon the right wing of the Hegelian school who were able and willing to integrate Hegel's speculative God-man with their orthodox Christology, there were others upon the left wing of the school who were not. The Hegelian heritage proved to be profoundly ambiguous. Where Marheineke regarded Hegel as a major ally in the church's struggle against unbelief, more perceptive observers noted the manner in which Hegel had reconstructed and redefined central theological ideas – such as incarnation – until they virtually disappeared from view, having been replaced by secular philosophical notions. It is the challenge posed to the Christology of Orthodoxy and of right-wing Hegelianism by the work of David Friedrich Strauss, Ferdinand Christian Baur, Ludwig Feuerbach and Karl Marx which we shall consider in the present chapter. First, we may consider the social context within which their ideas are to be located.

The Social Context of Left-Wing Hegelianism

As noted earlier (p. 17), during the period of the Enlightenment, the German universities came to be seen as centres of social protest against the conservativism of the *ancien régime*. They fostered the progressive and modernist ideology of the Enlightenment, in conscious opposition to that of the past. A critical attitude to the religious past was seen as an integral element of this programme of social protest: the emphasis on present religious experience and rational reflection was partly due to a determination that the authority of the past should not be allowed to intrude on the present. The need to deprive the old order of its intellectual and cultural weapons led to a sustained assault upon the notion that the past was endowed with any authority or insights currently denied to the individual thinker. A conscious decision to disarm the past of intellectual authority thus *preceded* the devising of academic strategies by which this goal might be achieved.

With occasional exceptions, on the other hand, the German churches, especially the Lutheran church, were usually regarded as sharing the vested interests of the established order. In part, this social development rests upon Martin Luther's 'Doctrine of the Two Kingdoms (*Zwei-Reich-Lehre*)', which emphasized the close links between church and state – and, in the view of at least some commentators, contributed in no small manner to the development of the 'German Church Crisis' of the 1930s, in which the Nazi Government was able to exercise considerable influence over the German Lutheran church. To a certain extent, the eighteenth-century Lutheran church in Germany justified its social position and religious views by an appeal to tradition – a Gordian knot which the Enlightenment felt able to cut. A clash of ideologies thus conditioned the theological disagreements between the academy and church of the period. They were seen as one specific conflict in the more general confrontation between the orders of the past and the future – a confrontation in which neutrality or inconsistency were generally regarded as unthinkable.

This tension did not disappear with the waning of the Enlightenment; it was, however, modified to a significant extent, in that the criticism of the established church and its doctrinal formulations extended beyond the universities. The post-Napoleonic period seemed to many merely to restore the same reactionary state of affairs as that which had existed in the mid-eighteenth century. The social unrest accompanying the new political activism of the 1830s led to a polarization between cultural and political radicalism on the one hand and conservatism on the other developing in the 1830s and 1840s. This was reflected in the emergence of right- and left-wing Hegelianism.

The strong cultural affiliations of Hegel's system (whether viewed from an idealist or materialist stance) inevitably meant that 'Hegelianism' was prone to echo cultural tensions. Karl Rosenkranz's (1805–79) comic drama of 1840 (in which the problem of succession within the Hegelian school was to be settled by a shooting match at Berlin) hints at the seriousness of the social and political divisions within German society at the time, which were echoed in the tensions within Hegelianism following Hegel's death. The sensation accompanying the publication of D. F. Strauss's *Leben Jesu* ('Life of Jesus', 1835), to be discussed presently, was partly due to its appeal to socially and religiously alienated progressive elements, who recognized it as a useful propaganda weapon in their concerted attack on each and every aspect of the German establishment. An important contemporary witness to this polarization is W. H. Riehl, who argued that the period witnessed the emergence of a new 'intellectual proletariat' which had broken with the old social and intellectual order, and saw themselves as the new church militant.

The evidence for this suggestion is considerable, especially in the case of theology. Of the total graduate output of German universities in the 1830s, two in every five were theologians. Ecclesiastical positions of any kind became increasingly difficult to find: despite the sharp increase in population which is so significant a feature of German social history in the 1830s, the number of ecclesiastical posts available decreased over the period 1815–40. Perhaps three or four theological graduates in every ten might hope to find employment of this nature.

The situation in the universities was even more bleak, with contractions, moratoria and salary cuts becoming a regular feature of academic life. Simultaneously, however, establishment figures (such as the landed aristocracy) were given particular preference in obtaining positions in the civil and ecclesiastical administration, causing intense anger among those outside this privileged section of the community. As a result, there were many disaffected and unemployed graduate theologians who saw themselves as members of the new 'intellectual proletariat', prepared to assault the civil and religious establishment. The emergence of a socially alienated, theologically literate, anti-establishment lay intelligentsia is one of the more significant consequences of the social history of Germany in the 1830s.

In turning to deal with the Christologies of left-wing Hegelian writers, their social context must not be ignored. There was a widespread reaction against institutional Christianity on the part of a 'Young Germany' which had expected the French Revolution to usher in a new and progressive period in German history. Nothing of the sort happened, and many young people were consequently disillusioned and alienated from the establishment, whether church or state. And if direct attacks upon the church were unrealistic, given the political situation of the time, then that church could nevertheless be attacked *indirectly*, by way of its foundational doctrines. If the existence of the church depended upon its central legitimating doctrines, such as the divinity of Christ, then an attack on the plausibility of such doctrines would serve to undermine the social credibility and status of the churches. The attraction of this possibility to a socially and religiously alienated group of intellectuals will be obvious. We may therefore begin our analysis by considering the views of David Friedrich Strauss (1808–74), whose *Life of Jesus* achieved precisely this effect for exactly these reasons.

D. F. Strauss

In his early phase, Strauss showed considerable interest in the writings of Schleiermacher, which appear to have functioned as a catalyst for his conversion to Hegelianism.[4] Nevertheless, the Hegelianism which Strauss espoused was considerably different from that of Marheineke. For Hegel, the necessity and actuality of the incarnation could be justified rationally, thus permitting the *Begriff* of the realization of the idea of divine-human unity to be harmonized with the *Vorstellung* of the incarnation of Christ. Strauss, however, pointed out that this left unanswered two crucial questions:

1. Must this idea necessarily be realized as one specific individual?
2. Is speculative philosophy in any position to establish whether a given individual (such as Jesus of Nazareth) is, in fact, the historical realization of this idea?

For Strauss, the answer to both these questions was an emphatic 'No', despite the protestations of right-wing Hegelians. The only way of establishing whether a specific individual was, in fact, the historical realization of the idea of divine-human unity was through critical-historical enquiry: the historical facts of the gospel narratives and their religious significance were not necessarily related. In order to establish the significance of Jesus of Nazareth, it was essential to undertake an empirical enquiry into the gospel narratives, independent of the presuppositions of speculative philosophy. One the one hand, this historical enquiry would not be capable of determining whether this idea necessarily found historical embodiment. Yet on the other, it would be capable of deciding whether any specific individual (such as Jesus of Nazareth) actually was the unique embodiment of that idea.

These ideas were developed with force in his celebrated *Life of Jesus* (1835). The remarkable impact of this books appears, as we have seen, to have been due as much to cultural as to theological consider-ations, in that it was widely perceived to be a challenge to the reaction-ary social and political establishment of Restoration Germany, of which the Lutheran church was a central pillar. However, the work also posed a serious challenge to contemporary orthodox Christology, for four reasons.

First, Strauss insisted that the Christian proclamation had to be treated as philosophical in nature. Hence it could not be regarded as having any essential or necessary connection with any historical event, or series of events, such as the existence of a God-man in general, or the assertion that this God-man was the historic figure of Jesus of Nazareth. In other words, the truth of dogmatic claims was not dependent upon, and could not be verified with reference to, the gospel accounts of Jesus of Nazareth. This conclusion follows directly from Strauss's Hegelian presuppositions.

Second, the investigation of the gospel accounts of Jesus of Nazareth must be regarded as an historical, rather than a theological, undertaking. Historico-critical exegesis alone may be permitted to establish the historical veracity of the gospel accounts: indeed, if the truth claims of Christianity are based upon the historical veracity of these accounts, the truth claims must be based upon the independent findings of historical science. As such, history is prior to dogma.

Third, the gospel writers must be regarded as sharing the mythical worldview (*Weltanschauung*) of their cultural situation. Strauss thus distances himself from Reimarus's suggestion that the evangelists distorted their accounts of Jesus of Nazareth, whether unconsciously or deliberately, and argues that mythical language is the natural mode of expression of a primitive group culture which had yet to rise to the level of abstract conceptualization. For Reimarus, the gospel writers were either telling the truth or lying (for whatever reason), his own researches having convinced him that the latter option was the more probable. Strauss's distinctive contribution to the debate was to introduce the category of *Mythos* ('myth'). Strauss understood the concept of 'myth' to be a reflection of the gospel writers' social conditioning and cultural outlook. To suggest that their writings were partly 'mythical' was thus not so much a challenge to their integrity, but simply an acknowledgment of the premodern outlook of the period in which they were written.

Fourth, Strauss argued forcefully that no absolutely perfect principle of religion can be actualized in history at any point. For Strauss, the very idea of an 'absolute religion' or an 'absolute personality' cannot be located in history without gross self-contradiction. Hegel's insistence upon this possibility (which had been welcomed by the exponents of traditional Christology) was thus to be disregarded.

Whereas both rationalist and supernaturalist accepted the gospel accounts as factual accounts of the history of Jesus of Nazareth (the former regarding miracles as misunderstandings of natural events, the latter as literal accounts of divine intervention), Strauss argued that the gospel accounts are heavily impregnated with mythical elements. Strauss understands 'myth' to be an expression of the religious imagination, located at the level of *Vorstellung* rather than *Begriff*. Indeed, Strauss is able to develop an Hegelian interpretation of myth as a primitive stage in the self-development of 'spirit' through its own history. In the third and fourth editions of the *Life of Jesus*, Strauss distinguishes three levels of myth:

> *Evangelical myth* is a narrative relating directly or indirectly to Jesus, which may be considered not as the expression of a fact (*Tatsache*), but as the impression of an idea of his earliest followers . . . *Pure myth* in the gospel has two sources . . . [one is] the Messianic ideas and expectations existing according to their several forms in the Jewish mind before Jesus, and independently of him; the other is that particular impression which was left by the personal character, actions and fate of Jesus, and which served to modify the Messianic idea of his people. *Historical myth* (*Mythus an der Geschichte*) has for its background a definite individual fact which has been seized upon by religious enthusiasm, and surrounded with mythical conceptions deriving from the idea of the Christ.[5]

The supernaturalists, according to Strauss, remained loyal to the gospel text, and as a result demanded belief in the incredible; the naturalists distorted the text beyond credible limits in an attempt to posit a natural event which might underlie the gospel account. For Strauss, the explanation lies in myth, the presence of which in a gospel passage was a positive criterion of its lack of historicity. Although Strauss does not deny that an historical event may lie behind myth, myths themselves are not to be regarded as historical formulations. Thus Strauss argues that although the presence of myth may be detected in practically every aspect of the gospel accounts of the history of Jesus of Nazareth, genuinely historical events may be supposed to underlie this history. Thus it may be stated that Jesus actually lived, that he had disciples, that he regarded himself as the Messiah, and that he was crucified.

Furthermore, Strauss concedes that the gospel accounts of Jesus' discourses are substantially correct. Nevertheless, for reasons which we noted above, this factual kernel at the heart of the mythical husk is of no significance. Also, at every point which might be deemed theologically significant by orthodox criteria (such as many details of the passion accounts, and the accounts of the resurrection and ascension), Strauss detects extensive mythical elements, thus indicating the unhistorical nature of these narratives. Thus, for example, he argues that because the idea of 'resurrection' includes the obviously supernatural idea of the return to life of a dead human being, a rational observer is compelled to conclude that 'either Jesus was not really dead, or he did not really rise again'. Strauss thus seemed to many of his contemporaries to destroy both the foundations of the supernaturalist citadel and the compromises of rationalism, and thus to oblige those who followed him to deal with the New Testament foundations of Christology in a new manner.

Strauss is thus able to eliminate the need to explain gospel passages such as the resurrection account on either supernatural or natural grounds: the account is ultimately an expression of the cultural consciousness of a primitive people. There is simply no possiblity of mediation between historico-critical investigation and Christian faith. As such, faith must either collapse, or else must be reinterpreted by dissociating the dogmatic principle of incarnation from the claim that this idea had been fully embodied in a concrete historical individual, Jesus of Nazareth. In effect, Strauss argues that the *Vorstellung* and *Begriff* of incarnation (that is, the unity of the divine and human spirit) can be kept strictly separate, and that the latter can replace the former, fulfilling the same religious need in a more adequate manner.

So what are the results of this approach? Strauss himself notes that the resurrection of Christ is of central importance to Christian faith:

The root of faith in Jesus was the conviction of his resurrection. He who had been put to death, however great during his life, could not, it was thought, be the Messiah: his miraculous restoration to life proved so much the more strongly that he *was* the Messiah. Freed by his resurrection from the kingdom of shades, and at the same time elevated above the sphere of earthly humanity, he was now translated to the heavenly regions, and had taken his place at the right hand of God.[6]

Strauss notes that this understanding of what he terms 'the Christology of the orthodox system' has come under considerable attack since the Enlightenment. However, the Christology offered by rationalism fails to satisfy at the religious level. 'For a Christ who is only a distinguished human being creates indeed no difficulty to the understanding, but is not the Christ in whom the Church believes.'[7]

What, then, of the approach adopted by Schleiermacher? Strauss describes this Christological style as 'eclectic': Schleiermacher has 'saved many in these days from the narrowness of Supranaturalism, and the emptiness of Rationalism'. Yet, as Strauss emphasizes, the cost of this is remarkably, perhaps even unacceptably, high:

> Its disagreement with the faith is the most conspicuous in the position, that the facts of the resurrection and ascension do not form essential parts of the Christian faith. For the belief in the resurrection of Christ is the foundation stone, without which the Christian church could not have been built.[8]

And what of Strauss's own position? Cryptic to the end, Strauss makes it difficult for his readers to define his own stance with any degree of certainty. However, it seems that the way of dealing with the resurrection that Strauss himself commends is that adopted by the theologian who, when preaching at Easter,

> ... will indeed set out from the sensible fact of the resurrection of Christ, but he will dwell chiefly on the being buried and rising again with Christ, which the Apostle himself has strenuously inculcated ... this is nothing else than the transition from the externally historical to the inward and spiritual. It is true, we must not overlook the distinction, that the orthodox preacher builds his moral on the text in such a way, that the latter remains as an historical foundation; whereas with the speculative preacher, the transition from the biblical history or the church doctrine to the truth which he thence derives, has the negative effect of annihilating the former.[9]

For Strauss, conceptual thinking is as existentially satisfying as, and considerably more precise than, symbolic or mythical forms of the religious imagination. This must be regarded as a significant departure from Hegel's insistence upon the necessity of the foundation of philosophy upon religious experience: the religious image (*Vorstellung*) gives rise to the speculative concept (*Begriff*), and the *Begriff* articulates the true meaning of the *Vorstellung*. In effect, Strauss's programme amounts to a severing of the Hegelian link between speculative thought and the religious imagination and historical experience, detaching theology from religious consciousness. Through his introduction of the category of 'myth', Strauss believed he had a means of destroying religious symbols, which rendered unnecessary the more difficult task of reinterpreting them. On the basis of this assumption, Strauss developed a form of monistic pantheism which had little, if any, connection with the historical figure of Jesus of Nazareth, whom he regarded as having little significance for modern humanity. The outcome of this development was perhaps inevitable: in 1872, Strauss published his *Der alte und der neue Glaube* ('The Old Faith and the New'), in which he declares that Jesus has no relevance for Christianity, and advocated a purely humanist ethic.

That judgment turned out to be radically provisional. By the end of the nineteenth century, Strauss was regarded within the German theological tradition as yesterday's scholar. As Adolf von Harnack remarked in 1900, 'Sixty years ago David Friedrich Strauss thought that he had almost entirely destroyed the historical credibility not only of the fourth but also of the first three Gospels as well. The historical criticism of two generations has succeeded in restoring that credibility in its main outlines.'[10] In any case, even those sympathetic to Strauss at the time regarded his more radical conclusions as untenable. One such contemporary was Ferdinand Christian Baur (1792–1860), to whom we may now turn.

F. C. Baur

As a young man, Baur had been deeply impressed by Schleiermacher's *Christian Faith*, which he regarded as ending the old and sterile debate between rationalism and supernaturalism.[11] However, Baur considered that Schleiermacher appeared to be unable to accommodate the historical and ecclesiastical dimensions of Christianity within the context of his *Glaubenslehre*, which appeared to be dominated by the philosophical and the idealistic. Nowhere, he argues, does Schleiermacher explain how he moves from the general consciousness of redemption to a specific historical individual as the ground of that consciousness. In fact, Schleiermacher appears to make the archetypal Christ (that is, the Christological interpretation of the subjective experience of redemption) prior to the historical Jesus, so that the person and work of Christ may be treated only as derivative functions of the religious consciousness.

Baur therefore develops a penetrating critique of the Christology of Schleiermacher's *Glaubenslehre* on the basis of its perceived failure to mediate between the archetypal Christ and the historical Jesus. Unless theology begins with the historical Jesus, in terms of a critical analysis of the gospel accounts (in which alone he may be encountered), he will never be found. Baur is particularly critical of the manner in which Schleiermacher infers his Christology from religious consciousness. The experience of pious consciousness within the Christian community is treated as the effect of the influence of a single individual, whose identity may be inferred by arguing backwards from effect to cause. For Baur, this is illegitimate: to understand an historical process, it is necessary to begin with the cause, and thence to follow through its effects.

In the case of Schleiermacher's argument, there is no historical necessity that the cause of religious consciousness should be a single individual, nor that it be the specific historical individual Jesus of Nazareth. Baur's conclusion may be stated as follows: Schleiermacher's argument from the ideal or archetypal Christ to the historical Jesus fails to demonstrate the possibility of an authentically historical Jesus. The direction of the argument (the inference of the cause from the effect) does not demonstrate the necessity of an historical Jesus. Baur himself argued that the foundations of Christology must be regarded as historical in character, and had already established the techniques which he felt were necessary for this undertaking. It was the study of the events of the past, rather than the religious experience of the present, which held the key to Christological reconstruction.

During the period at which he taught classics at the Blaubeuren seminary (1817–26), Baur became familiar with the new source-critical methods discussed in B. G. Niebuhr's (1776–1831) *Römische Geschichte* ('Roman History', 1811–12), and developed an interest in ancient religion through reading G. F. Creuzer's (1771–1858) *Symbolik und Mythologie der alten Völker* ('Symbolism and Mythology of Ancient Peoples', 2nd edn, 1819–23). The need for a conceptual philosophy and critical history in dealing with the Christian tradition was clearly identified in his own *Symbolik und Mythologie* ('Symbolism and Mythology', 1824–25), although it would be a decade before Baur committed himself to Hegelianism as the philosophy capable of reviving history from its 'eternally deaf and dumb' state. The catalyst for this development was the publication of Strauss's *Life of Jesus*.

As noted above, Strauss drew the conclusion that the historical Jesus has at best only an accidental connection with the ideal or archetypal Christ, thus denying the significance of the historical individual Jesus of Nazareth for Christian faith. Furthermore, Strauss's radical criticism of the relationship between *Vorstellung* and *Begriff* effectively eliminated any means by which the historical Jesus could be employed as a means of verifying the interpretation which the Christian community had placed upon him. Baur's task was therefore to distinguish between the critical-historical and speculative philosophical viewpoints, without destroying their inherent interconnection.

For Baur, Strauss engaged in historical criticism solely in order to destroy the Christian tradition: it is for this reason that he characterized Strauss's *Glaubenslehre* as the 'most striking example' of the rationalism of the eighteenth century. For Strauss, 'the true criticism of dogma is its history'; for Baur, the strongly anti-dogmatic approach to the history of dogma was more concerned with the destruction of dogma than the investigation of its history. The key to a correct understanding of the significance of Jesus of Nazareth thus lay in a critical study of Christian origins.

The most significant and immediate casualty of this approach was the Fourth Gospel, regarded as an historical source by Schleiermacher. For Schleiermacher, the Fourth Gospel was the most nearly continuous, complete and historically reliable portrait of Jesus, giving insights into his personality, and a thoroughly spiritual and religious interpretation of his identity and mission, tinged only to a slight degree with apocalyptic messianic supernaturalism. The traditional interpretation of the *Vorstellung* of the incarnation, to name but one significant Christian doctrine, was derived practically in its totality from the Fourth Gospel. The historicity of that gospel had been called into question, although on somewhat weak grounds, by Strauss: it was, however, through the massive critical studies of Baur that its peculiar character was first established on critical grounds.

In an important study of 1837, Baur attempted to compare the relation of Socrates to Platonism with the relation of Jesus to Christianity.[12] His purpose in doing so was to attempt to cast light upon the origins of Christianity, especially the relation of Christianity to the person of its founder. In that study, he treated the Fourth Gospel as a relatively reliable historical source, primarily concerned with Christ's higher nature and immediate divinity. By 1847, however, Baur had concluded that the narratives and discourses of the Fourth Gospel were so controlled by an idealizing *Weltanschauung* that they could not by regarded as historical. The Fourth Gospel was thus a source for the theology of the early church (how early being a matter of debate), rather than a source for the history of Jesus of Nazareth.[13] Noting that the narratives and discourses of this gospel were all made subservient to the theme of the incarnation of the Word, Baur argued that the rejection of the historicity of the Fourth Gospel was tantamount to the rejection of the dogma of the incarnation of the Logos. He thus proceeded to construct a purely historical Jesus on the basis of a purely historical method.

For Baur, it was possible and necessary to go behind the Christ of faith, on the presupposition (his criticism of Strauss being obvious at this point) that there existed an inextricable connection between the two. However, it should be added that Baur was not prepared to accept the identity or coincidence of the Jesus of history and the Christ of faith, *contra* orthodoxy. It is in this respect that Baur's divergence from Hegel is perhaps at its clearest. For Hegel, Christianity was primarily about a concept (*Begriff*), so that it was not necessary to go behind the Christ of faith to consider the 'historically factual objective reality' underlying faith; for Baur, Christianity was primarily about a person. Thus his account of the historical figure of Jesus of Nazareth is of decisive significance for his Christology, as well as for his theology in general.

It is, however, possible to misunderstand seriously Baur's attitude to Hegel. Baur does not suggest that Hegel severs all essential or internal connections between the Christ of faith and the Jesus of history, but merely draws attention to the inadequate manner in which he formulates their relationship. For Baur, 'the unity of the divine and human nature first became concrete truth and self-conscious knowledge in Christ, and was expressed and taught by him as truth'. By making this significant assertion, Baur is able to provide an integral connection between the historical and the ideal, which he found lacking in Hegel. Having made this step, Baur is then able to avoid the historically unjustifiable compromise of Schleiermacher, and the philosophically untenable and ungrounded assertions of Marheineke and Daub, all of whom resorted to identifying the archetypal Christ with the historical figure of Jesus of Nazareth.

Baur insists that the two are integrally and inextricably interrelated, and that the latter is absolutely indispensable to faith. However, despite a careful analysis of Baur's writings, we are forced to the conclusion that Baur's antithesis between the Jesus of history and the Christ of faith represents an unresolved dualism, bequeathed to his successors within the Tübingen school for further critical investigation. Nevertheless, we are not primarily concerned with the ambiguities of Baur's Christology, but with the significance of his historical approach to it, which has such important consequences for Schleiermacher's Christology in general, and the theological method of the *Glaubenslehre* in particular.

It is clear that Baur's historical critique of Schleiermacher's causal argument concerning the relationship between the archetypal Christ and historical Jesus, and supremely his rejection of the use of the Fourth Gospel as a source for the history of Jesus of Nazareth, have devastating consequences for Schleiermacher's *Christusbild*. A perhaps still more significant criticism was, however, yet to come, again arising from Hegelian idealism – the anti-theology of Ludwig Feuerbach (1804–72).

Ludwig Feuerbach

The matrix within which Feuerbach's thought emerged was the philosophical radicalism of the so-called 'Young Hegelians', a somewhat diffuse group of thinkers prominent in Berlin in the 1830s and 1840s. Although initially a defender of Hegel against his critics, by 1839 Feuerbach had come to share many of their misgivings concerning him.[14] Many of the insights which are incorporated into the substance of his celebrated and controversial work *Wesen des Christentums* ('The Essence of Christianity', 1841) may be shown to date from this earlier period. The publication of this work caused a sensation, evoking the admiration of thinkers such as Strauss and Engels, and is rightly regarded as a milestone in the development of religious criticism in the nineteenth century. In view of the importance of this work in relation to Schleiermacher, we propose to consider it in some detail.

In the foreword to the first edition of his work, Feuerbach states that the purpose of the work is 'to show that the supernatural mysteries of

religion are based upon quite simple natural truths'. The leading idea of
the work is deceptively simple: human beings have created the gods,
who embody their own idealized conception of their aspirations, needs
and fears. Nevertheless, to suggest that Feuerbach merely reduces the
divine to the natural is to inhibit appreciation of his full significance.
The permanent significance of the work lies not in its repetition of the
reduced theology of Xenophanes (sixth century BC) or Lucretius (c.
99–55 BC), but in its detailed analysis of the means by which religious
concepts arise within the human consciousness. The thesis that human
beings create the gods in their own image is but the conclusion of a
radical and penetrating critique of concept formation in religion, based
on the Hegelian concepts of 'self-alienation' and 'self-objectification'.

The Hegelian analysis of consciousness requires that there be a
formal relation of subject to object. The concept of 'consciousness'
cannot be isolated as an abstract idea, in that it is necessarily linked with
an object: to be 'conscious' is to be conscious of something, so that
there is a latent differentiation within consciousness between its subject
and object. When Hegel introduces the phenomenological concept of the
'other Being of consciousness (*das Anderssein des Bewusstsein*)', he
intends us to understand the process by which the human consciousness
identifies its object, thus transferring the object from its 'abstract' to its
'concretized' form. Whatever the object may be in itself, it is an object
in consciousness only to the extent that it is an object for some
conscious subject. The process by which the conscious subject identifies
the object of that consciousness is defined as 'objectification
(*Vergegenständlichung*)' or 'externalization (*Entäusserung*)'. It is this
process of 'objectification' which is taken up by Feuerbach, and
developed in an anti-theological direction. It is therefore necessary to
point out that his English admirer George Eliot (1819–80) has seriously
impeded the proper understanding of Feuerbach on this point by
translating *Vergegenständlichung* as 'projection', thus obscuring the
Hegelian background to his thought.

For Feuerbach, the process of the self-objectification of human
consciousness requires that the 'other Being' (*Anderssein*) of consciousness must be like the conscious subject, but distinct from it. In other
words, to develop Feuerbach's point, the 'other Being' must be a You,
rather than an I, but identical in species (*Gattung*) to the subject. For
Feuerbach, the culmination of a dialectical phenomenology is human
self-knowledge as a species being, as will be explained shortly.

With this point in mind, we are in a position to develop Feuerbach's 'anthropotheism'. Human consciousness of feelings, such as fear or love, leads to their objectification and thus to externalization of these feelings. Although they are not mistaken in the attribution of such predicates to external objects, they may be mistaken in relation to the object to which they attribute them. It is possible to treat natural objects (such as trees) or fantasy objects (such as ghosts) as if they were human, so that they serve as surrogates of humanity in the attribution of feelings such as love or fear. In other words, they are examples of the real but mistaken objectification of human feelings. The predicates which are thus objectified are properly conceived, but misapplied: properly speaking, they can be applied only to the human species, and not to non-human or imaginary human objects. By objectifying such human emotions in inappropriate manners, the subject has simply made a species or category mistake, applying predicates which properly belong to humanity (considered as *Gattung*) to inappropriate objects. As God cannot be included in the human *Gattung*, such emotions cannot be objectified in relation to him.

Divine predicates are thus recognized to be human predicates, precisely because the processes of *Entäusserung* and *Vergegenständlichung* cannot be applied to God. Whereas Hegel understood the subject of the dialectic of self-differentiation to be the Absolute Idea (in order to rationalize the manner of its unfolding), Feuerbach took it to be humans as a species. With this dramatic shift in the point of reference, a universal pantheism became little more than an atheism:

> Consciousness of God is human self-consciousness; knowledge of God is human self-knowledge. By the God you know the human, and conversely, by the human, you know the God. The two are one. What God is to a person that too is the spirit, the soul; and what the spirit, the soul, are to a person, that is the God. God is the revealed and explicit inner self of a human being. . . The historical progress of religion consists therefore in this: that what an earlier religion took to be objective, is later recognized to be subjective; what formerly was taken to be God, and worshipped as such, is not recognized to be something human. What was earlier religion is later taken to be idolatry: humans are seen to have adored their own nature. Humans objectified themselves but failed to recognize themselves as this

69

object. The later religion takes this step; every advance in religion is therefore a deepening in self-knowledge.[15]

It is obvious that Feuerbach tends to use the terms 'Christianity' and 'religion' interchangeably throughout *The Essence of Christianity*, thus glossing over the fact that his theory has some difficulty in accounting for non-theistic religions. Nevertheless, it is clear that his reduction of Christian theology to anthropology is of considerable significance in relation to the solution to the Christological dilemma developed by Schleiermacher.

The most important epistemological analysis in *The Essence of Christianity* is concerned with the role of feeling in the process of religious concept-formation, and has important consequences for the *Gefühl*-centred approach of Schleiermacher. For Feuerbach, Christian theology has tended to interpret the externalized image of 'feeling' or self-consciousness as a wholly other, absolute essence, whereas it is in fact *das selbstfühlende Gefühl*, a 'self-feeling feeling', which cannot be objectified in any manner save in the form of the human species. The instrument by which the improper objectification of *das selbstfühlende Gefühl* takes place is the religious imagination. In other words, imagination is the instrument of human consciousness which interprets feelings as a concrete sensory representation – and in doing so, is prone to make species or category errors. For Feuerbach, every act of *das religiöse Gefühl* is nothing more than an expression or an embodiment of the feeling that human beings have for their own sensible nature. As such, they are liable mistakenly to objectify *das Gefühl* as God: 'If feeling is the essential instrumentality or organ of religion, then God's nature is nothing other than an expression of the nature of feeling . . . The divine essence, which is comprehended by feeling, is actually nothing other than the essence of feeling, enraptured and delighted with itself – nothing but self-intoxicated, self-contented feeling.'

For Schleiermacher, the nature of the religious self-consciousness was such that the existence of the Redeemer could be inferred from it; for Feuerbach, this species self-consciousness was nothing more and nothing less than human beings' awareness of themselves. It is experience of oneself, not of God. Whereas Baur had challenged Schleiermacher's argument from consciousness to its origins in terms of its logic, Feuerbach effectively reduced it to the inevitable delusion of self-objectification and self-externalization. Humans merely objectify themselves in religion. Although those who might care to defend Schleiermacher in the face of this critique could conceivably appeal to the fact that Schleiermacher appeals to the corporate, rather than the individual, self-consciousness, Feuerbach had already cut the ground from under this objection by his insistence that the dialectical process has as its subject human self-knowledge as a species being.

Thus for Feuerbach, the incarnation enshrines the insight that God is human, and enables human beings to value their own humanity as they would otherwise value deity. 'Religion is the reflection, the mirroring of human nature in itself.' What is most emphatically not permissable, according to Feuerbach, is the argument from human feeling or self-consciousness to the existence of a different species, distinct from humanity. 'God-consciousness' is merely human self-awareness, not a distinct category of human experience. Although Feuerbach does not make this point, it may be stated that, on the basis of his analysis of human concept-formation, the 'dominant God-consciousness' which Schleiermacher ascribes to Jesus of Nazareth can only be regarded as a deluded self-consciousness. Where Schleiermacher speaks of God, he is merely making unconscious anthropological statements. Even if Feuerbach did not totally reduce theology to anthropology, he at least succeeded in making it an anthropological epiphenomenon, with devastating effects for any theology which began with human feelings and inferred the existence of external or objective realities from them.

As we stressed in the previous chapter, Schleiermacher's theological system rests upon an analysis of human experience, supremely the experience of being dependent upon another (which is interpreted as being dependent upon God).[16] Whatever the undoubted merits of this approach might be, it has the effect of making the reality of God dependent upon the religious experiences of the pious believer. Theology becomes anthropology, as an understanding of God becomes reduced to an understanding of human nature.

Feuerbach's analysis represents a brilliant critique of this approach, which continues to be influential in Western liberal Christianity. The existence of God is held to be grounded in human experience. But, as Feuerbach emphasizes, our human experience might be nothing other than our own experience of *ourselves*, rather than of God. We might simply be projecting our own experiences, and calling the result 'God', where we ought to realize that they are simply experiences of our own human natures. Feuerbach's approach represents a devastating critique of anthropocentric or experience-centred ideas of Christianity.

Feuerbach's critique of religion loses much of its force when dealing with non-theistic religions, or theologies (such as that of Karl Barth, see pp. 123–43) which claim to deal with an divine encounter with humanity from outside.[17] However, when applied to a theistic construction or interpretation of human emotional or psychological states, it is in its element. Has anyone really spoken about God or Christ? Or have we simply projected our longings and fears on to an imaginary transcendent plane, or on to a distant historical figure about whom we know so little? The growing conviction that Christology must be objectively grounded in the history of Jesus of Nazareth (especially prominent, for example, in the writings of Wolfhart Pannenberg, see pp. 187–98) is at least due in part to Feuerbach's critique of religion. The very idea of 'God' was, according to Feuerbach, an illusion which we can in principle avoid, and, with sufficient progress in self-knowledge, could discard altogether. It is, of course, a small – and perhaps an inevitable – step to proceed from this assumption to the Marxist view that religious feeling is itself the product of an alienated social existence – to which we may now turn.

Feuerbach's Legacy: Marx and Freud

In his 1844 political and economic manuscripts, Karl Marx (1818–83) develops an approach to religion which rests upon ideas demonstrably due to Feuerbach. Religion has no real independent existence. It is a reflection of the material world. 'The religious world is but the reflex of the real world.'[18] Marx argues that 'religion is just the imaginary sun which seems to humans to revolve around themselves until they realize that they themselves are the centre of their own revolution'.[19] In other words, God is simply a projection of human concerns. Human beings 'look for a superhuman being in the fantasy reality of heaven, and find nothing there but their own reflection'.[20]

The notion of alienation is of central importance to Marx's account of the origins of religious belief.[21] 'Humans make religion; religion does not make humans. Religion is the self-consciousness and self-esteem of people who either have not found themselves or who have already lost themselves again.'[22] Religion is the product of social and economic alienation. It arises from that alienation, and at the same time encourages that alienation by a form of spiritual intoxication which renders the masses incapable of recognizing their situation, and doing something about it. Religion is a comfort, which enables people to tolerate their economic alienation. If there were no such alienation, there would be no need for religion. The division of labour and the existence of private property lead directly to the introduction of alienation and estrangement within the economic and social orders.

Materialism, according to Marx, affirms that events in the material world bring about corresponding changes in the intellectual world. Religion is thus the result of a certain set of social and economic conditions. Change those conditions, so that economic alienation is eliminated, and religion will cease to exist. It will no longer serve any useful function. Unjust social conditions produce religion, and are in turn supported by religion. 'The struggle against religion is therefore indirectly a struggle against *the world* of which religion is the spiritual fragrance.'[23]

Marx thus argues that religion will continue to exist, as long as it meets a need in the life of alienated people. 'The religious reflex of the real world can . . . only then vanish when the practical relations of everyday life offer to man none but perfectly intelligible and reasonable relations with regard to his fellow men and to nature.'[24] Feuerbach had argued that religion was the projection of human needs, an expression of the 'uttered sorrow of the soul'. Marx agrees with this interpretation. However, his point is more radical. It is not enough to explain how religion arises on account of sorrow and injustice. By changing that world, the causes of religion can be removed. It is important to note that Marx regards Feuerbach as correct in his analysis of the origins of religion, even if he failed to discern how an understanding of those origins might lead to its eventual elimination. It is this insight which underlies his often quoted eleventh thesis on Feuerbach: 'The philosophers have only interpreted the world, in various ways; the point, however, is to change it.'[25]

Feuerbach's basic ideas found new life in the writings of the psychoanalyst Sigmund Freud (1856–1939).[26] In fact, it is probably fair to say that the 'projection' or 'wish-fulfilment' theory is best known today in its Freudian variant, rather than in Feuerbach's original version. The most powerful statement of Freud's approach may be found in *The Future of an Illusion* (1927), which develops a strongly reductionist approach to religion.[27] For Freud, religious ideas are 'illusions, fulfilments of the oldest, strongest and most urgent wishes of humanity'.[28] Religion represents the perpetuation of a piece of infantile behaviour in adult life, being little more than an immature response to the awareness of helplessness, by going back to one's childhood experiences of paternal care: 'My father will protect me; he is in control.' Belief in a personal God is thus little more than an infantile delusion. Religion is wishful thinking, an illusion.

This exploration of the manner in which Feuerbach's approach was developed will serve to emphasize the severe weaknesses of Schleiermacher's experiential approach to Christology. It will be helpful to return to the 1830s to summarize the implications of the Hegelian critique for the future of Schleiermacher's Christological style.

The Aftermath of the Critique of Schleiermacher

The developments which took place in the decade after Schleiermacher's death in 1834, and which posed so effective a challenge to his solution to the Christological problem, may be summarized as follows.

1. The historicity of the Fourth Gospel was called into question, so that it could no longer be treated as a source for the history of Jesus of Nazareth, but only as a source for the history of the early church. This development is associated initially with Strauss, and was subsequently championed by Baur. Schleiermacher's *Christusbild* was constructed on the assumption of the historicity of the Fourth Gospel: for Schleiermacher, the markedly spiritual content of the gospel indicated that its author was a witness to the events it portrayed. From this point onward, the question of the historical Jesus had to be discussed solely with reference to the synoptic gospels.

2. In the case of the synoptic gospels themselves, the researches of Strauss had called into question the historical character of a substantial number of passages, generally in contexts of significance for orthodox theology (such as the narrative of the resurrection), on the grounds of their including 'mythical' material. Whereas it had been generally assumed up to this point that the gospel records were true accounts of the history of Jesus of Nazareth (the difference between supernaturalists and naturalists lying primarily in the manner in which miracles were interpreted), Strauss argued that they incorporated a substantial quantity of non-historical material. On the basis of this conclusion, he effectively restricted the source material for the history of Jesus of Nazareth to that

small section of the gospel material which he regarded as significant.

3. The rise in historical thinking particularly associated with the Tübingen school led to an emphasis being placed upon the methodological priority of the origins of Christianity over its present-day manifestations. In other words, the question of the significance of Jesus of Nazareth, and particularly his relation to the 'archetypal Christ', had to be answered by seeking that significance in his history, and not by inferring such significance from the present-day pious consciousness of the community of faith. Schleiermacher's appeal to present-day Christian religious experience was inadequate as an approach to Christology. This new emphasis upon the study of Christian origins was complemented by a devastating attack on the manner in which human experience was to be interpreted, as our final point indicates.

4. Feuerbach's critique of religion called into question the propriety of inferring the existence or nature of 'God' from religious feeling, in that this feeling could only be interpreted anthropologically, and not theologically. It was no longer reasonable to ignore the possibility that the traditional Christian understanding of the relation between the 'archetypal Christ' and the Jesus of history might be purely illusory, resulting from the erroneous objectification and externalization of human aspirations. The unsatisfactory foundation which Schleiermacher established for this relation was thus exposed, and shown to be severely – perhaps even fatally – inadequate.

As we noted in the previous chapter, Schleiermacher must be regarded as founding an era, rather than a school. The Hegelian critique of Schleiermacher seemed to leave his approach in utter ruins, having undermined both its historical foundations and its experiential analysis. However, history has a way of picking up its pieces, and putting them back together again. Although Schleiermacher's original Christological method now appeared to be seriously inadequate, it was not totally beyond salvage. In the following chapter, we shall indicate how a new *Christusbild* arose from the ashes of the old.

4

The Liberal Picture of Christ: from Ritschl to Harnack

By the 1840s, German Protestant theology was in a state of flux. There was general agreement in advanced circles that the old Christological ideas were beyond salvage. But what could replace them? Although the vision of Enlightenment rationalism still exercised something of its former force, and the notion of an all-competent human reason continued to retain at least some of its potency, in many quarters doubts were growing concerning the viability of the entire Enlightenment undertaking. Rationalism seemed to be quietly dying. But what could replace it? The great Hegelian synthesis was widely considered to have fallen apart; where Hegel had been able to hold together the spiritual and material sides of life, his followers regarded this as little more than philosophical posturing. Although Schleiermacher's legacy continued to receive a sympathetic reception, anxiety concerning its historical and philosophical foundations was being expressed by many. The way ahead seemed unclear. So important was the reaction against and general disillusionment with Hegelianism, which probably reached its climax in the 1850s, that we must consider it in some detail before proceeding any further.

The Reaction against Hegelianism

The challenge posed to the Hegelian 'philosophy of nature *(Naturphilosophie)*' by the new empirically-grounded 'science of nature

(Naturwissenschaft)' dates from the opening of the nineteenth century, and is especially associated with the astronomical discoveries of the period. In his *Dissertatio philosophica de orbitis planetarum* (published in 1801, although written earlier), Hegel had argued, on the basis of idealist presuppositions, that the number of planets was necessarily restricted to seven, and that no planet existed between Mars and Jupiter. This bold assertion of the astronomical competence of reason was rudely discredited, even as Hegel's book was in the course of its production. On 1 January 1801, as the new century dawned, the astronomer J. E. Bode (1746–1826) discovered the planetoid Ceres, and established that its orbit fell between that of Mars and Jupiter.

The same pattern could be seen in the field of botany. F. W. J. Schelling's (1775–1854) *Naturphilosophie*, which showed little concern for observation of nature, exercised considerable influence in the field of botany until the second half of the century. At that point, Wilhelm Hofmeister (1824–77) finally managed to displace it with an empirically grounded plant morphology. The successes of the 'exact sciences' – of which the discovery of Ceres, and subsequently of Neptune a few decades later, were typical – led to a widespread reaction against idealism. The somewhat elusive Hegelian thesis of the manifestation of the Absolute and Infinite in the finite and relative conditions of human history appeared fatuous in the light of the concrete, empirical and verifiable knowledge deriving from the natural sciences.

Yet the growing disillusionment with Hegelianism did not lead to the immediate adoption of a philosophical alternative. No Christological consensus, nor even a common pattern, emerges in the 1840s and 1850s. The period is perhaps best regarded as a time of experimentation and exploration, rather than of positive system-building. This is not to say that the period is without significance, but merely to note the absence of general trends at the time. The restlessness of the period is well illustrated from the writings of Richard Rothe (1799–1867), perhaps one of the most important German speculative theologians of the nineteenth century (although little known in the English-language world). In many ways, Rothe's writings show the influence of Enlightenment rationalism, such as its characteristic concern for morality and hostility to the metaphysical categories of traditional Christology. Thus he argues that the doctrine of the two natures of Christ is to be abandoned as compromising the simplicity of Scripture, and makes the basis of Christ's relationship to God physical rather than moral.

A similar position is taken by Alexander Schweitzer (1808–88), in *Die christliche Glaubenslehre* ('The Christian Doctrine of Faith', 1863). In common with many at the time, Rothe argued that the permanent significance of Jesus lay in his ethical example, and supremely his act of self-giving on the cross. Yet his emphasis upon the moral personality of Jesus, and his idiosyncratic understanding of the ascension of Christ as his transition from a purely historical existence to a continuing personal presence in the church, marks him off from the narrow confines of a purely rationalist Christology, and places him closer to Schleiermacher.

The Re-emergence of Christology, 1850–70

The second half of the nineteenth century witnessed both a growing reaction against the philosophical idealism of the earlier part of the century, as noted above, and a growing conviction that Christology was of decisive importance within the context of Christian dogmatics. An integral aspect of the new Christological style to emerge during this period of reconstruction was a concern for the religious personality of Jesus. A number of developments may be regarded as laying the foundations for this new style.

First, a renewed emphasis upon the importance of the religious and theological importance of Jesus of Nazareth developed. This is clearly seen within the writings of Gottfried Thomasius (1802–75), especially his *Christi Person und Werk* ('The Person and Work of Christ'), published in three parts over the period 1852–61. Thomasius opens this massive work with a robust assertion of the centrality of Christ to the Christian faith. The person and work of Christ are the centre of the Christian religion, constitute the essential content of the Christian faith, and are the object of Christian knowledge, including theological speculation. Similarly, in his *Christliche Dogmatik* (1869) A. E. Biedermann (1819–85) insisted that 'the Christian religion has its historical basis and fountainhead in the person of Jesus'.

Second, a developing appreciation for the humanity of Jesus, especially his religious personality, can be discerned during the period. Thus Biedermann stated that 'the religious principle of Christianity is to be more precisely defined as the religious personality of Jesus, that is, that relation between God and humanity which, in the religious self-consciousness of Jesus, has entered into the history of humanity as a new religious fact with the power to inspire faith'. The roots of this idea can be argued to lie in German Pietism, especially in the form this takes in the writings of Nikolaus von Zinzendorf (1700–60), whose 'religion of the heart' laid particular emphasis upon an intimate personal relationship between the believer and Christ. It was developed and redirected by Schleiermacher, who regarded himself as a '*Herrnhuter* [that is, a follower of Zinzendorf] of a higher order'. Schleiermacher's understanding of the manner in which Christ is able to assimilate believers into his fellowship has strong parallels with Zinzendorf's analysis of the role of religious feelings in the spiritual life, and their grounding in the believer's fellowship with Christ.

Nevertheless, the importance attached to the human personality of Jesus left a number of theological loose ends. What about the divinity of Christ? Where did this come into things? Was not the emphasis upon Christ's humanity equivalent to a neglect of his divinity? Such questions and suspicions were voiced within more orthodox circles during the 1840s and early 1850s. However, during the later 1850s an approach to Christology was mapped out which seemed to have considerable potential in this respect. At one and the same time, it defended the divinity of Christ, yet justified an emphasis upon his humanity. The approach in question is known as 'kenoticism', and is especially associated with Thomasius (see above). Thomasius first developed these ideas (in what has to be described as a rather tentative manner) in his *Beiträge zur kirchlichen Christologie* ('Essays on ecclesiastical Christology', 1845), before giving them fuller (and more confident) expression in his *Christi Person und Werk*. Thomasius here argues that the incarnation involves *kenōsis*, the deliberate setting aside of all divine attributes, so that, in the state of humiliation, Christ has voluntarily abandoned all priviliges of divinity. It is therefore entirely proper to stress his humanity, especially the importance of his suffering as a human being.

This understanding of *kenōsis* must be distinguished from that of an earlier stage in German theology. During the early seventeenth century, a controversy developed between Lutheran theologians based at the universities of Giessen and Tübingen. The question at issue can be stated as follows. The gospels make no reference to Christ making use of all his divine attributes (such as omniscience) during his period on earth. How is this to be explained? Two options seemed to present themselves to these Lutheran writers as appropriately orthodox solutions: either

Christ used his divine powers in secret, or he abstained from using them
gether. The first option (*krypsis*) was defended vigorously by Tübingen;
the second (*kenōsis*) with equal vigour by Giessen.

Yet it must be noted that both parties were in agreement that Christ
possessed the central attributes of divinity – such as omnipotence and
omnipresence – during the period of the incarnation. The debate was
over the question of their use: were they used in secret, or not at all?
Thomasius' approach was more radical. The incarnation involves
Christ's *abandoning* of the attributes of divinity. They are set to one side
during the entire period from the birth of Christ to his resurrection.
Basing himself on Philippians 2:6–8, Thomasius argues that in the
incarnation, the second person of the Trinity was reduced totally to the
level of humanity. A theological and spiritual emphasis upon the
humanity of Christ is thus entirely justified.

This approach to Christology was criticized by Isaak August Dorner
(1809–84), on the grounds that it introduced change into God himself.
The doctrine of the immutability of God was thus compromised by
Thomasius' approach.[1] Interestingly, this *aperçu* contains much truth,
and can be seen as an anticipation of the twentieth-century debate over
the question of the 'suffering of God' (see pp. 205–10).

Dorner is also of importance in another respect – as a shrewd
observer of new trends in Christology. Writing in 1856, he correctly
noted that the Christological dogma had come to the fore as a consequence of the critical questions with which German theology was
faced in the wake of the subjectivity of the Enlightenment.[2] In part, this
may be seen as a reflection of Schleiermacher's call for a Christocentric
principle – that everything in theology should be directly related to the
redemption accomplished in Jesus of Nazareth. In his celebrated later
work, published after his death, *System der christlichen Glaubenslehre*
('System of Christian Doctrine'), Dorner states the importance of the
Christological dogma as follows:

> It must be said that, in the present century, our dogma has
> again, in its exegetical, historical and dogmatic aspects, come to
> the fore, and been affected by more profound change than at
> any time since the first centuries. The most vital concern is to
> gain a true and living view and knowledge of the person of
> Christ.

On the basis of his massive researches into the development of the Christological dogma, Dorner concludes that a third major epoch in 'that development began around the year 1800, on the basis of assumptions unknown to the first eighteen hundred years of church history'. In its earlier phase, that epoch had been dependent upon idealist assumptions which were increasingly abandoned during the second half of the nineteenth century. Thus A. E. Biedermann, whilst retaining the Hegelian concept of *Vorstellung*, insisted that the constitutive element in religion was not *Vorstellung* itself (for that would be to reduce religion to a purely theoretical relation to God), but the 'whole personal relation of the individual to God, which is carried out in a unified manner in human thinking, feeling and willing'. Biedermann exemplifies the reaction against Hegelianism by insisting that the 'Christ-principle' (*Christusprinzip*) was understood metaphysically or anthropologically, rather than as an expression of piety:

> The error of all previous speculative Christologies, which correctly understand the essential content of the dogma to be an idea newly emerging in human history in his person, rather than a personal definition of the single person Jesus, has been that they did not define this idea as specifically religious, whose content immediately constituted the essence of the religious personality of Jesus and from this historically constituted the essence of Christian piety. Rather, they understood the content of this idea as a universal metaphysical truth concerning the abstract relation of the absolute and the finite (universally cosmically) or of the divine and the human (anthropologically).

Against Hegel, Biedermann maintained that philosophy could never take the place of religion: there was a fundamental distinction to be made between religion and philosophy, with the former addressing human needs in a manner that the latter could not. Like Dorner, Biedermann was highly critical of the neo-Lutheran kenotic Christologies of Gottfried Thomasius and W. F. Gess (1819–91), which called the basis of this principle into question, without supplying a viable alternative in its place. Finally, that lacuna was filled by the approach of Albrecht Benjamin Ritschl (1822–89), to which we may now turn.

A. B. Ritschl

It is widely believed that the key to Ritschl's success lies in the gradual collapse of confidence in Hegelianism, noted earlier, and the failure of any rival system to achieve widespread support. It is not clear precisely what factors led to the remarkable and general decline of Hegelianism in the 1850s. It is certainly true that there were serious tensions within the Hegelian school itself, which inevitably weakened it. Perhaps more significant, however, were the remarkable advances being made in the natural sciences at the time, which led many to conclude that advancement in knowledge was more likely to come about through the meticulous observation and analysis of natural phenomena. The origins of liberal theology may be seen in this growing disillusionment with Hegelian idealism, which left an ideological vacuum at a critical phase in German intellectual history. It was within this vacuum that the highly influential liberal theology of Ritschl developed. Like so many others of his generation, Ritschl began life as a Hegelian, only to become gradually disillusioned with its solutions to the intellectual and spiritual riddles of life – theology included.[3]

It will be helpful to state the differences between Ritschl and Schleiermacher on the one hand, and between these two thinkers and rationalism on the other. One of the reasons for doing this is that Ritschl and Schleiermacher are often uncritically linked together as the 'leading representatives of liberal theology'. It is necessary to map out their divergences, in order to appreciate the quite distinct approaches adopted by the two writers, and the very different styles of 'liberalism' associated with them. Ritschl restores an emphasis upon *ethics*, which he believes to have been lost through Schleiermacher's emphasis upon 'feeling'. In Ritschl's view, an emphasis upon 'feeling' leads to introspection: religion comes to be a matter between the individual (or, at best, the *community* of believers) and God, which leaves out any reference to the world. Religion is not about introspection, but about life in human society. It is about culture, not mysticism or Pietism.

This emphasis upon ethics might seem to ally Ritschl with at least part of the programme of Enlightenment rationalism. And it must be conceded immediately that a Kantian agenda, probably mediated through the influence of his Göttingen colleague, Hermann Lotze (1817–81), may well lie behind Ritschl's thinking at this point. This is especially the case in relation to his attempt to exclude metaphysics from theology, and bringing religion into close relation with ethics. Yet there are fundamental differences between Ritschl and the Enlightenment. For example, rationalism argued that Jesus had nothing that was both *right* and *new* to say. Where he was right, he merely agreed with what sound human reason always knew to be the case. If he said anything that was new (that is, hitherto unknown to reason), this would, by definition, be irrational and hence of no value. Ritschl disgrees. Jesus of Nazareth brings something new to the human situation, something which reason had hitherto neglected. 'Jesus was conscious of a *new and hitherto unknown relation to God.*'[4] Where rationalists believed in a universal rational religion, of which individual world religions were at best shadows, Ritschl argues that this was little more than a dream of reason, an abstraction without any historical embodiment. Christianity possesses certain definite theological and cultural characteristics as a historical religion, partly due to Jesus of Nazareth.

For Ritschl, the nature and function of religion are inherently pragmatic, with a strong ethical bias reflecting his conviction that Christianity is primarily concerned with action in relation to God and to humanity in the world. As we noted above, this is one consideration which distinguishes him sharply from Schleiermacher. At other points, Ritschl appears to be in agreement with Schleiermacher, as in his suggestion that the facts of Christian experience constitute the proper starting point for theological reflection; nevertheless, he insists that the 'experience' in question is the consequence of objective data, open to critical empirical investigation. The empiricism which has been detected in Ritschl's *Weltanschauung* may reflect the fact that the University of Göttingen, to which Ritschl was called as a professor in 1864, was by then regarded as a leading centre of scientific research and speculation. His most important work is the three-volume *Die christliche Lehre von der Rechtfertigung und Versöhnung* ('The Christian Doctrine of Justification and Reconciliation'), published in the five-year period 1870–4. The first of these three volumes deals with the development of the Christian doctrines of justification and reconciliation (or atonement: the German term *Versöhnung* bears both meanings) in the Christian theological tradition; the second with its biblical foundations; and the third with the positive exposition of the doctrine, in which Ritschl's personal views are expounded and defended.

By 1870, the date of the publication of the first such volume, Ritschl had concluded that the proper starting point for theological speculation was the 'moral effects of the life, passion, death and resurrection of Christ towards the founding of the church'. Christian theology is, for Ritschl, a discipline which is carried out within the sphere of the Christian church, and presupposes the commitment of the theologian to certain soteriological principles (the 'idea of the forgiveness of sins, justification and reconciliation'), which 'had been called into existence by Jesus as the founder of the Christian church, and maintained by the apostles as its earliest representatives'. However, this idea was taken up in the consciousness of the Christian community, and its peculiar theological status derives from its perceived significance within that specific community:

> The material of the theological doctrines of forgiveness of sin, justification and reconciliation is to be sought not so much directly in the words of Christ, as in the correlative representations of the original consciousness of the community. The faith of the community that it stands to God in a relation essentially conditioned by the forgiveness of sins is the immediate object of theological cognition. So far, however, as this benefit is traced back to the personal action and passion of Christ, his proved intention to adopt such means makes the mediation of the community more intelligible.[5]

It is, in effect, axiomatic for Ritschl that there is no direct or immediate relationship between the believer and God, in that the presence of God or Jesus Christ is always mediated through the community of faith. But in what sense is Christ 'present' in the community of faith?

The supernatural interpretation of this concept of the presence of Christ is rigorously excluded by Ritschl. Indeed, it can be pointed out that Ritschl consistently declines to become involved in ontological discussions, apparently on the basis of the assumption that such notions were unintelligible to the modern educated bourgeoisie. The 'presence of Christ' is to be understood as the spatio-temporal extension of the ideas and principles represented in the person of Jesus within the community of faith – in other words, the 'tradition of Christ propagated in the church (die in der Kirche fortgepflanzten Überlieferung von Christus)'. This 'tradition' is essentially empirical and historical, referring to a general ethical and religious principle or idea first embodied in the historical Jesus. This idea was then taken up and propagated by the community of faith, and made available to this day:

> Christ comes to act upon the individual believer on the one
> hand through the historical recollection of him which is possible
> in the church, on the other hand as the permanent author of all
> the influences and impulses which are due to other people, and
> like in nature to himself . . . To believe in Christ implies that
> we accept the value of the divine love, which is manifest in his
> work, for our reconciliation with God, with that trust which,
> directed to him, subordinates itself to God as his and our
> Father.[6]

As a consequence, Christ occupies a unique position towards all
those within the community of faith, expressed in a religious judgment
concerning his status. Those who 'believe in Christ' (in Ritschl's sense
of the phrase) participate in the kingdom of God, and are therefore
reconciled to God, participating in the same qualitative relationship to
God as the founder of their religion. In terms of its material content, the
calling (*Beruf*) of Christ was 'the establishment of the universal ethical
fellowship of humanity (*die Gründung der universellen sittlichen
Gemeinschaft der Menschen*) as the objective in the world which rises
above all conditions included in the notion of the world'.

Although Ritschl is severely critical of the Christologies of the
Enlightenment, it is very difficult to avoid the conclusion that he regards
Christ as an archetypally significant and unsurpassable individual, whose
significance cannot be articulated in any categories other than those of
humanity in general. This point becomes particularly clear from Ritschl's
discussion of two questions: in what sense, if any, is Christ 'unique', and
in what manner did this putative 'uniqueness' arise? Ritschl's replies to
these questions are widely regarded as unsatisfactory. For him, Christ's
'uniqueness' is primarily to be articulated in terms of his being the
founder of the Christian community, thus possessing temporal priority
over those who followed after. Ritschl argues that, although it is
conceivable that another individual could arise, equal in his religious and
ethical status to Christ, 'he would stand in historical dependence upon
Christ, and would therefore be distinguishable from him'.[7]

The concession, however, is significant, in that it indicates that
Christ's 'uniqueness' is understood historically rather than ontologically,
a first among equals whose primacy arises through the historical accident

of his being the unique founder of the Christian church. To use Emil Brunner's distinction, noted in a later chapter (see pp. 144–5), Christ is *einzigartig*, rather than *einmalig*. The fact that the community of faith is historically dependent upon the person of its founder is a remarkably weak defence of his uniqueness, and prompts even the most uncritical reader of Ritschl's *Hauptwerk* to ask whether this 'uniqueness' cannot be grounded in terms of Christ's relationship to God, and whether this 'uniqueness' can be determined by objective scientific investigation, or is only a subjective value-judgment (*Werturteil*) made by faith.

For Ritschl, this is an improper question, as Christ's person must be determined from his work – in other words, from his historic function of establishing the kingdom of God. The basic datum upon which Christology is based is the historical priority of Christ over believers in establishing and ruling the kingdom of God:

> One must avoid all attempts to go behind this datum, that is to determine in detail how it has come into being and empirically how it has come to be what it is. These attempts are superfluous because they are ineffectual; and it is dangerous to give oneself to these attempts since they are superfluous.[8]

It is difficult to avoid the conclusion that Ritschl considers Jesus to be nothing more than the historical point of departure for a self-sufficient idea. The 'divinity' of Christ is thus not true in any objective sense of the term, as had been suggested by the theologians of Orthodoxy, but is a value-judgment evoked by, and conveyed in, the proclamation of the community of faith. Although Jesus may be regarded objectively as a human being, faith recognizes him as having the religious value of God. The doctrine of the divinity of Christ is a value-judgment on the part of Christians, who recognize him as the unique bearer of the values of the kingdom of God. Jesus of Nazareth was divine, in that he, and he alone, was given the 'vocation (*Beruf*)' of being the perfect embodiment of the values of the kingdom of God on earth.

Nevertheless, Ritschl's discussion of the manner by which this 'divinity' can be recognized is, as we have indicated, unsatisfactory. It is, in fact, hard to avoid the conclusion that Ritschl understood Christ to have introduced into history certain ideas, such as that of the 'kingdom of God' (which ultimately derive from God, and hence may be regarded as 'divine' in a restricted sense of the term). However, in doing so,

Ritschl appears to have made himself vulnerable to the results of the increasingly dominant critical-historical method.

Ritschl's heavy dependence upon the Fourth Gospel at points of importance was also open to critical challenge, particularly from the Tübingen school to which he had once belonged. However, as his later followers, such as Wilhelm Herrmann (1846–1922), demonstrated, it was possible to adopt a negatively critical attitude towards the New Testament without destroying the powerful personal influence which the perfection of Christ's personality, reflected in the gospels, had upon the sincere believer. The tradition concerning Jesus is merely the medium through which the historical reality of the man Jesus is conveyed to the believer, and is not in itself a constitutive factor of Christian experience. For Herrmann, faith is essentially concerned with finding God in one's own spiritual life, through encountering another who inspires certainty and trust. For this reason, we may turn to consider the ideas of Herrmann in a little more detail.

Wilhelm Herrmann

Herrmann may be regarded as continuing and developing the Ritschlian approach to the religious life in general, and to Christology in particular.[9] Like Schleiermacher and Ritschl before him, he insists upon the close relationship of Christology and soteriology: who Christ is becomes known through his effect upon us. 'If we understand by "God" a power which so affects us that we, through this experience, gain strength to overcome the world, it is self-evident that we can know this God only in so far as he reveals himself to us by this work in us.'[10] This also points to a central theme of Herrmann's thought – the notion of revelation, which at points appears to become synonymous with 'the work of God within us'. It must, however, be stressed that Herrmann does not understand revelation to mean a generally valid knowledge; rather, he takes it to mean a human experience, in which one becomes aware of a divine, life-giving power.

This takes place through the encounter of the individual with the 'tradition about Jesus in the books of the New Testament', which portrays the person of Jesus with such force that it becomes the ground of faith. Herrman thus draws his celebrated distinction between the ground of faith (Jesus) and the content of faith (Christ). The existence of the man Jesus of Nazareth is an undoubted reality, adequate in itself as the basis of personal faith. The starting point of Christian faith, and hence also of Christian theology, must be with the historical Jesus with whom the believer is confronted in the gospel narratives, whose inner life (rather than metaphysical dogmas about his person) becomes the revelation of God. The 'inner life' of Jesus of Nazareth confronts the inner life of the believer directly and compellingly, and transforms it. Christological dogmas represent an unnecessary intrusion into this process.

Although Herrmann uses the category of revelation in history, of central importance to Christology, it is deployed in a thoroughly Ritschlian manner. 'Revelation in history' does not refer primarily to God's self-revelation through some past historical event; rather, it has reference to a religious experience in the transcendent dimension of an individual's life in the present. An aspect of the past becomes revelation only if the individual allows it to have this function. One can know history only in so far as one is sympathetically and actively involved in it.[11] For this reason, the revelational status of Jesus relates to, and is ultimately grounded in, the believer's apprehension of the religious personality of Jesus, as experienced in and mediated through the life of the Christian community.

Once more, it is the 'inner life of Jesus' which is regarded as being of decisive importance to faith. The 'religious personality of Jesus' is seen as something that is compelling, capable of being assimilated by believers, and something that is hitherto without parallel in the religious and cultural history of humanity. There are obvious resonances with the Christological ideas developed by Schleiermacher. Although Herrmann tends to avoid the language of 'absolute dependence', it is clear that he understands Jesus to have made *known* and made *available* something that is new, and that this *novum* is thence made known in the inner life of the Christian. It is the 'impression of Jesus' which the believer gains from the gospels which is of decisive importance; this gives rise to a personal certainty of faith, which is grounded in an inner experience rather than by an appeal to the hard facts of history. 'There arises in our hearts the certainty that God himself is turning towards us in this experience.' Perhaps the most significant statement of such views are found in the 1892 essay 'Der geschichtliche Christus der Grund unseres Glaubens' ('The Historical Christ the Ground of our Faith'), a study of the manner in which the historical figure of Jesus can function as the basis of faith. Here, Hermann drew a sharp distinction between the 'historical fact of the person of Jesus' and the 'fact of the personal life of Jesus', understanding by the latter the psychological impact of the figure of Jesus upon the reader of the gospels.[12]

It may be helpful to summarize the basic features of Herrmann's Christology in terms of three fundamental statements:

1. The religious importance of Jesus resides in his religious personality, specifically his 'inner being', and the impact which this makes upon the heart of the believer.

2. It is possible to arrive at a certainty of faith, not on the basis of critical-historical research, but upon the subjective impression which the Jesus of the gospels makes upon the sensitive reader.

3. The eschatological aspects of Jesus' preaching are de-emphasized, with the kingdom of God being treated as 'the true lordship of God over personal existence, especially in human souls and in their fellowship with one another'.

Such insights are developed and refined in the later writings of Adolf von Harnack (1851–1930), and require to be explored in detail.

Adolf von Harnack

The most influential presentation of the liberal picture of Christ appeared in the year 1900, even as its foundations were near to collapse through the impact of a growing body of historical and theological criticism (see pp. 99–115). Adolf von Harnack's *Das Wesen des Christentums* ('What is Christianity?') originally took the form of a series of open lectures to students of all the faculties at the University of Berlin. Although not intended for publication, the lectures were taken down in shorthand by one of the students present, to become a publishing sensation. Their portrait of Christ is widely regarded as the definitive culmination of the liberal school in nineteenth-century Germany, and it is necessary to appreciate the critical-historical insights underlying the work if its full significance is to be apprehended.

The background to the work lies in Harnack's massive researches into *Dogmengeschichte*, or 'the history of dogma' (to use the conventional English translation of the term). His careful studies of the manner in which Christian doctrine developed convinced Harnack that an essentially simple gospel message concerning the significance of Jesus had become distorted through the importation of alien ideas, deriving from Greek (or 'Hellenistic') philosophy. 'Dogma' in general (especially dogmas relating to the person of Christ) was thus regarded by Harnack as representing a distortion of the gospel.

Harnack's massive *History of Dogma* was intended to demonstrate the unacceptable manner in which dogma originated and developed, in order to bring about its more rapid elimination, while at the same time enabling the historian to identify the essential features of the Christian faith in its historic forms. For Harnack, the origins of dogma were to be sought in the 'activity of the Hellenistic spirit upon the gospel soil', as the early church attempted to make the gospel comprehensible to the Hellenistic world within which its early expansion took place:

> The gospel entered into the world, not as a doctrine, but as a joyful message and as a power of the Spirit of God, originally in the forms of Judaism. It stripped off these forms with amazing rapidity, and united and amalgamated itself with Greek science, the Roman Empire and ancient culture, developing, as a counterpoise to this, renunciation of the world and the striving after supernatural life, after deification. All this was summed up in the old dogma and in dogmatic Christianity.[13]

Harnack thus replaces the traditional dogmatic criterion of the *doctrines* of Christianity with the historical criterion of the *nature* of Christianity, by which the fundamental principles (*Grundzüge*) of the gospel may be established and verified through a critical-historical analysis which isolates the distinctive essence (*das Wesen*) of Christianity from the temporary historical forms in which it manifested itself. In many respects, Harnack may be regarded as bringing the historical theology of Enlightenment writers such as J. S. Semler (1725–91) to a state of near-perfection.

On the basis of his historical studies of the development of Christian doctrine, Harnack argues forcefully that the transition of the gospel from its original Palestinian milieu (dominated by Hebraic modes of thought and rationality), to an Hellenistic milieu (characterized by radically different modes of thinking), represented a decisive turning point in the history of Christian thought. The notion of dogma, Harnack argues, owes nothing to the teaching of Jesus Christ, or to primitive Christianity in its original Palestinian context. Rather, it is due to the specific historical location, characterized by Hellenistic modes of thought and patterns of discourse, within which the dogmatic statements of the early church were developed and subsequently formulated:

> What Protestants and Catholics call 'dogmas' are not only
> ecclesiastical teachings, but also (1) conceptually expressed
> theses which, taken collectively, form a unity. These theses
> establish the contents of the Christian religion as knowledge of
> God, of the world, and of sacred history as demonstrated truths.
> Furthermore, (2) these theses have emerged at a definite stage
> in the history of the Christian religion. Both in the manner in
> which they are conceived and in many of their details, they
> demonstrate the influence of this stage (the Greek period), and
> they have preserved this character in all subsequent epochs,
> despite qualifications and additions.[14]

For Harnack, the gospel is nothing other than Jesus Christ himself.
'Jesus does not belong to the gospel as one of its elements, but was the
personal realization and power of the gospel, and we still perceive him
as such.' Jesus himself *is* Christianity. In making this assertion, however,
Harnack implies no *doctrine* of Jesus; the basis of the assertion is partly
historical (based on an analysis of the genesis of Christianity), and partly
a consequence of Harnack's personalist religious assumptions (Jesus'
significance resides primarily in the impact he has upon individuals).
Nevertheless, the transmission of the gospel within a Hellenistic milieu,
with its distinct patterns of rationality and modes of discourse, led to the
attempt to conceptualize and give metaphysical substance to the
significance of Jesus.[15]

In the first edition of the *Dogmengeschichte* ('History of Dogma'),
Harnack illustrates this trend with reference to Gnosticism, the Apolo-
gists, and particularly the Logos-Christology of Origen.[16] To a certain
extent, the development of doctrine may be likened, in Harnack's view,
to a chronic degenerative illness. In the specific case of Christology,
Harnack detects in the shift from soteriology (an analysis of the personal
impact of Jesus) to Christology (an exercise in speculative metaphysics)
a classical instance of the Greek tendency to retreat from the concrete
world of personal experience into the abstract world of ideas.

This may be regarded as an extension of Ritschl and Herrmann's
theoretical criticism of metaphysics to the historical plane. Ritschl
regarded the assertion of the priority of soteriology over Christology as
a means of confining superfluous theological speculation, and restricting

theology to an account of the impact of Jesus of Nazareth upon history
and culture:

> What we substantiate religiously as the activity of God or Christ
> within us authenticates the presence . . . of the author of our
> salvation . . . *Hoc est Christum cognoscere, beneficia eius*
> *cognoscere, non quod isti (scholastici) docent, eius naturas,*
> *modos incarnationis contueri.* Therefore the substance and
> worth of Christ should be understood in the beneficient actions
> upon us Christians, in the gift of blessedness which we sought
> in vain under the law – not in a previously held general concept
> of his divinity.[17]

(The Latin quotation – 'This is to know Christ, to know his benefits, not
[as those scholastics teach] his natures and modes of incarnation' – is
taken from a seminal work of early Lutheran dogmatics, Philip
Melanchthon's *Commonplaces* of 1521.) Harnack supplements this
theological assertion with three historical observations:
1.   A Christology is no part of the proclamation of Jesus of Nazareth.
Jesus' own message is not a Christology; it includes no self-referring
affirmations. It is this point which underlies Harnack's famous, and often
totally misunderstood statement, that *'the gospel, as Jesus proclaimed it,
has to do with the Father only and not the Son'.*[18]
2.   In the history of Christian thought, a concern with Christology was
both chronologically and conceptually posterior to a concern with
soteriology.
3.   The concern with Christology arose within a Hellenistic culture,
which echoed a characteristic Greek concern for abstract speculation.
   Nevertheless, Harnack does not regard these developments as
historically irreversible. Athanasius is viewed as correcting the Hellenistic excesses of Origen; Augustine is seen as a reformer of Greek
speculative theology in general; and Luther is declared to be the
reformer of the post-Augustinian Western theological tradition. The role
assigned to Luther by Harnack is of particular interest, in that the
German reformer is regarded as directing fundamental criticism against
speculative and moral conceptions of God, Christ and faith. Harnack
clearly saw the science of the history of dogma as performing a
comparable task in the modern period. In a letter of March 1879,
Harnack states that the object of his programme of historical investiga-

tion was the reversal of the trend towards 'philosophical evaporation of our saviour'. Dogma is thus to be corrected by history.

Although recent critics of Harnack have cast considerable doubt on the value of his historical analysis of the patristic period, especially his rather uncritical use of the very broad category of 'Hellenism', his insistence that history should be the critic of dogma remains significant, at least in one major respect. If it can be shown, on historical grounds, that some aspect of Christian doctrine does not naturally and legitimately arise from Scripture, it may reasonably be regarded as of questionable validity. For Harnack, the doctrine of the incarnation was a case in point: he regards it as being the direct result of Greek metaphysics, with no place in the gospel itself.[19] The reliability of this particular judgment is highly questionable; nevertheless, Harnack must be considered correct in his demand that we interrogate the Christian doctrinal tradition closely concerning its intellectual pedigree, in order to eliminate those components which are clearly reiterations of Greek metaphysical axioms rather than evangelical insights. The importance of this point will become clear later (see pp. 204–10) when we return to the question of whether God can suffer, and the manner in which this is related to modern Christology.

For Harnack, the history of early Christianity is that of the gradual adulteration of an essentially simple message concerning Jesus, in order that it could assimilate itself to, and thus survive within, new cultural situations:

> The gospel did not enter into the world as a positive statutory religion, and cannot therefore have its classic manifestation in any form of its intellectual or social types, not even in the first. It is therefore the duty of the historian of the first century of the church, as well as that of those which follow, not to be content with fixing the changes of the Christian religion, but to examine how far the new forms were capable of defending, propagating, and impressing the gospel itself. It would probably have perished if the forms of primitive Christianity had been scrupulously maintained in the church; but now primitive Christianity has perished in order that the gospel might be preserved.[20]

It must be stressed that Harnack does not believe that it is possible to distil an historically abstracted 'essence of Christianity'. Christianity is a living thing, like a plant, which changes, and is influenced by its environment. Culture provides the clothing in which the gospel grows. The image of a growing tree has obvious attractions for Harnack: the sap of Christianity needs to be united with bark, if a viable tree is to result. 'Religion does not struggle up into life free and isolated, but grows up, so to speak, in coverings of bark and cannot grow without it.'[21] Harnack uses a famous – indeed, one might say infamous – analogy to clarify his point concerning the cultural accretions and distortions to Christianity, arising from its transference from a Palestinian to a Hellenistic culture. While discussing developments in the third century, he remarks that Christianity had

> . . . already developed a husk and a covering; to penetrate through to it and grasp the kernel had become more difficult; it had also lost much of its original life. But the gifts and the tasks which the gospel offered still remained in force, and the fabric which the church had erected around them also served many a person as the means by which they attained to the thing itself.[22]

The 'kernel of the matter' thus received new and transitory historical forms, with which it became encrusted, and from which it must ultimately be disentangled. Yet this process of disentanglement would not lead to an historically disembodied form of the gospel (which Harnack regards as impossible); rather, it allows the gospel to become firmly embodied in our own culture, shorn of the cultural encumbrances of an alien one. It is this programme of identifying and isolating the kernel from the husk that Harnack expounded to great effect in *What is Christianity?* (1900), to which we may now turn in more detail.

In this important work, Harnack states explicitly that he proposes to analyse the question of what Christianity fundamentally is historically, thus excluding apologetic or philosophical responses. Noting the multiplicity of historical forms which Christianity has taken during its development, and the radical departure of the later from the primitive forms, Harnack concludes: 'There are only two possibilities here: either the gospel is in all respects identical with its first form, in which case it came with its time and has departed with it; or else it contains something which is of permanent validity, in historically changing forms. The latter is the correct view.'[23] It is thus the task of the historian, having established the historical phenomena, to apprehend what is essential in them, and to distinguish the kernel from the husk.

For Harnack, the gospel 'has only one goal – that the living God might be found, and that all persons should discover him as their God, and thus gain strength and joy and peace'. The gospel is thus not a Christology as such, but a soteriology, concerned with the realization of the Fatherhood of God. How this aim was achieved in the course of history is of secondary importance. The irreducible element in the gospel has, in the course of history, become overlaid with unnecessary (although not therefore necessarily incorrect) hypotheses arising primarily from the influence of speculative Hellenistic philosophy. The 'Logos Christology', the dogma of the 'Incarnation' and the concept of salvation as 'deification' are all cited as examples of the Hellenization of the gospel during the first three centuries of its existence.[24] Indeed, Harnack foreshadows the celebrated remark of A. N. Whitehead (1861–1947), that 'Christianity is a religion seeking a metaphysic', when he asserts that the gospel presupposes no philosophy of nature, no specific metaphysical outlook, and is 'doctrine' only to the extent that it proclaims the reality of God the Father. But how does the historical figure of Jesus of Nazareth enter into Harnack's historical analysis of the essence of Christianity?

In view of the numerous, and influential, misunderstandings of Harnack's Christology, it is necessary to consider this question in some detail. For Harnack, the gospels are evangelistic rather than historical documents. They are insufficient for a biography of Jesus, although they provide information upon three important points:

> In the first place, they offer us a plain picture of the preaching of Jesus, both of its main features and of its individual application; in the second place, they describe how his life issued in the service of his vocation; in the third place, they describe to us the impression which he made upon his disciples, and which they transmitted.[25]

Although Harnack identifies the main elements of Jesus' teaching and analyses these elements in some detail, he does not reduce the gospel to the teaching of Jesus or absolutize it in this form. Harnack was too sophisticated an historian to suppose that the earliest recorded form of the gospel could be treated as its sole legitimate expression, or to overlook the historical impact which the gospel initially made, as a result of which certain aspects of Jesus' teaching were passed over. For Harnack, 'the gospel, as Jesus proclaimed it, has to do with the Father alone, and not with the Son'. Nevertheless, this version of the gospel cannot be permitted to be considered as normative or constitutive; it is merely one of many historical forms which the gospel has taken. As Harnack emphasizes, 'within two generations of his death Jesus Christ was already spoken of in the highest terms humanly possible', so that the Son was subsequently an element of the gospel proclamation. Harnack's important distinction between the 'Easter message' and the 'Easter faith' is significant in this respect.

Those who suggest that Harnack identified the gospel with the teachings of Jesus seriously misunderstand him. Harnack was far too good an historian, by the standards of his age, to lapse into such a crude positivism. For Harnack, Jesus' teaching was of enormous significance, but, like every historical manifestation of the gospel in its history, it contained elements which were peripheral rather than central, husk rather than kernel. The subsequent development of Christianity in the apostolic era revealed a significantly different understanding of the total teaching of Jesus, and of the relation between his life and death, which is no less important an aspect of the historical manifestation of the gospel. It is for this reason that Harnack asserts that the gospel, as the New Testament proclaims it, contains two elements: (1) the preaching of Jesus, and (2) the proclamation of Jesus as the Christ who died and rose again for the sake of sin and who gives assurance of forgiveness and eternal life.

On the basis of his historical approach to the development of Christianity, Harnack is able to build up a series of profiles: the gospel as proclaimed by Jesus himself; the gospel as proclaimed by Paul; the gospel as proclaimed by Augustine; the gospel as proclaimed by Luther; and so forth – and none of these may be identified with the essence of the gospel itself. For Harnack, it is impossible for the historian to define Christianity; indeed, Harnack never portrays the 'essence' of Christianity as an historical phenomenon. Harnack insists that the proper task of the historian is to document historical forms which Christianity has taken down the ages, *none of which may be absolutized or treated as normative*. Jesus' significance therefore ultimately lies elsewhere than in his being the teacher of the 'higher righteousness'.

Harnack summarizes his understanding of the permanent significance of Christ as follows: 'Jesus does not belong to the gospel as one of its elements, but *was the personal realisation and power of the gospel, and we still perceive him as such.'*[26] Although it is clear that Harnack has the highest possible estimation of Christ, he insists that the irreducible element of the gospel concerns our relationship to God the Father. Such a faith in God the Father is linked to Jesus Christ historically, not theologically. The peculiar significance of Christ in relation to Christianity resides in the power of his religious personality:

> Whoever receives the gospel, and tries to recognize the one who brought it to us, will testify that here the divine appeared as purely as it can appear on earth, and that Jesus was himself the power of the gospel for his followers. What they experienced and recognized in him, however, they have proclaimed, and this proclamation is still a living force.[27]

It will therefore be clear that Harnack's Christology rests upon assumptions which he justifies inferentially, with reference to their historical development. Two of these are particularly important. First, the 'Logos Christology' and 'incarnational' modes of thought are identified as arising from extra-biblical and secular Hellenistic philosophical intrusions into Christian thought. Second, the connection between the gospel of 'eternal life in the midst of time, by the strength of and under the eyes of God' and Jesus of Nazareth is demonstrated to be historical rather than theological.

It can be argued that Harnack's importance to our study lies not in his Christology itself, but in the means he employed to derive it. Harnack's distinctive contribution to the development of our theme is largely the result of his insistence that the historical orgins of traditional Christological formulations should be subjected to a rigorous critical examination. Nevertheless, this critical-historical approach to traditional Christology was supplemented by Harnack's own approach to the theme. Harnack was concerned to do more than correct the past; he wanted to construct the future. By adopting the methodologically legitimate procedure of permitting the history of Christianity itself to define the questions to be answered, Harnack believed he would be capable of developing an 'undogmatic' Christology, suited to the dawning brave new world of the twentieth century. In a reminiscence of his student days in 1894, Theophil Wurm (1868–1953) reported that Harnack suggested the following structure for a work of dogmatic theology:

Part I: The teachings of Jesus and their apostolic interpretation.

Part II: Mysteries.

To this second part Harnack assigned everything usually included in a work on dogmatic theology – especially Christology.

The 'liberal portrait of Christ' may not have reduced Christ totally to the stereotype of a German professor, as its more forceful critics were wont to suggest. Nevertheless, it effectively prohibited any normative pronouncements concerning his significance, and simultaneously seemed to legitimate an astonishingly wide range of Christological opinions. Even as late as 1925, Harnack himself suggested that the irreducible Christological affirmation was that Jesus was the 'mirror of God's fatherly heart'.[28] His critics were not slow to suggest that the only reflection to be seen in that mirror was that of a liberal Protestant face, looking remarkably like Harnack himself. This was certainly the view of the English modernist George Tyrrell (1861–1909), whose scathingly caustic remarks concerning Harnack's historical approach were published posthumously in 1909: 'The Christ that Harnack sees, looking back through nineteen centuries of catholic darkness, is only the reflection of a liberal Protestant face, seen at the bottom of a deep well.'[29]

By then, however, the historical approach to Christology had been undermined to such an extent that Harnack's *aperçu* attracted little notice. We now return to the final decade of the nineteenth century, to consider the rise of the ideas which would eventually destroy even the most genial liberal portrait of Christ.

The Collapse of the Liberal Christology: from Weiss to Troeltsch

The rise of the Ritschlian school in the final quarter of the nineteenth century led to a new interest in the religious personality of Jesus, and hence to renewed attention being paid to the nature of the New Testament sources upon which the life of the historical Jesus could be constructed. The intense interest which developed in the 'Synoptic Problem' was thus partly a consequence of the perceived dogmatic need to establish facts concerning the historical Jesus, in order to bring out the unique nature of his religious personality. It was widely believed that the new literary approach to the New Testament in general, and to the synoptic gospels in particular, would permit scholars to establish a 'firmly drawn and life-like portrait which, with a few bold strokes, should bring out clearly the originality, the force, the personality of Jesus'.[1] It was this enterprise which has been poetically described in English as the 'quest of the historical Jesus', and more prosaically in German as the '*Leben-Jesu-Forschung* (life of Jesus research)'.

The assumption underlying the 'life of Jesus movement' in the later nineteenth century was that the remarkable religious personality of Jesus, whose contours could be delineated by thoroughgoing historical inquiry, would provide a solid historical foundation for faith. The firm ground of historical truth upon which Christian faith depended was thus not supernatural or anti-rational (a perceived weakness of traditional Christology), but merely the religious personality of Jesus, a fact of history open to scientific investigation. The impression which he made upon his contemporaries could be reproduced in his followers of every age. The first-century legendary embellishments to the gospel stories could thus be discarded, as could the anachronistic dogmatic formulations of a later age concerning him. The remarkable number of 'lives of Jesus' produced in the later nineteenth century in England, America and France, as well as Germany itself, is an adequate testimony to the popular appeal of the ideas underlying the 'life of Jesus' movement. Through it, the religious personality of the 'far-off mystic of the Galilean hills' – to use Lord Morley's famous phrase – could be brought into the present, uncluttered by cultural irrelevancies, in order to form the basis of faith for the coming generation.

It was, of course, inevitable that the portrayals of the religious personality of Jesus were radically subjective, so that the rediscovered Jesus of history turned out to be merely the embodiment of an ideal figure by the progressive standards of the nineteenth century. George Tyrrell, whose views on Harnack we noted earlier (p. 98), summarizes the aims of liberal Protestant writers as follows:

> They wanted to bring Jesus into the nineteenth century as the incarnation of its ideal of divine righteousness, i.e. of all the highest principles and aspirations that ensure the healthy progress of civilisation. They wanted to acquit him of that exclusive and earth-scorning otherworldliness, which had led men to look on his religion as the foe of progress and energy, and which came from confusing the accidental form with the essential substance of his gospel.[2]

There was a widespread tendency to assume that 'Jesus of Nazareth as he actually was (*wie er eigentlich gewesen war*)' coincided with 'Jesus of Nazareth as he may be reconstructed by means of the objective historical method'. The assumption that lay beneath the liberal picture of Christ was that the 'Jesus of history who lived in first century Palestine' could be precisely defined in terms of dates, places, events, sequences, causes and effects – in other words, on the basis of a very superficial view of history which fails to take account of the deeper levels of historical actuality, as it is now understood.[3] Indeed, it is possible to argue that the fundamental defect in the liberal picture of Christ, underlying both the criticisms we have just made, was a failure to recognize the historicity of the historian's own situation, so that the historically relative was misunderstood as the historically absolute. The relativity of historical research was not immediately obvious to the nineteenth-century 'life of Jesus' movement, whose adherents regarded themselves as practitioners of the objective historical method, rather than as an historically conditioned phenomenon of which they themselves were a part. Earlier writers had laboured under misunderstandings; their successors in German theological faculties had access to the most sophisticated historical methods and resources, which allowed them access to the authentic history of Jesus. The liberal Protestant writers of the nineteenth century certainly saw Jesus as he had never been seen before; sadly, they believed that they saw him as he actually was.

The illusion could not last. The most sustained challenge to the 'life of Jesus' movement developed on a number of fronts during the final decade of the nineteenth century, and may be argued to date from the foundation of the 'history of religions school (*religionsgeschichtliche Schule*)' in 1890. Originally known as the 'little Göttingen faculty (*kleine Göttinger Fakultät*)', this school was destined to exercise considerable influence over biblical scholarship and Christological speculation in the first third of the twentieth century.[4] At this early stage, the school was characterized primarily by little more than its hostility towards the Göttingen master, Albrecht Ritschl.

However, other characteristics soon began to emerge. From its outset, the school proved itself to be of major importance in relation to both Old and New Testament studies, on account of its insistence that the religious developments of both Old and New Testaments, as well as those of the early church, had to be seen in the context of other religions. Biblical religion was not something distinct in its own right; its origins could be understood in terms of general developments in religious thinking at the time. Thus Hermann Gunkel's (1862–1932) *Schöpfung und Chaos* ('Creation and Chaos', 1895) derived much of the Old Testament's themes of creation and chaos from Babylonian mythology, while Wilhelm Bousset's (1865–1920) *Kyrios Christos* (1913) considered the development of early Christian ideas in terms of their Hellenistic-Jewish context. An important series of studies from within this school, as well as several from outside it, called the foundations of the liberal 'quest of the historical Jesus' into question.

Broadly speaking, four main criticisms of the *Christusbild* of liberal Protestantism emerged in the period 1890–1911:
1. The *apocalyptic critique*, primarily associated with Johannes Weiss

(1863–1914) and Albert Schweitzer (1875–1965), which maintained that the strongly eschatological bias of Jesus' proclamation of the kingdom of God called the static liberal interpretation of the concept into question. The 'kingdom of God (*Reich Gottes*)' was not to be seen as a settled realm of liberal moral values, but as a devastating apocalyptic moment which overturned human values.

2. The *sceptical critique*, associated particularly with William Wrede (1859–1906), which called into question the historical status of our knowledge of Jesus in the first place. History and theology were closely intermingled in the synoptic narratives, and could not be disentangled.

3. The *dogmatic critique*, due to Martin Kähler (1835–1912), which challenged the theological significance of the reconstruction of the historical Jesus. The 'historical Jesus' was an irrelevance to faith, which was based upon the 'Christ of faith'.

4. The *historicist critique*, developed by Ernst Troeltsch (1865–1923), which raised fundamental questions concerning the accessibility and relevance of Jesus of Nazareth. This was supplemented by a theory, grounded in the social psychology of the day, concerning the need for a central cultic figure within a religious system, which, Troeltsch believed, explained the place of Jesus within Christianity.

In the present chapter, we shall consider these four criticisms of the liberal picture of Christ, and assess their theological significance.

Johannes Weiss

In 1892, Johannes Weiss published *Die Predigt Jesu vom Reich Gottes* ('Jesus' Proclamation of the Kingdom of God'), a work of a mere 67 pages, occasioning a crisis within liberal Protestantism in doing so. The idea of the 'kingdom of God' was understood by the Ritschlian school to mean the exercise of the moral life in society, or a supreme ethical ideal. In other words, it was conceived primarily as something subjective, inward or spiritual, rather than in spatio-temporal terms. For Weiss himself, Ritschl's concept of the kingdom of God was essentially continuous with that of the Enlightenment, primarily a static moral concept without eschatological overtones. The rediscovery of the eschatology of the preaching of Jesus called into question not merely this understanding of the kingdom of God, but also the liberal portrait of Christ in general.[5]

As noted earlier (pp. 33–5), H. S. Reimarus had suggested that Jesus was essentially an apocalyptic visionary whose ideas had been radically modified in a non-political direction by his disciples. This idea found little favour at the time, although it was taken up sporadically in the century following its appearance. In 1891, two monographs appeared from the presses of E. J. Brill in Leiden on the subject of the eschatological character of the 'kingdom of God' in Jesus' preaching – Ernst Issel's *Die Lehre vom Reich Gottes im Neuen Testament* ('The Doctrine of the Kingdom of God in the New Testament') and Otto Schmoller's *Die Lehre vom Reich Gottes in den Schriften des Neuen Testament* ('The Doctrine of the Kingdom of God in the Writings of the New Testament)'. As Weiss indicates, the publication of these books provided the necessary stimulus for him to publish his own, in which the radical difference between the biblical and Ritschlian concept of the kingdom of God was first exposed. The former was eschatological in character, in marked contrast to the settled and static concept developed by Ritschl.

Weiss records that he was disturbed at an early phase of his career by the 'clear perception that Ritschl's idea of the kingdom of God and the corresponding idea in the preaching of Jesus were two very different things'. Weiss therefore undertook investigation of two distinct, although clearly related, questions, of which the first is historical and the second theological in nature. First, what did Jesus teach concerning the kingdom of God? Second, what is the relationship between this understanding of the kingdom of God and that of the church subsequently? Although it is clear that Weiss's interest lies primarily with the first question, the significance of the second could hardly be overlooked. For Weiss, Jesus understood the kingdom of God in charateristically apocalyptic and eschatological terms. The career of Jesus, and especially his teaching, may be explained on the basis of late Jewish apocalyptic, with its expectation of the imminent end of the world and its hope of the coming of the Messiah, the Son of Man, who would transform the world and inaugurate the kingdom of God. The kingdom of God is thus radically other-worldly and belongs to the future:

> The interpretation of the kingdom of God as an innerworldly ethical idea is a vestige of a Kantian ideal, and does not stand up before a more precise historical examination . . . The kingdom of God, as Jesus thought of it, is never something subjective, inward or spiritual, but always the objective messianic Kingdom, which is usually portrayed as a territory

into which one enters, a land in which one has a share, or a treasure which comes down from heaven.[6]

For Jesus, the kingdom of God was an event, to be brought about by God himself in the imminent future. Jesus cannot be thought of as having initiated the kingdom of God: his preaching was essentially the proclamation of a penitential ethic by which his followers might be prepared for the impending advent of the kingdom. The 'new righteousness' which Jesus required of his disciples must be understood eschatologically, as the condition for entrance into the coming kingdom of God, rather than as an end in itself. The kingdom of God is thus the motive for ethics, rather than its embodiment. Weiss states this as follows:

> The kingdom of God, as Jesus conceived it, is a radically otherworldly entity which stands in diametric opposition to this world. This is to say that there can be no talk of an inner-worldly development of the kingdom of God in the mind of Jesus! On the basis of this observation, it seems to follow that the dogmatic religious-ethical application of this idea in more recent theology (an application which has stripped away the original eschatological-apocalyptical meaning of the idea) is unjustified.[7]

The kingdom of God, as Jesus conceived it, thus does not come about as the result of a long period of human development within the world, on the basis of insights first enunciated by Jesus, but comes as a catastrophe from heaven. The demands which it makes on humanity are so radical and absolute that it overthrows, rather than confirms, human understandings of civilization and morality. It might therefore be thought that Weiss abandoned Ritschlianism. In fact, Weiss remained attached to the Ritschlian theology, despite his radical critique of its religious-ethical foundations. Where Herrman regarded Jesus as the object of trust, Weiss regarded him as an example to be imitated. However, the little book brought one era to an end, and began another.[8] The destructive effect of his *Kingdom of God* was reinforced considerably through the appearance of Albert Schweitzer's *Das Messianitäts- und Leidensgeheimnis* ('The Mystery of the Kingdom of God') in 1901.

Albert Schweitzer

As we noted, Weiss remained Ritschlian in outlook even after the publication of the second edition of his *Kingdom of God* (1900). He was able to maintain this apparently impossible position by insisting that the apocalyptic element was absent from certain parts of Jesus' preaching, thus permitting these non-eschatological elements to have a permanent significance where the eschatological elements did not. Thus the command to 'love God and one's neighbour' was non-eschatological, and constituted the centre and focus of Jesus' preaching. For Schweitzer, however, the whole character of Jesus' ministry was conditioned and determined by his apocalyptic outlook. It is this idea which has become familiar to the English-speaking world as 'thorough-going eschatology', although the more obvious English equivalent 'consistent eschatology' perhaps conveys the sense of the German *konsequente Eschatologie* more readily. Where Weiss regarded a substantial part (but not all) of the teaching of Jesus as being conditioned by his radical eschatological expectations, Schweitzer argued for the need to recognize that every aspect of the teaching and attitudes of Jesus was determined by his eschatological outlook. Where Weiss believed that only part of Jesus' preaching was affected by this outlook, Schweitzer argued that the entire content of Jesus' message was consistently and thoroughly conditioned by apocalyptic ideas – ideas which were quite alien to the settled outlook of western Europe, as it entered the twentieth century.

The result of this consistent eschatological interpretation of the person and message of Jesus of Nazareth was a portrait of Christ as a remote and strange figure, with dark anxieties and fears, an apocalyptic and wholly unworldly figure, whose hopes and expectations finally came to nothing. Far from being an incidental and dispensable 'husk' which could be discarded in order to establish the true 'kernel' of Jesus' teaching concerning the universal Fatherhood of God, eschatology was an essential, dominant and inalienable characteristic of his *Weltanschauung*. Jesus thus appears to us as a strange figure from an alien first-century Jewish apocalyptic milieu, so that, in Schweitzer's famous words, 'he comes to us as one unknown'.[9] Although Weiss and Schweitzer alike appear to have evaded the dogmatic consequences of their eschatological approach to the historical Jesus, it was inevitable that historical consistency would triumph over dogma. It was thus necessary to attempt to develop some new means of approaching the history of Jesus of Nazareth, which could address the apocalyptic dimension of his context. As Julius Kaftan (1848–1926) observed, 'If Johannes Weiss is right, and the conception of the kingdom of God is an eschatological one, it is then impossible to make use of this concept in dogmatics.'

We have already noted the importance of Schweitzer's work on the apocalyptic aspects of Jesus' ministry, and will return presently to consider its further implications. However, Schweitzer had another contribution to make to the debate, which, with the benefit of hindsight, may be seen to have been the more significant. The publication of Schweitzer's *Geschichte der Leben-Jesu-Forschung* ('Quest of the Historical Jesus') in 1906 may be regarded as the final and most cruel exposure of the inadequacy of the pseudo-historical theology of liberal Protestantism. Although the book was, in many respects, unoriginal, it succeeded in highlighting the deficiencies of the 'Life of Jesus' movement in a manner which was more thorough-going than anything that had been seen before.

Schweitzer, by bringing together the results of the critical study of the life of Jesus, erected a monument to the 'Life of Jesus' movement which proved to be its gravestone, precisely because the full coherence of the case against the movement was now obvious. Schweitzer did not, in fact, add to the history which he so carefully documented; rather, he brought it to an end by demonstrating its inner tensions and contradictions. Schweitzer did not need to employ extensive dogmatic arguments (such as those of Kähler, to be considered presently) in reaching his conclusions: the case was established simply on the basis of the history of the *Leben-Jesu-Forschung* itself.

With great force and persuasiveness, Schweitzer relentlessly posed the three great questions of 'Either-Or' which the 'Life of Jesus' movement could not ignore:

> The first was posed by Strauss: either purely historical or purely supernatural; the second was fought out by the Tübingen school and Holtzmann: either synoptic or Johannine; and now the third: either eschatological or non-eschatological.

In every case, Schweitzer himself effectively demonstrated the necessity to adopt the first of the two positions: it was necessary to adopt a purely historical approach to the synoptic gospels, recognizing the full weight which had to be given to their eschatological cast and presuppositions. The full recognition of the eschatological character of the historical *Christusbild* of the synoptic gospels inevitably led to the rejection of the decidely non-eschatological, Kantian *Christusbild* of liberal Protestanism. Writing in 1962, Ernst Käsemann (see pp. 184–7) assessed the theological impact of the rediscovery of primitive Christian apocalyptic as follows:

> The history of theology in the last two generations demonstrates that the rediscovery of primitive Christian apocalyptic, and the recognition of its significance for the entire New Testament (especially due to Kabisch, Johannes Weiss and Albert Schweitzer), was a shock to its discoverers and their contemporaries beyond our imagination. Weiss promptly fell back upon the liberal *Christusbild*, Schweitzer bravely drew the consequences from his theses about the historical Jesus (untenable theses, as it happened), and the remainder paid enthusiastic attention to the fields of religious history, cultic piety and mysticism. Barth's Romans commentary brought 'consistent eschatology' out of its shadowy existence, and made it the dominant programme of the exposition of the New Testament (although in a variety of interpretations) in Germany.

So how was this new appreciation of the importance of apocalyptic on the one hand, and the inadequacy of the liberal Protestant interpretative framework on the other, to be handled? Three new approaches to the interpretation of apocalyptic would be developed within the German Protestant Christological tradition in the twentieth century, and will be discussed at appropriate points later in this work. They are:

1. The *apocalyptic* approach of the young Karl Barth, especially in his commentary on Romans, which appeals to the apocalpytic element in Jesus' preaching to emphasize his *otherness*, in the face of the characteristic liberal Protestant tendency to assimilate him to bourgeois cultural ideals. The way was thus cleared for rediscovering God as he has chosen to make himself known, rather than projecting bourgeois values on to the distant historical figure of Jesus (see pp. 123–9).

2. The *demythologizing* approach of Rudolf Bultmann, which argues for the need to abstract the gospel proclamation from its first-century

context, saturated with apocalyptic ideas, and transfer them to a twentieth-century worldview, which is concerned with fundamental questions of human existence (see pp. 160–2).

3. The *interpretative* approach of Wolfhart Pannenberg, which treats the apocalyptic context of Jesus' preaching and existence as a hermeneutical framework for the interpretation of his life, and supremely his resurrection (see pp. 188–92).

All this, however, lay far in the future. As liberal Protestants gloomily surveyed the latest findings from the biblical scholars, the outlook seemed bleak indeed. If Christianity was to be focused on the religious personality of Jesus, what could be done if that 'personality' was saturated and conditioned by beliefs and expectations which were absurd in the eyes of the cultured late nineteenth-century German bourgeoisie? And, as subsequent events were to prove, things moved from bad to worse. On the same day as Schweitzer's *Mystery of the Kingdom of God* was published at Tübingen, Wrede's *Das Messiasgeheimnis in den Evangelien* ('The Messianic Secret') appeared at Göttingen.

William Wrede

Although the significance of Wrede's *Messianic Secret* would not be fully appreciated until immediately after the First World War, the immediate challenge which it posed to liberal Christology could not be ignored. It was widely believed within the liberal school that the resolution of the literary question concerning the gospels, which had led to the conclusion that Mark was the oldest of the synoptic gospels, also amounted to the resolution of the literary question concerning the most reliable source material for the construction of a 'life of Jesus'. The studies of writers such as Heinrich Holtzmann (1832–1910) had established the literary priority of Mark. The acceptance of the *literary* priority of Mark seemed to many to imply its *historical* priority. There was thus a widespread interest in the *Christusbild* of the Second Gospel, which was held to be a reliable source for details of Jesus' ministry and for insights into his religious personality.

The concept of a growing recognition on the part of Jesus that he was indeed the Messiah was fundamental to many representatives of the 'life of Jesus' movement. The 'developing Messianic consciousness' hypothesis was heavily dependent upon Mark for both its chronology and its factual basis. Furthermore, even Schweitzer himself assumed the basic accuracy of Mark's historical sequence: his critique of the older 'quest of the historical Jesus' was essentially that it had failed to take the apocalyptic element in Jesus' thought sufficiently seriously. At no point does he suggest that the whole enterprise of producing a 'developmental life of Jesus' was, by its very nature, impossible. The significance of Wrede's *Messiasgeheimnis* lies chiefly in the fact that he demonstrated that the old developmental view of the life of Jesus cannot be sustained on the basis of Mark's gospel. Wrede was able to demonstrate that Mark was writing not with the objectivity of the interests of the modern theologian, but rather as a theologian of the *Messiasgeheimnis* (which could be translated 'messianic mystery', as well as the customary 'messianic secret').

According to Wrede, Mark was painting a theological picture in the guise of history, imposing his theology upon the material which he had at his disposal.[10] The Second Gospel was thus not objectively historical, but was actually a creative theological reinterpretation of history. It was thus impossible to go behind Mark's narrative and reconstruct the history of Jesus, in that – if Wrede is right – this narrative is itself a theological construction, beyond which one cannot go. The 'quest of the historical Jesus' thus comes to an end, in that it proves impossible to establish an historical foundation for the 'real' Jesus of history.

The gospel writers in general, according to Wrede, thus had to be understood in the social context of the communities in which they lived and wrote, and which both shaped and modified the materials they used. Although one of Wrede's chief conclusions was that the so-called 'messianic secret' was not part of the history of Jesus, but arose within the community of faith (indeed, it may be suggested that, far from being a conclusion drawn from a study of Mark, it was a presupposition with which he approached it!), it was the general approach Wrede adopted which proved the more devastating for the liberal portrait of Christ. The synoptic gospels could at best be considered as secondary sources for the life of Jesus, as they were primary sources only for the views of the evangelists and the communities they represented.

Wrede's contribution to the destruction of the liberal picture of Christ is considerably greater than Schweitzer's, although this point has been obscured by uncritical English evaluations of Schweitzer's study of the development of the 'quest of the historical Jesus'. Wrede identified three radical and fatal errors underlying the liberal *Christusbild*.[11]

First, although the liberal theologians appealed to later modifications of an earlier tradition when faced with unpalatable features of the synoptic accounts of Jesus (such as miracles, or obvious contradictions between sources), they failed to apply this principle consistently. In other words, they failed to realize that the later belief of the community had exercised a normative influence over the evangelist at every stage of his work.

Second, the motives of the evangelists were not taken into account. The liberal theologians tended simply to exclude those portions of the narratives they found unacceptable, and contented themselves with what remained. By doing so, they failed to take seriously the fact that the evangelist himself had a positive statement to make, and substituted for this something quite distinct. The first priority should be to approach the gospel narratives on their own terms, to establish what the evangelist wished to convey to his readers, and thence to make this the foundation of critical historiography.

Third, the psychological approach to the gospel narratives tended to confuse what was *conceivable* with what *actually took place*. In effect, liberal theologians were likely to find in the gospels precisely what they were seeking, on the basis of a 'sort of psychological guesswork' which appeared to value emotive descriptions more than strict accuracy and certainty of knowledge. This was hardly an adequate foundation for historical reconstruction.

Although it is possible to argue that Wrede actually based his analysis of Mark upon his own *a priori* reconstruction of the nature of the beliefs of primitive Christianity, it is impossible to deny the cumulative force of his critique of the methodology underlying the liberal 'quest of the historical Jesus'. Particularly significant in this respect is the all too frequently overlooked divergence of opinion between Schweitzer and Wrede on the dogmatic content of the Marcan tradition. For Wrede, the *Messiasgeheimnis* exemplified the unhistorical character of the tradition in general; in the view of Schweitzer, the dogmatic element was genuinely historical, and might be explained on the basis of Jesus's eschatological milieu.[12] For Schweitzer, the only ways forward were his own consistent eschatology, and the so-called '*Wredestrasse*' – consistent scepticism. *Tertium non datur*: there was no alternative. Schweitzer does not, however, appear to have recognized the significance of a little essay published by Martin Kähler in 1892, originally delivered as a lecture to the Wuppertal pastoral conference, and expanded in 1896. This essay indicated a third possible approach to the issues surrounding the relation of faith and history, the exploration of which would prove to be one of the most fertile and significant areas of twentieth-century Christology.

Martin Kähler

Martin Kähler's *Der sogenannte historische Jesus und der geschichtliche, biblische Christus* ('The So-Called Historical Jesus and the Historic, Biblical Christ'), appeared in 1892. The work, which was a mere 45 pages in length, may be regarded as an attempt to establish an 'invulnerable area (*sturmfreies Gebiet*)' of faith in the midst of the crisis which he correctly perceived to be developing in the final decade of the century. Kähler rightly saw that the dispassionate and provisional Jesus of the academic historian cannot become the object of faith. Yet how can Jesus Christ be the authentic basis and content of Christian faith, when historical science can never establish certain knowledge concerning the historical Jesus? How can faith be based upon an historical event without being vulnerable to the charge of historical relativism? It was precisely these questions which Kähler addressed in this famous work.

Before considering his response, it is appropriate to consider a difficulty encountered in translating its title. An important distinction is drawn between two senses of 'historical', which cannot be adequately reproduced in English. The term *historisch* is used to refer to Jesus as the object of critical-historical investigation, whereas the term *geschichtlich* is used to refer to Jesus as the object of faith. Of the various suggested English equivalents for the word-pair *historisch -geschichtlich*, two may be noted:

1. *Historisch* may be translated as 'objective-historical', and *geschichtlich* as 'existential-historical': this brings out the distinction between the objective empirical facts of history, and their perceived significance for the individual.[13]

2. Alternatively, *historisch* may be translated 'historical', and *geschichtlich* as 'historic': this translation emphasizes the distinction between an event which is *located* in history and an event which *makes* history.[14]

To avoid confusion, we propose to translate both German terms as 'historical' and to indicate which of the two terms is being translated.

Kähler has been seriously neglected within the English-speaking world, largely through the absence of translations of his principal works. (It may be noted, incidentally, that the writings of the British Congregationalist theologian Peter Taylor Forsyth [1848–1921] are heavily dependent upon Kähler's writings. Forsyth is often described as the English Barth. He is nothing of the sort; if anything, he is the English Kähler.) Despite its neglect within English-language scholarship, Kähler's celebrated *Die Wissenschaft der christlichen Lehre* ('The Science of Christian Doctrine') is often cited by German scholars as the greatest single-volume dogmatic work to appear in the period between Schleiermacher and Barth. This work develops a number of central themes, including the need for an objective basis for faith.

Kähler was increasingly alarmed by the subjectivism of his contemporaries, such as Schleiermacher, J. C. K. von Hoffmann (1810–77), Ritschl and Herrmann, and attempted to rectify this in a number of important works published in the period 1892–1917. Kähler, it may be emphasized, was a dogmatic theologian, rather that a New Testament scholar, whose interest in the New Testament was primarily a consequence of his dogmatic interest in the question of the grounds of faith. It is for this reason that his approach differs so sharply from that of Wrede and Schweitzer, even if their conclusions at times coincide. Kähler effectively challenges the Christology of the Enlightenment and liberal school (or 'Jesuology', as he styles their Ebionitism) on the grounds of its implicit (and apparently unacknowledged) dogmatic presuppositions. *The So-Called Historical Jesus* of 1892 was intended as a critique of the theological foundations of the 'life of Jesus' movement.

Kähler states his two objectives in this work as follows: first, to criticize and reject the errors of the 'life of Jesus' movement; and second, to establish the validity of an alternative approach, this latter being by far the more important. For Kähler,

> The historical Jesus of modern writers conceals the living Christ from us. The Jesus of the 'life of Jesus' movement is merely a modern example of a brain-child of the human imagination (*eine moderne Abart von Erzeugnissen menschlicher erfindlicher Kunst*), no better that the notorious dogmatic Christ of Byzantine Christology. They are both equally far removed from the real Christ. In this respect, historicism is just as arbitrary, just as humanly arrogant, just as speculative and 'faithlessly

Gnostic', as that dogmatism which was itself considered modern in its own day.[15]

Kähler concedes immediately that the 'life of Jesus' movement was completely correct in so far as it contrasted the biblical witness to Christ with an abstract dogmatism. He nevertheless insists upon its futility, a view summarized in his well-known statement to the effect that the entire 'life of Jesus' movement is a blind alley. His reasons for making this assertion are complex, foreshadowing those of Wrede and provoking charges of 'morbid scepticism' from his critics.

The most fundamental reason is that Christ must be regarded as a 'supra-historical' (*übergeschichtlich*) rather than a merely 'historical' (*geschichtlich*) figure, so that the critical-historical method cannot be applied in his case. The critical-historical method could not deal with the supra-historical (and hence supra-human) characteristics of Jesus, and hence was obliged to ignore or deny them. In effect, the critical-historical method could lead only to an Arian or Ebionite Christology, on account of its latent dogmatic presuppositions. This point, made frequently throughout the essay, is developed with particular force in relation to the psychological interpretation of the personality of Jesus, and the related question concerning the use of the principle of analogy in the critical-historical method.

Kähler notes that the psychological interpretation of the personality of Jesus is dependent upon the (unrecognized) presupposition that the distinction between ourselves and Jesus is one of degree (*Grad*) rather than kind (*Art*), which Kähler suggests must be criticized on dogmatic grounds. More significantly, Kähler challenges what he regards as an improper use of the principle of analogy in the interpretation of the New Testament portrayal of Christ. This, he argues, inevitably leads to Jesus being treated as analogous to modern human beings, and hence to a reduced or degree Christology. If it is assumed from the outset that Jesus is an ordinary human being, who differs from other humans only in degree and not in nature, then this assumption will be read back into the biblical texts, and dictate the resulting conclusion – that Jesus of Nazareth is a human being who differs from us only in degree. In fact, precisely this point would underlie Kähler's later criticisms of Harnack's *What is Christianity?*, which he argued reduced piety from worship of God to admiration of a hero.

Second, Kähler argues that 'we do not possess any sources for a life of Jesus which an historian could accept as reliable and adequate'. This is not to say that the sources are unreliable and inadequate for the purposes of *faith*. Kähler is rather concerned to emphasize that the gospels are not the accounts of disinterested, impartial observers, but rather accounts of the faith of believers, which cannot be isolated, either in form or content, from that faith: the gospel accounts 'are not the reports of alert impartial observers, but are throughout the testimonies and confessions (*Zeugnisse und Bekenntnisse*) of believers in Christ'. In that 'it is only through these accounts that we are able to come into contact with him', it will be clear that the 'biblical portrait of Christ' is of decisive importance for faith.

What is important for Kähler is not who Christ was, but what he presently does for believers. The 'Jesus of history' lacks the soteriological significance of the 'Christ of faith'. The thorny problems of Christology may therefore be left behind in order to develop 'soterology', a term which Kähler introduces to designate 'the knowledge of faith concerning the person of the saviour'. (It should be noted that 'soterology' – that is, the 'study of the *saviour*' – should not be confused with the similar and widely-used term 'soteriology', or 'the study of *salvation*'. Kähler's term has not found general acceptance within the scholarly community.) In effect, Kähler argues that the 'life of Jesus' movement has done little more than create a fictitious and pseudo-scientific Christ, devoid of existential significance. For Kähler, 'the real Christ is the preached Christ (*der wirkliche Christus ist der gepredigte Christus*)'. Christian faith is not based upon this *historische Jesus*, but upon the existentially significant and faith-evoking figure of the *geschichtliche Christus*.

As Kähler emphasizes, the New Testament proclamation of Christ does not presuppose or necessitate a distinction between 'the memory of the days of his flesh and the confession of his eternal significance (*Erinnerung an die Tage seines Fleisches und Bekenntnis zu seiner ewigen Deutung*)'. This means that the New Testament itself contains an irreducible dogmatic element, which cannot be eliminated without gross historical distortion. It is for this reason that Kähler feels able to assert that, even in those circles in which 'apostolic dogma' is depreciated, 'one finds a dim reflection of that dogma, namely the knowledge of a certain incomparable evaluation of Jesus within the church, and the mediation of his portrait for attention and approval'. The *biblische, geschichtliche Christus* is thus the total Christ, rather than the fictitious and soteriologically deficient *historische Jesus.*

By accepting the distinction between the 'Jesus of history' and the 'Christ of faith', Kähler is thus able to argue that, as a matter of fact, Christian faith is based upon the latter, rather than the former. The 'life of Jesus' movement has thus little significance for faith, in that the 'historical Christ' (*geschichtliche Christus*) cannot be reduced to a mere biography or intellectual analysis of the 'historical Jesus' (*historische Jesus*). For Kähler, the historical method cannot objectively demonstrate (or, indeed, negate) the revelation upon which faith stands – and as such, has little ultimate significance for faith. The saving significance of the historical figure of Jesus of Nazareth is encapsulated in the biblical portrait of Christ, which is immeasurably richer, and which alone evokes and sustains faith. It is this biblical portrait of Christ as saviour which, for Kähler, constitutes the invulnerable foundation of faith.

Kähler was, of course, heavily criticized by his contemporaries. In the same year as the publication of Kähler's essay, Wilhelm Herrmann argued that Kähler's approach made it utterly impossible to ascertain whether the 'historical Christ (*geschichtliche Christus*)' – supposedly the basis of faith – was not, in fact, merely a product of faith rather than an historical actuality.[16] In the following year, Otto Ritschl (1860–1944) argued that Kähler had misunderstood and unnecessarily depreciated the results of the application of the critical-historical method.[17] Nevertheless, Kähler's dogmatic point concerning the priority of the 'biblical, historical (*geschichtlich*) Christ' over the 'historical (*historisch*) Jesus' did not go unnoticed, and was destined to exercise considerable influence over later discussion of the relationship between faith and revelation, particularly in the writings of the dialectical theologians.

That, however, lay in the future. On the eve of the First World War, a very different approach was developed in the writings of Ernst Troeltsch. Although sharing the common disillusionment of the period with Ritschlianism, Troeltsch developed an approach significantly different from any considered up to this point, which drew attention to the importance of historicism in matters of theology.

Ernst Troeltsch

The most consistent and radical application of *das religionsgeschichtliche Denken* to Christian dogmatics in general, and to Christology in particular, is associated with Ernst Troeltsch.[18] To many, Troeltsch appeared to have completely undermined the foundations of constructive theology, his radical application of the historical method leading to the total dissolution of dogmatics. It is therefore necessary to understand how the historical method, exploited to such effect by writers such as Harnack, could come to be turned against them.

Writing in 1911, Troeltsch stated that he regarded his teacher Albrecht Ritschl as having correctly identified the programme by which the Christian tradition could be accommodated to the modern situation. This programme consisted of the correlation of the dogmatic tradition of Protestantism with the demands of the modern situation. For Troeltsch, Ritschl's mistakes were to be located in his analysis of these two elements, rather than in his essential programme itself. In his doctoral dissertation on the relationship between reason and revelation in Philip Melanchthon (1497–1560) and Johann Gerhard (1582–1637), Troeltsch emphasized the discontinuity between modern theology and that of the period of the Reformation (exemplified by Melanchthon) or of Orthodoxy (exemplified by Gerhard). Troeltsch thus corrected Ritschl's historical analysis, effectively concluding that the Ritschlian theology could not be justified with reference to the dogmatic tradition of Protestanism.

In his early period (up to about 1895), Troeltsch's approach could be described as a liberalism which has been tempered by the influence of the 'history of religions' school. Jesus' preaching, for example, is argued to show important parallels with contemporary Jewish literature. However, Jesus stood in a unique relation to God, as demonstrated in his 'wonderful religious personality'.[19] However, Troeltsch's growing interest in the implications of the critical-historical method caused a gradual break from the dominant outlook of liberal Protestantism over the next decade, while raising a series of major issues for Christology in general, and liberal Christology in particular.

The origins of Troeltsch's break with the Ritschlian school may be seen in the aftermath of the publication in 1897 of Gustav Ecke's (1855–1920) study of the Ritschlian school. In this study, Ecke documented the division between the right and left wings of the school (regarding Harnack, Herrmann, Friedrich Loofs (1858–1928) and Ferdinand Kattenbusch (1851–1935) as representatives of the former, and Bousset, Gunkel, Troeltsch, Weiss and Wrede as representatives of the latter). In July of the following year, Troeltsch responded both to the book itself, and to reviews by Harnack and Kattenbusch (the latter of which had been particularly critical of Troeltsch's 'modern' tendency to deny the supernatural). Troeltsch, speaking as a representative of the 'younger generation' of Ritschlians, argued that the original successes of the Ritschlian theology was a direct consequence of the cultural situation in the 1850s, in the aftermath of the collapse of the Hegelian speculative systems which had dominated the first half of the century. Ritschl's anti-speculative and empirically grounded theology was thus ideally placed to exploit the cultural situation of the period, and thus to base itself upon such ideas as the absoluteness of Christianity or supernaturalism.

In the meantime, however, culture had not remained unchanged: intellectual interest, in the universities and elsewhere, had shifted away from speculative philosophy to historical analysis, thus highlighting the deficiencies of the older Ritschlian approach. The early period of Troeltsch's development can be regarded as an increasingly tentative Ritschlianism coming into conflict with the ideas developed by Weiss on the one hand, and the history of religions school on the other.

The general lines of Troeltsch's mature historical approach to Christianity can be seen in his 1898 article on the relation between history and metaphysics. In this essay, Troeltsch suggests that the fundamental difference between himself and old-style Ritschlians is that the latter based themselves upon a discredited supernaturalism, whereas he based himself upon a consistent historicism. The general trend within the Ritschlian school, which grounded theology in the unique historical revelation in Jesus Christ, is, according to Troeltsch, an instance of the now discredited dogmatic method, exemplifying the persistent tendency of the Ritschlians to deal with specific individual problems raised by the critical-historical method, without coming to terms with the underlying presuppositions of that method.

For Troeltsch, the critical-historical method itself is the 'much more fundamental ground upon which the disintegration of the Christian complex of ideas actually originates'. It is this method itself which is a 'leaven which, once applied to biblical science and church history, alters everything until it finally explodes the entire structure of theological methods employed until the present'. No area of history can be regarded as exempt from the critical-historical method. It is this development of a 'theology of historicism' which is recognized to be one of Troeltsch's most distinctive contributions to modern German theology.

For Troeltsch, 'dogmatic' or 'supernaturalist' understandings of the nature of Christianity had been discredited by the rise of the critical-historical method. If one is to think historically, one is committed to the principles and presuppositions of the historical method, in that it is impossible to 'think without and against this method'. For this reason, Troeltsch holds that it is impossible to make exclusive claims concerning Christianity: all religions must be regarded as historical phenomena, characterized by the intermingling of the human and the divine spirit. As such, the same methods may be applied to the study of Christianity as to the study of other religions, or other historical phenomena in general. If Christianity is unique, 'this uniqueness lies in the content of its object, not in special methods of study or demonstration', and should therefore be open to critical investigation by purely secular historical methods, unfettered by supernaturalist assumptions or subjective value-judgments.

In his 1900 essay on 'historical and dogmatic methods of theology',[20] Troeltsch thus argues that the critical-historical method is characterized by three fundamental and interrelated principles:

1. The principle of *criticism* recognizes that historical judgments are matters of probability, rather than truth or falsity, and are thus open to correction and refinement. The absolute historical judgments of Christianity concerning Jesus of Nazareth are thus unrealistic. 'Historical criticism brings a measure of uncertainty to every single fact . . . it thus becomes impossible to base religious fact on any single fact.'

2. The principle of *analogy* states that such historical judgments are based upon the presupposition that the events of the past are similar to the events of the present. As such, supernatural elements must be rigorously excluded from any interpretation of the historical figure of Jesus of Nazareth. The history of Judaism and Christianity alike are to be recognized as 'analogous to all other history'. Troeltsch notes a growing trend to recognize this point, although he recognizes that many would wish to place 'the moral character of Jesus and the resurrection' in a separate category, immune from such historical investigation. It is not clear from the text itself whether Troeltsch is merely noting this hesitation, or subjecting it to destructive criticism; the direction his thought was to take suggests, but does not prove, that it was the latter.

3. The principle of *correlation* recognizes that historical phenomena are interrelated in such a manner that events must be interpreted in terms of their antecedents and consequences. The historically conditioned character of the history of Jesus of Nazareth must therefore be conceded. For Troeltsch, these three principles combined to raise serious difficulties

for any 'portrait of Christ' based upon historical analysis, including that of the Ritschlian school.[21] By 1911, he was speaking openly of the intolerable contradictions within the Ritschlian Christology.

It is difficult to understand fully the nature of Troeltsch's positive Christological stance. In part, this difficuly rests in the dense and occasionally obscurantist nature of his writings, which make their interpretation a painful process for all but the most dedicated of scholars.[22] It is, however, also due to an apparent reluctance on his part to allow that Christological doctrines which he subjects to criticism can be restated; Troeltsch appears to believe that they ought to be abandoned, in the light of his comments. This is especially clear in his discussion of the doctrine of the incarnation, which he treats dismissively. As Coakley demonstrates, Troeltsch's critique of the doctrine can be brought together under three general headings:[23]

1. Troeltsch's precommitment to relativism leads him to reject the idea of an 'absolute' revelation of God in history: 'the Absolute lies beyond history and is a truth that in many respects remains veiled . . . It belongs to the future, and will appear in the judgment of God and the cessation of earthly history'.

2. Troeltsch's doctrines of God, revelation and redemption exclude the notion of an incarnation in history. For example, he declares that history (at least, as he understands it) cannot accommodate 'a cosmic salvific intervention of God into the world'. Sadly, Troeltsch treats this as a self-evident truth, which requires no justification, leaving the critical reader with the impression of a series of dogmatic assertions about the nature of history, where argument is so obviously needed.

3. Troeltsch's reflections on Christology itself. Of particular importance is his appeal to a 'social psychological' understanding of the origins of the central place of Christ within the Christian tradition, which we shall consider below.

Yet, when all is said and done, Troeltsch appears to assume that these assertions and arguments oblige Christendom to abandon the notion of incarnation. There is no serious attempt to engage the patristic tradition, to give one especially alarming omission from his analysis, to inquire what pressures led the early church to express its Christological beliefs in a specifically incarnational form. Equally, the doctrine of the incarnation has always been open to reformulation along non-metaphysical lines – for example, in terms of revelational presence (Karl Barth) or personal dialogue (Emil Brunner). Troeltsch makes no attempt to consider or anticipate such obvious possibilities.

Despite these serious weaknesses in his approach, Troeltsch has raised a number of difficulties for Christologies which rest upon an appeal to the 'religious personality of Jesus'. We have rehearsed those relating to the provisionality of historical scholarship; perhaps a more significant proposal relates to his arguments concerning the psychological necessity for a Jesus-figure, which first becomes important in his writings dating from 1911.

The background to this development lies in 1909, when the Karlsrühe controversialist Arthur Drews (1865–1935) published *Die Christusmythe*.[24] This sensationalist piece of writing, which argued for the non-existence of Jesus on grounds as spurious and inconsequential as those which later came to be associated with the British writer John Allegro, set off a furious controversy. While this controversy is not without interest, our attention is claimed by the important essay on the historical existence (*Geschichtlichkeit*) of Jesus that was published by Troeltsch as a contribution to this remarkably vigorous debate. In this work, Troeltsch argues that the liberal portraits of Christ, as presented by Ritschl and Herrmann, are nothing more than *Mischformen*, or 'hybrids', which unsuccessfully attempt to mediate between the historicization of reality and the old supernaturalism of Orthodoxy. This is not to say that Troeltsch rejects the possibility of such mediation, in that he readily concedes that a purely historical and pedagogical interpretation of the meaning of the person of Jesus is devoid of warmth. Rather, he locates the correct mediating position in the cultic life of the Christian community, for which the portrait of Christ is a focal point.[25] Troeltsch undergirds this social psychological approach to the person of Christ with a critique of a dogmatic understanding of that person. Following Harnack, Troeltsch argues that the preaching of Jesus gave absolute priority to the kingdom of God. However, the early church transferred this absoluteness to the person of Jesus himself. As a result, the person of Christ came to be absolutized, and supported by all kinds of arguments and proofs.[26]

For Troeltsch, the continuity of a community is not governed by doctrines or ideas, but by 'cult and community'. There is a 'social psychological necessity' for a central figure, who functions as a central locus for reflection on the part of its members. The figure of Jesus thus fulfils a number of important social functions, including those of *cohesion* (by giving the community a focus and identity) and *edification* (by providing a vision or paradigmatic personality as an inspiration to the community as a whole).

The Christian community thus lives by constant recollection of the memory of its head, Christ. In this, Troeltsch may be regarded as developing the theological programme of Schleiermacher: for the latter, Christ's significance within the community of faith was to be explained religiously; for Troeltsch, it was to be explained sociologically and psychologically. The centrality of Christ within the Christian community may thus be justified upon grounds of socio-psychological utility, which may be defended against Orthodoxy and the Enlightenment alike. The tradition deriving from Schleiermacher, Ritschl and Harnack grasped the significance of Jesus' person as the formative factor in the creation of the Christian community, but tended, according to Troeltsch, to accommodate its Christological claims to the accepted modes of dogmatic expression: for Troeltsch, those claims are to be articulated in terms of general social phenomena. The importance of Jesus to the church is thus to be explained upon *sociological* rather than specifically *theological* grounds. The necessity of the actual historical existence of Jesus for the Christian community may be maintained, according to Troeltsch, on the basis of his assumption that the *Christuskultus* requires foundation in historical actuality (*die Wurzelung in geschichtlicher Tatsächlichkeit*).

This leads to what is probably the most disconcerting paradox of Troeltsch's position. He castigates the Ritschlian tradition for its argument that the Christian faith would be immeasurably impoverished 'without the elevating or suggestive impression of the person of Jesus'; yet he himself argues that faith needs to find support in the knowledge that 'a real man thus lived, struggled, believed and conquered'.[27] Although Troeltsch is thus prepares to ascribe a position of historical and sociological honour to Jesus, he seems reluctant to consider what the theological conseqences of this position might be. For example, the following statement from the seminal 1910 lecture 'On the Possibility of a Liberal Christianity' unquestionably makes unacknowledged and implicit metaphysical claims concerning the significance of Jesus in the course of affirming his historical and cultural relevance:

Jesus is the embodiment of superior religious power, embellished in ever new ways in the course of thousands of years, whose heartbeat is felt through the whole of Christendom . . .

That is why he himself will always keep on living . . . and why (Christian belief) will rise to its full power . . . only by having such a person to look up to. But if this is so, then the figure of Jesus will remain alive and inseparable from the power of the Christian belief in God.[28]

But if this is true about the historical place and importance of Jesus, what is true about him metaphysically? Troeltsch's confident rhetorical statement about the permanent place of Jesus in culture or history needs metaphysical justification, unless it is to be viewed as an exaggerated overinterpretation of a contingent historical phenomenon.

Doubtless Troeltsch's agenda remains significant for modern theology, including its emphasis upon the importance of historicist considerations for any Christology. Within the German theological tradition with which we are concerned, however, Troeltsch was widely regarded as marking an end point. The Ritschlian tradition was seen to have too many theological and historical loose ends for comfort.

It will therefore be clear that by the year 1911, the liberal mediating Christology of the Ritschl–Herrmann–Harnack tradition was widely regarded as discredited. Although there remained those who were convinced that it remained viable, there was a growing recognition of its pseudo-historical foundations and latent dogmatic presuppositions. It was not entirely clear in what direction Christology could now develop: the apocalyptic approach to the gospel *Christusbild* yielded a strange and distant figure, ill-suited to the perceived needs of Christian piety and worship; the *religionsgeschichtlich* approach appeared to many to destroy, rather than merely recast, the traditional Christian understanding of the person of Christ; the consistent sceptical approach appeared to reduce Christology to silence, lest it overstate itself. As it happened, the new direction in which Christology would develop was largely determined by an historical event, rather than scholarly reflection upon the nature of the historical process of which it was unquestionably a part. On 1 August 1914, the First World War broke out.

6

The Dialectical Christologies: Barth and Brunner

On the evening of 4 August 1914, as the First World War began to embed itself in the consciousness of the German nation, perhaps her greatest contemporary theologian drafted an appeal on behalf of the Kaiser to his people in support of the war effort. The same theologian shortly afterwards added his signature to those of 92 other intellectuals, addressing a similar public appeal to the 'world of culture'.[1] That theologian was Adolf von Harnack, and he was joined in that appeal by theologians of the stature of Adolf Deissman (1866–1937), Wilhelm Herrmann, Adolf von Schlatter (1852–1939), Friedrich Naumann (1860–1919) and Reinhold Seeberg (1859–1955). It seemed that the German theological establishment, liberal and conservative alike, was committed to the war effort, with all that this entailed. The 'manifesto of the intellectuals' was widely seen as representing the collapse of the bourgeois idealism of the nineteenth century, and the theological programme it had engendered. There were many who wondered what would happen next. One of them was Karl Barth (1886–1968).

Karl Barth

Barth is unquestionably one of the most significant theologians of the twentieth century. In part, his achievement relates to his emphasis upon the centrality of Jesus Christ for Christian theology, giving Christology a central normative role in his *Church Dogmatics*. This emphasis upon the centrality of Christ was partly due to his reaction against the liberal

123

theological tradition, which he regarded as totally discredited by its support for the Kaiser's war policies:

> For me personally, one day in the beginning of August of that year stands out as a black day, on which ninety-three German intellectuals, among whom I was horrified to discover almost all of my hitherto revered theological teachers, published a profession of support for the war policy of Kaiser Wilhelm II and his counsellors. Amazed by their attitude, I realised that I could no longer follow their ethics and dogmatics, or their understandings of the Bible and history, and that the theology of the nineteenth century no longer had any future for me.[2]

As a student, Barth had come to 'absorb Herrmann through every pore', and his publications over the period 1908–16 demonstrate the influence of the great Marburg liberal, particularly in relation to the theological significance of the critical-historical method. A theological student beginning his or her studies in Germany in the first decade of the twentieth century could scarcely have failed to encounter the tension between the historical theology of Troeltsch and the ahistorical theology of Herrmann, which we explored in previous chapters. It must thus be appreciated that, despite all the differences between Barth, Gogarten and Herrmann, they remain united in their hostility to historicism in general, and that of Troeltsch in particular. Writing to his colleague and fellow-pastor Eduard Thurneysen on 1 January 1916, Barth admitted

> ... how frightfully indifferent historical questions have become to me. Of course, this is nothing new for me, as even under the influence of Herrmann, I always regarded (historical) criticism merely as a means of achieving freedom in relation to the tradition, rather than a constitutive factor in a new liberal tradition, as Wernle and company apparently want it to be.[3]

The strongly ahistorical character of the early 'dialectical theology' has often been noted, and it is therefore important to observe that, at least in this respect, there is a significant continuity between Herrmann and the 'dialectical theology' of Barth and Gogarten.

In 1919, Barth published the work which was to establish his reputation and signal the development of a significant new element in

European theology. His commentary on Romans represented a savage prophetic attack upon the Marburg liberalism he had once espoused. This work, written while a pastor at the little Swiss village of Safenwil, is prophetic in tone, stressing the utter inability of humanity to discover or conceptualize God unaided, and the utter inability of human culture to mirror or image God. It created both a sensation and a new term – 'dialectical theology'. (The term reflects Barth's emphasis upon the dialectic between God and humanity, which stands in sharp contrast to the liberal notion of the enculturation of God.)

For many of Barth's critics, the 'theology of crisis' was merely an uncritical emotional reaction to the aftermath of the First World War – at that stage known as the 'Great War', in the absence of any knowledge that a second such war was less than twenty years distant. Yet, in response to this, it is necessary to point out that European culture, weary with liberalism and disillusioned by its optimistic and evolutionary theory of human progress, was ready for a change in religious key. The new pessimism of the period, nourished by political and economic crises and the collapse of bourgeois idealism, was unquestionably extraordinarily receptive to the 'theology of crisis (*Theologie der Krisis*)'. It seems, however, that this new cultural atmosphere merely provided a 'point of contact' for the new theology, establishing a context within which the full force of 'dialectical theology' could be felt.

The impact of the First World War upon European culture cannot be overstated. The years 1918–22 saw remarkable alterations in Western European self-consciousness. Although the publication of Oswald Spengler's (1880–1936) *Decline of the West* in 1918 – which drew heavily upon the degenerative theories of Max Nordau (1849–1923) and Cesare Lombroso (1836–1909) – is probably the most celebrated sign of this shift in culture, others soon followed. On 29 May 1919, observation of a solar eclipse confirmed two of the three crucial predictions of Albert Einstein's special theory of relativity. The third was subsequently confirmed in 1923. The concept of a 'relativistic universe' appeared to be as revolutionary to the twentieth century as the Newtonian mechanical universe was to the eighteenth, calling existing human understandings of the world into question. On 23 June 1919, Marcel Proust (1871–1922) published *A l'ombre des jeunes filles*, a radical literary experiment with subliminal sexual emotions and disjointed time. J. B. Bury (1861–1927) poured scorn upon the idea of continuous development of human culture, civilization and ideas in his *Idea of*

Progress, published in 1920. In that same year, the ideas of Sigmund Freud suddenly broke free of their captivity within specialized medical and psychiatric circles with the founding of the first psychiatric polyclinic at Berlin, and the launching of the *International Journal of Psycho-Analysis*. James Joyce's (1882–1941) *Ulysses* appeared in 1922, shocking the literary world, and causing the Anglo-American literary critic and writer T. S. Eliot (1888–1965) to remark that it 'destroyed the whole world of the nineteenth century'.

It is thus no exaggeration to state that the immediate post-war years were widely perceived as witnessing the final collapse of the cultural heritage of the nineteenth century, with shock-waves which were felt in every sphere of intellectual and creative activity. The theological consequences of this shift in cultural attitude may be seen in the reaction to Franz Overbeck's (1837–1905) controversial work *Christentum und Kultur* ('Theology and Culture', published posthumously in 1919). The 'theology of crisis' thus developed within, rather than as a result of, the cultural situation of the post-war period.[4] It may also be pointed out that a number of theological factors conspired to bring about a rediscovery of the deity of God. Among these, the Luther renaissance and the publication of Rudolf Otto's (1869–1937) *Das Heilige* ('The Idea of the Holy') (1917) were probably the most significant, in addition to the widespread dissatisfaction with the pseudo-historical theology of the liberal school noted in the previous chapter. In every sphere of thought, the situation was ripe for radical new development. Barth's commentary on Romans – often referred to simply as his *Römerbrief* – happened to be the occasion of that development in the sphere of Christian theology.

The Christology of the Romans Commentary (1919)

The origins of the great turning point in modern Christology are generally agreed to lie in Barth's commentary on Romans. Perhaps the work may be regarded as a midwife to a new theological trend rather than its cause; there is considerable evidence for the cumulation of considerable dissatisfaction with liberal theology in the period 1914–19, and Barth's work may simply have triggered off a looming anti-liberal reaction. The Romans commentary, first published in 1919, is often regarded as a work of prophecy rather than theology. Although its main impact appears to date from the publication of its heavily rewritten second edition (1922), even the first edition caused a mild sensation.

Now that dialectical theology is an aspect of the history of Christian thought, rather than a contemporary theological force, it is perhaps difficult for the modern scholar to appreciate the full force of this violent work when it broke upon an unprepared theological world. It was perhaps through this work that the full power of Søren Kierkegaard's (1813–55) critique of Hegelian historical pantheism was first channelled into the German theological consciousness. Time and time again in this work, Barth turns to stress the Kierkegaardian 'infinite qualitative distinction' *(unendliche qualitative Unterschied)* between God and human beings.

Like an Old Testament prophet, Barth emphasizes God's total holiness, and his remoteness from humanity in general, and from human culture and religion in particular. God 'stands over and against humanity and everything human in an infinite qualitative distinction *(in unendlichem qualitativem Unterschied dem Menschen und allem Menschlichen gegenüberstehend)*, and is never, ever *(nie und nimmer)* identical with anything which we name, experience, conceive or worship as God'. God cannot and must not be constructed or conceived in human terms, as if he were some kind of projection of human culture, reason or emotion. Time and time again Barth emphasizes the vastness of the gulf fixed between God and humanity, and the impossibility of bridging this gulf from our side. Barth substitutes for Lessing's *garstige breite Graben* ('ugly great ditch') of history the *Gletscherspalte* ('crevasse') of time and eternity. God is *totaliter aliter*, wholly and absolutely different from us. How, then, may mediation between God and humanity take place? Barth's answer, stated in the preface to the second edition of the Romans commentary (1922), is significant:

> If I have any system, it is restricted to bearing in mind, as much as possible, what Kierkegaard called the 'infinite qualitative distinction' between time and eternity, in its negative and positive aspects. 'God is in heaven, and you are on earth.' For me, the relation of this God and this person, the relation of this person and this God, is, in a nutshell, the theme of the Bible and the totality of philosophy. The philosophers term this crisis of human knowledge the prime cause; the Bible sees Jesus Christ at this cross-roads *(Kreuzweg)*.[5]

It is perhaps worth noting that Barth replaces Kierkegaard's existential dialectic between the temporal and the eternal with a corresponding eschatological dialectic, in which time is annihilated by eternity. The emphasis placed by Weiss and Schweitzer upon the eschatological aspects of the preaching of Jesus, so studiously ignored by Herrmann and Harnack, comes to its full theological expression in the early writings of Barth. The eschatology of that preaching utterly prevents the theologian from reducing God to a settled bourgeois set of values, or to fashioning Christ in the image of human cultural norms. *Christentum, das nicht ganz und gar und restlos Eschatologie ist, hat mit Christus ganz und gar und restlos nichts zu tun!* ('A Christianity which is not totally and utterly eschatology, has totally and utterly nothing to do with Christ!') Any possibility of interpreting Jesus' relationship to God in terms of liberal Protestantism is ruthlessly destroyed. Human religious consciousness can only be the consciousness of our abandonment by God. God remains unknown and unknowable, and all that may be seen of the reality of this unknown God in the history of the world or of Jesus of Nazareth are his effects, rather that that reality itself (Barth, with the battlefields of the First World War in mind, refers to these effects as *Einschlagstrichter und Hohlraüme* – 'shellholes and craters').[6]

God cannot be thought of as 'entering into' history, in that his revelation is a 'non-historical' event (*unhistorisches Ereignis*), which impinges upon human history only as a tangent touches a circle – at a 'mathematical point'. God's revelation can no more be pinned down in human history than a bird in flight, concealing more than it reveals (in that it reveals the 'otherness' of God in the chasm fixed between God and humanity), having no 'stationary point (*Standpunkt*)'. Revelation comes 'perpendicularly from above (*senkrecht von oben*)'. In Jesus, God becomes a secret, making himself known as the unknown, speaking in eternal silence. The concept of 'incarnation' is thus utterly inconceivable, in that God cannot be seen as entering into history.

The impact of the Barthian emphasis upon the absolute (*schlechthinnig*) distinction between God and the world may be judged from the exchange of views between Barth and the ageing Adolf von Harnack in the January and February issues of the journal *Christliche Welt* for 1923. In many ways, the Barth–Harnack correspondence may be seen as symbolic, representing an encounter not merely between two different schools of thought, but two different theological eras, with irreconcilably opposed ways of speaking and thinking about God. In this exchange,

Harnack put fifteen questions to the 'despisers of intellectually defensible theology', of which the fourteenth identifies the central Christological issue thrown up by the rise of dialectical theology:

> If the person of Jesus Christ stands at the centre of the gospel, how can the foundation for a reliable and generally accepted knowledge of that person (*die Grundlage für eine zuverlässige und gemeinschaftliche Erkenntnis dieser Person*) be gained other than through critical-historical investigation, in order that an imagined Christ (*erträumte Christus*) is not substituted for the real one? What else, other than scientific theology, is able to undertake such a study?[7]

In many respects, Harnack's question to Barth is similar to Herrmann's question to Kähler, discussed earlier (see p. 115), and relates to precisely the same issue – the relationship between the Jesus of history and the Christ of faith. For Barth, as for Kähler, it is the risen Christ, rather than the historical Jesus, who is central to theology. The historical Jesus is not of decisive importance to faith. As Barth states this in his reply to Harnack:

> The 'reliable and generally accepted' knowledge of the person of Christ as the centre of the gospel can only be that of faith awakened by God. Critical-historical study represents the deserved and necessary end (*das verdiente und notwendige Ende*) of those 'foundations' of this knowledge (that is, the knowledge of faith). Such foundations do not exist except where they are laid by God himself. Whoever does not know that we do not know Christ according to the flesh any more – and this applies to all of us! – should let the critical study of the Bible tell him so. The more radically he is terrified, the better it is for him and for the subject in question. This could well be the service which 'historical science' can render to the real task of theology.

In effect, Barth may be regarded as emphasizing the dogmatic consequences of the critical-historical studies of the gospel tradition (such as those of Weiss, Wrede and Schweitzer), in a manner similar to, although more consistent and radical than, Martin Kähler. It is thus significant that Barth suggests, in an essay of 1925, that even Herrmann himself implicitly adopted the risen Christ of faith as the point of departure for his Christological speculation: Herrmann's fault was merely a lack of consistency.[8]

In 1920–21, Barth was publicly joined in his reaction against both historicism and *Kulturprotestantismus* by Friedrich Gogarten (1887–1967) and Emil Brunner (1889–1966). The former delivered his celebrated lecture on 'the crisis of our culture' to the *Freunden der Christlichen Welt* at the Wartburg in 1920, causing a mild sensation by doing so. His great emphasis upon the 'annihilating and creative act of God (*Gottes vernichtender, schaffender Tat*)' in the present crisis of European civilization, by which the distinction between God and the world was brought home as it had never been brought home before, reminded many of his audience of some of the more forceful pronouncements of Luther, and horrified Troeltsch, who saw in the lecture a programmatic critique of the relation between religion and culture.[9] Gogarten's essay *Zwischen den Zeiten* ('Between the Times'), published in 1920, was widely recognized as a theological manifesto, setting out the programme which dialectical theology would undertake in the years ahead. In the following year, the movement gained a new supporter in the person of Emil Brunner, who identified the enemies of the new theology as *Historismus* and *Psychologismus*, two characteristics of the later writings of Ernst Troeltsch. (In fact, the first major specifically Christological work to emerge from the school of dialectical theology was due to Brunner: *Der Mittler* – 'The Mediator' – appeared in 1927.)

By 1925, dialectical theology had established itself as a leading force in German theology – despite its Swiss pastoral origins. By 1935, however, it was clear that there were serious tensions within the movement, particularly between Barth and Brunner. Despite their common theological presuppositions, the leading figures of the dialectical theology movement developed Christologies which were different to the extent of near-incompatibility. In a later section (see pp. 143–53), we shall analyse the main features of the Christology of Emil Brunner; our attention is, however, at present claimed by Barth's mature Christology, in which a distinctive new Christological style, differing from his iconoclasm of the early 1920s, emerged. The negative and destructive approach of this earlier period gave way to solid theological reconstruction, and the publication of one of the most significant theological works of the twentieth century – the *Church Dogmatics*.

The Christology of the Church Dogmatics

Barth's later works may be regarded as an attempt to unfold the objective knowledge given to humanity in a real historical event, whereas he earlier disregarded the unique revelation of God in Christ in favour of what can only be termed a general theological agnosticism. It is this later approach which is to be found in the more explicitly Christological sections of the *Kirchliche Dogmatik* ('Church Dogmatics'). We are obliged to qualify 'Christological' in this manner, in that Barth frequently emphasizes that the entire contents of the *Dogmatics* may be regarded as Christological:

> When Holy Scripture speaks of God, it concentrates our attention and thoughts upon one single point . . . And if we look closer, and ask: who and what is at this point upon which our attention and thoughts are concentrated, which we are to recognise as God? . . . then from its beginning to its end the Bible directs us to the name of Jesus Christ.[10]

All theology necessarily possesses an implicit Christological perspective and foundation, which it is the task of theology to make explicit, in the manner of *fides quaerens intellectum*, 'faith seeking understanding', a theological programme associated with the eleventh-century writer Anselm of Canterbury, to which Barth became increasingly attracted in the 1930s. By definition, Christological thinking constitutes the unconditional basis for all theological thinking, in that Jesus Christ is the *fundamentum* upon which all theology must ultimately be recognized to be grounded, and by which it is controlled.

Reacting against approaches to Christology such as that represented by A. E. Biedermann (see p. 81), Barth explicitly rejects any deductive Christology based upon a 'Christ-principle' in favour of one based upon 'Jesus Christ himself as witnessed to in Holy Scripture'. Every theological proposition in the *Church Dogmatics* may be regarded as Christological, in the sense that it has its point of departure in Jesus Christ. It is this feature of Barth's later thought which has led to it being described as 'Christological concentration' or 'Christomonism'. Barth, it must be noted, is not suggesting that the doctrine of either the person or work of Christ (or both, if they are deemed inseparable) should stand at the centre of a Christian dogmatics, nor that a Christological idea or principle should constitute the systematic speculative midpoint of a deductive system. Rather, Barth is arguing that the act of God which is Jesus Christ underlies theology in its totality. A 'Church Dogmatics' must be 'Christologically determined' in that the very possibility and reality of theology are determined in the first place by the actuality of the act of divine revelation, by the speaking of the Word of God, by the event of Jesus Christ.

To think theologically is thus essentially to take seriously the fact that the being of God is prior to the enterprise of human theological speculation and questioning. It is to recognize that God's being in its character as 'being in motion' both establishes the foundation and directs the subsequent course of theology. Christology must be presupposed from the outset, rather than arrived at subsequently. Christological doctrine can at best approximate to the greater truth of the event of Jesus Christ, which Barth is reluctant to objectify propositionally. Barth's fundamental contention is that Christology is essentially the obedient orientation of the theologian towards the being and act of God: his apparent failure to remain consistent to this principle (evidenced by his obvious committment to a specific Christology) should not be permitted to obscure this point. Jesus Christ constitutes the perspective from which all of theology may and must be surveyed. But what, it may be asked, does Barth understand by the phrase 'Jesus Christ'?

In his earlier dialectical phase, Barth understood Christology to encapsulate the paradoxical nature of theology, providing a brilliant illustration and defence of the paradoxical situation of the theologian, as he had identified it in the 1922 essay *Das Wort Gottes als Aufgabe der Theologie* ('The Word of God as the Task of Theology'). One of the most important sentences of this work summarizes the dilemma of the theologian, as Barth sees it, succinctly: 'As theologians, we should speak about God. We are, however, human beings, and as such are unable to speak about God.' This 'theology of paradox' served only to infuriate his critics, such as Erik Peterson. In 1925, Peterson published a penetrating critique of dialectical theology, based upon Barth's 1922 essay, in which he illustrated the total futility of the 'dialectical' approach to theology with particular reference to the incarnation:

> To speak of the incarnation . . . as a 'dialectical possibility' actually means not to speak of it at all. And that is precisely what Barth does. For when he says that the impossible has itself

become the possible, that death has become life, that eternity has become time, or that God has become man, all that he has said in these different variations is exactly the same – basically, nothing whatsoever. Thesis and antithesis are brought together in a formal and empty synthesis, in which everything and yet nothing is said.[11]

There are clear indications, however, that Barth was moving away from this purely dialectical and paradoxical approach to Christology even before his seminal work on Anselm of Canterbury's theological method. The idea of paradox is now replaced by the idea of analogy. Barth, however, insists that this analogy be understood as *analogia revelationis* ('analogy of revelation') or *analogia fidei* ('analogy of faith'), rather than *analogia entis* ('analogy of being'). Whereas the *analogia entis* establishes a correlation between God and the world on the basis of a doctrine of creation, the *analogia fidei* establishes it on the basis of divine self-revelation. In other words, an analogy between God and the world is not discerned by human insight (which would be to constitute theology anthropologically), but is itself caused by God's being and action in revelation, which creates a correspondence in the creaturely realm to God. The analogy always leads from the creator to the creature, and never from the creature to the creator. Nevertheless, despite this important qualification, it is clear that Barth has moved away from the idea of the paradox of grace to the idea of an all-embracing – although God-given – analogy between God and humanity, nature and grace, and creation and redemption.[12] By the year 1932, in which the first half-volume of the *Kirchliche Dogmatik* ('Church Dogmatics') appeared, Barth had moved away from his earlier Kierkegaardian 'Christology of protest' towards his mature 'Christology of the Word', based upon the concept of the Christological concentration of the divine revelation to humanity.

It is important to appreciate that Barth's later Christology is totally integrated within a trinitarian context. In asserting that Barth's thought is totally Christological, it is necessary to add that this has as its corollary that it is totally trinitarian. The entire panorama of the history of salvation is surveyed from the standpoint of the Trinity. Barth thus does not begin his theological reflection from the history of Jesus of Nazareth, or even from the doctrine of the incarnation. The proper starting point for such speculation is eternity, with the pre-existent Christ, as the second person of the Trinity. Viewed from this standpoint, the history of Jesus Christ is recognized not merely as a 30-year episode in time and space, but as an event encompassing and embracing the entire history of God and humanity, beginning from eternity and stretching into eternity. History is thus *theatrum gloriae Dei*, 'a theatre of the glory of God' (a phrase of Calvin's which Barth gladly borrows and extends), an arena within which the glory of God may be discerned and recognized.

This discernment and recognition, however, is not to be seen as a purely human insight. Rather, it is to be treated as a revelatory act of God himself. Barth insists that humans are to be seen as passive epistemic objects, rather than active subjects. It is God who is active, and human beings who are passive, in revelation. For Barth, *Erkenntnis* ('knowledge') is thus *Anerkenntnis* ('recognition'), and *Denken* ('thinking') is *Nach-Denken* ('contemplation'). By thus splitting this latter word, Barth suggests that 'contemplation' should be interpreted as 'thinking afterwards': our knowledge of God is moulded by God himself, a process in which God is active and we are passive. The locus of this recognition, however, is defined by Barth in exclusively Christological terms. Hans Urs von Balthasar (1905–88) illustrates this 'Christological concentration' by comparing it to an hour-glass, in which the sand pours from the upper to the lower section through a constriction. Similarly, the divine revelation proceeds from God to the world, from above to below, only through the central event of the revelation of Christ, apart from which there is no link between God and humanity.

One could perhaps say that Barth regards theology as an ascending spiral constructed around the self-expression of God in time, in that Barth's Christology is essentially concerned with the contemporaneity of 'above' and 'below' in the history of the humiliation of Christ on the cross. Incarnation and reconciliation (and readers are reminded that the German term *Versöhnung* may be translated as either 'reconciliation' or 'atonement') are different sides or aspects of the one movement or action of God in Jesus Christ. The diverse aspects and elements of the question of the person and work of Christ are inextricably interwoven, in that God is merely declaring to us what he had consummated in eternity, by a decree which anticipates everything temporal. In these different ways, Barth develops the manner in which the reconciliation of God and humanity in Christ is made known – but it must be stressed that Barth's emphasis is unquestionably upon the making known, or revealing, to humanity of something which has already happened from all eternity. This point is of sufficient importance to warrant further discussion.[13]

We have already noted the trinitarian dimension of Barth's Christology. That trinitarian dimension is particularly linked with the human-ward divine movement of revelation. Distinguishing between the revealer, the revelation, and the 'revealedness (*Offenbarsein*)', Barth argues that the revelation of God the Father is totally determined and constituted by the person of the revealer, Jesus of Nazareth, in that the content of this revelation cannot be separated from its form. In this way, Barth is able to avoid a total detachment of Christology from the historical figure of Jesus of Nazareth. Equally, however, Barth avoids the suggestion that God is ontologically bound up with and conditioned by the facticity of human existence by his insistence that God is 'antecedently in himself' what he reveals to us. God does not require to create anything in order to realize or to interpret himself.

It is for this reason that Barth refers to revelation as the *repetitio aeternatis in aeternitate*, an eternal recapitulation of what God already is. In Christ, God reveals himself as himself, as he already is, without introducing the need for any created arena within which such potentiality may be actualized. This would introduce an anthropologically conditioned necessity into God where it is, for Barth, clearly out of place. The subjectivity of God precludes any such anthropological intrusions into what is, properly speaking, theological territory. The history of Jesus Christ can therefore only recapitulate in time what has already happened antecedently in eternity.[14]

We have made this point at some length because of its inherent Christological importance. Barth's reluctance to engage with historical questions – evident in the commentary on Romans – can be shown to have culminated in the *Church Dogmatics*, with the result that a Christology is constructed with only the most superficial of contacts with human history. As we have emphasized, Barth's concept of the divine freedom in revelation necessitates that the ensuing revelation merely recapitulates its eternal antecedents. The incarnation, death and resurrection of Christ merely declare what has already happened eternally. These events, so central to Christian theology as a whole (and two of which are unquestionably central to the New Testament *kerygma*), are thus minimized in their significance, in that the emphasis is seen to have shifted from God's revelation in time to the eternal antecedent of that revelation. Barth effectively proceeds from the pre-existence of Christ, thus seeing Christ as equally present at every stage in the historical process. Barth thus seems to distance himself from the specifically *historical* nature of revelation. The consequences of this are considerable.

Perhaps the most surprising conclusion which must be drawn from this analysis is that, despite all differences in substance and emphasis, Barth's Christology seems to be located within precisely the same framework as that of the Enlightenment, and the nineteenth century in general – namely, a concern for a 'right knowledge' of our situation. To appreciate the importance of this point, we may consider a crucial question, posed by Martin Kähler in his influential *Lehre von der Versöhnung* ('Doctrine of Reconciliation', 1898). Surveying the different manners in which the doctrine of the atonement has been interpreted, Kähler asks: 'Has Christ merely provided us with insights concerning an existing state of affairs, or is he the founder of an new state of affairs?' Kähler has no hesitation in assigning the theories of atonement associated with Enlightenment writers, and also some of their later liberal followers (including both Schleiermacher and Ritschl), to the first such category. Such theories, he argues, portray Christ as making available insights concerning a situation which already exists. Christ is presented as a 'surety or a symbol of the grace of God towards sinners'.

Against this, Kähler argues for the second option, which he associates with the writers of the Reformation. Christ introduces a totally new element into the situation, in that he brings about a change in the way things are. Christ does not present us with insights concerning the existing situation; he makes possible and inaugurates a *new* situation.

Although Barth inverts the nineteenth century subject-object relation in respect to God and humanity, his central interest remains the question concerning human knowledge of our situation. Christ is the locus in which the true knowledge of the human situation is disclosed, the *speculum* or mirror in which we see ourselves reflected. For Barth, Christ's incarnation, passion, death and resurrection cannot in any way be said to *change* the relationship between God and us; they merely *disclose* the Christologically determined situation to us. Although it may come as something of a surprise, given Barth's well-known hostility to the humanity-centred theologies of the Enlightenment, it is beyond doubt that Barth actually belongs to the first category identified by Kähler. In his life, death and resurrection, Christ discloses a situation which has already been determined; he does not establish anything that can be described as fundamentally *new*.

This point is confirmed by Barth's tendency towards a doctrine of universal salvation. Christ makes known the unilateral triumph of grace. It appears impossible for human beings to avoid being saved, whether they know it or not, whether they wish to be saved or not.[15] Those who find this conclusion questionable should consider what, according to Barth, it is necessary for us to do in order *not* to be saved. Barth's discussion of predestination (*Church Dogmatics*, II/2) is of direct relevance here. It is based upon two central Christological affirmations, which indicate the centrality of Christology to Barth's discussion of salvation:

1. Jesus Christ is the electing God;
2. Jesus Christ is the elected human being.

This strongly Christological orientation of predestination is maintained throughout his analysis of the doctrine. 'In its simplest and most comprehensive form, the doctrine of predestination consists of the assertion that the divine predestination is the election of Jesus Christ. But the concept of election has a double reference – to the elector and the elected.'

So exactly what is it that God has predestined? Barth's answer to this question has several components, of which the following two are of especially importance for our purposes in this discussion.

1. God elected to bear totally the pain and cost of redemption. God chose to accept the cross of Golgotha as a royal throne. God chose to accept the lot of fallen humanity, especially in suffering and death. God chose the path of self-humiliation and self-abasement, in order to redeem humanity.

2. God elected to take from us the negative aspects of his judgment. God rejects Christ in order that we might not be rejected. The negative side of predestination, which ought, Barth suggests, properly to have fallen upon sinful humanity, is instead directed towards Christ, the electing God and elected human being. God willed to bear the 'rejection and condemnation and death' which are the inevitable consequences of sin. Thus 'rejection cannot again become the portion or affair of humanity'. Christ bore what sinful humanity ought to have borne, in order that they need never bear it again.

In so far as predestination contains a No, it is not a No spoken against humanity. In so far as it involves exclusion and rejection, it is not the exclusion and rejection of humanity. In so far as it is directed to perdition and death, it is not directed to the perdition and death of humanity.

Barth thus eliminates any notion of a 'predestination to condemnation' on the part of humanity. The only one who is predestined to condemnation is Jesus Christ who, 'from all eternity willed to suffer for us'.

The consequences of this approach are clear. Despite all appearances to the contrary, humanity cannot be condemned. In the end, grace will triumph, even over open unbelief. Barth's doctrine of predestination eliminates the possibility of the rejection of humanity. In that Christ has borne the penalty and pain of rejection by God, this can never again become the portion of humanity. Taken together with his characteristic emphasis upon the 'triumph of grace', Barth's doctrine of predestination points to the universal restoration and salvation of humanity – a position which has occasioned a degree of criticism from others who would otherwise be sympathetic to his general position. Emil Brunner is an example of such a critic:

> What does this statement, 'that Jesus is the only really rejected person', mean for the situation of humanity? Evidently this: that there is no possibility of condemnation . . . The decision has already been made in Jesus Christ – for all of humanity. Whether they know it or not, believe it or not, is not so important. They are like people who seem to be perishing in a stormy sea. But in reality they are not in a sea in which one can drown, but in shallow waters, in which it is impossible to drown. Only they do not know it.[16]

This is unquestionably one of the most controversial aspects of Barth's theology. Controversy, however, does not centre upon the nature of Barth's teaching at this point, but over its lack of theological orthodoxy and fidelity to Scripture. It is perfectly clear what Barth believes; controversy centres upon the consonance of this viewpoint with the Christian tradition, which has tended to take a very different position. It is beyond question that Barth believes that everyone will eventually be saved. Setting to one side for our present purposes the orthodoxy of this position, what are its implications for Barth's Christology?

Given that Barth believes that all of humanity will be saved, it is understandable that his emphasis should fall upon the present knowledge of the real situation. His tendency to use terms such as *Kenntnis* ('knowledge') and cognates where one would expect *Heil* ('salvation') or *Versöhnung* ('atonement') may easily be explained upon this basis. Thus in his discussion of both the positive and negative aspects of the judgment and sentence of God executed and revealed in the death and resurrection of Jesus Christ, Barth's emphasis falls upon the *knowledge of our election* thus made available to us:

> In the mirror of Jesus Christ who was offered up for us and who was obedient in this offering, it becomes known (*wird offenbar*) who we ourselves are . . . we are exposed and known (*erkannt*), and have to know (*erkennen*) ourselves, as the proud creatures who ourselves want to be God and Lord . . . The knowledge (*Erkenntnis*) of the grace of God, and the comfort which flows from it in this sentence, the knowledge (*Erkenntnis*), therefore, of its positive sense, is bound up with the fact that we do not cease to know (*erkennen*) ourselves as those who are condemned.[17]

It is on the basis of the present temporal knowledge of the eternally actualized situation (that is, of the reconciliation of the world to God through Jesus Christ) that the community of faith stands or falls:

> If there is no knowledge (*Erkenntnis*) of the overruling righteousness of God, or knowledge only in the form of a mistaken apprehension (*Verkennen*), distorted by partial or total misunderstandings, how can the community escape error or decay, how can faith be kept from doubt and dissolution into all types of unbelief and superstition?

If we do not know what has already happened in eternity, we cannot act upon its basis. The crucial emphasis is therefore not so much upon what has happened, as upon what must yet happen – our coming to know or recognize the real Christologically determined situation. Despite all Barth's protests to the contrary, there are excellent reasons for supposing that he regards human knowledge and insight, rather than God's activity, as constituting the centre of theological reflection, precisely because that 'activity' belongs to eternity, rather than time.

The temporal recapitulation of that 'activity' can only be regarded as the 're-presentation' of what has already taken place in eternity, in order that we may learn of what has already happened. This 'eternalization' of revelation, which is necessary for Barth on the basis of his presupposition of both the divine freedom and the exclusion of anthropological considerations from theology, has a significant consequence. The emphasis is now shifted decisively from that revelation itself to the human recognition and appropriation of that revelation – and hence from God's activity to human insights and knowledge (or, more accurately, to human epistemic capacities and incapacities). As God 'is in revelation what he is antecendently in himself', it is impossible to speak of revelation 'happening' in time unless one refers to the event of the human appropriation of that revelation *qua* revelation. It is significant that Barth's doctrine of the person and work of Christ makes no reference to any engagement with sin or evil (unless these are understood in the epistemically reduced sense of human 'ignorance' or 'confusion' concerning our true situation).[18] Barth has simply *inverted* the liberal Christology, without, it seems, in any way altering its fundamental point of reference or its preoccupations.

A further difficulty arising from Barth's 'eternalization' of revelation relates to the critical-historical questions raised since the time of Lessing concerning the 'ugly great ditch' of history. How can Barth avoid the difficulties which eventually proved fatal to Harnack? Like his great teacher, William Herrmann, Barth appears to dismiss them as being of little significance, and appears reluctant to engage with the central questions of faith and history, such as those raised by Lessing:

> The problem does indeed have this temporal or spatial aspect. It has the form of the problem of the historical (*geschichtlich*) distance between the being and activity of Christ in its own place and ours, in a different place. That there is this difference cannot be denied . . . This distance-problem, however, which has become of such interest to modern Protestantism is, all things considered, more of a technical or conceptual difficulty rather than a spiritual, or a genuine theological, problem.[19]

But while Barth's insistence that revelation is not a predicate of history, linked with his conceptual distinction between the contemporaneous and coextensive 'secular form' and the 'divine content' of revelation, might seem to render him immune from such critical-historical questions, the reality is actually rather different.

Precisely because of the epistemic significance of human recognition of revelation for what it is, the question of how the 'secular form' – let alone the 'divine content' – of that revelation may be discerned within the historical continuum becomes acutely pressing. If revelation demands historical predicates, as Barth insists it does, the question of how those predicates may be recognized within the historical nexus cannot be evaded. It does not matter if revelation is merely 're-presentation' or 'recapitulation' of the Christologically determined situation: once the necessity of historical predicates is conceded, the full challenge of the critical-historical method must be faced. Although Eberhard Jüngel (see pp. 211–19) has argued with some force that the relationship between the 'form' and 'content' of revelation is not arbitrary, the fact remains that the circumstantial historical act 'with and under' which revelation occurs must be open to critical-historical inquiry if it is an historical event. Barth simply has not succeeded in freeing his Christology from the critical questions raised by the modern period.

It is therefore significant that Barth is often presented as the exponent of a 'classical Christology', reverting to the great themes of patristic Christology and their medieval and Reformation developments. Barth tends to enter into debate with the theology of medieval and Reformed scholasticism on matters of Christology, rather than with the Christologies of the modern period. Of particular importance in this respect is Barth's discussion of the distinction between anhypostatic and enhypostatic humanity. Barth appears to have encountered this distinction for the first time during his Göttingen period, and to have seen in the latter a means of safeguarding the essential unity of Jesus Christ with God. Similarly, Barth's frequent insistence that God is the subject of Jesus Christ's actions is articulated in terms of the patristic concept of the 'carrier' or 'bearer' (*Träger*): 'The Word became flesh: not an abstract human nature in general, but the carrier of our human essence.'[20]

Barth's unhesitating affirmation that Christ assumed fallen human nature (in other words, that the Word became 'flesh' as well as 'humanity') has caused disquiet among some of his critics, in view of its unorthodox historical associations. According to this view, God performs the actions of Jesus through the fallen human nature which he 'carries', this human nature not being an agent in itself. Barth emphasizes that God acts directly, rather than indirectly, in Christ. It is not a question of God acting vicariously through Christ, or delegating Christ to act on his behalf with his authority: Christ is God, and as such God may be said to act when Christ acts:

> We deal with God himself when we deal with this human being (*Mensch*). God himself speaks when this human being speaks in the words of humanity. God himself acts and suffers when this human being acts and suffers as a human being. God himself triumphs when this one triumphs as a human being. The human speaking and acting and suffering and triumphing of this one human being directly concerns us, in that his human history is ours, the salvation-history which, because God himself is its human subject in his Son, changes the entire human situation.[21]

Whereas the 'carrier' of the human nature in humanity is an individual human, Barth refuses to acknowledge the existence of any human carrier in the hypostatic union: the human nature is carried by the Word of God. In his polemic against the Christology of Lutheran Orthodoxy (as well as certain older representatives of Reformed Orthodoxy), Barth argues that the human nature of Christ may be thought of as a temple within which God dwells:

> Can one describe this in any way other than Calvin (*Inst.* II.14.1): *e virginis utero templum sibi delegit in quo habitaret?* Is 'temple' or 'dwelling' – a dwelling filled with Godhood, and exclusively and totally claimed and sanctified by God, but still a dwelling! – not really enough to describe what has to be said about human essence in relation to Jesus Christ and to the history which took place in him?[22]

This point is important, in that it illustrates Barth's tendency to treat Christ's humanity as a vehicle for his divinity, in a manner similar to John Calvin and the Alexandrian tradition (which Calvin follows at this point). It is passages such as the above which may be interpreted as indicating that Barth constructs his Christology 'from above', and expose Barth to the criticism that he presupposes the divinity of Christ: whereas this presupposition might be permissible for pre-modern thinkers such as Athanasius (c. 296–373) or John Calvin (1509–1564), since the time of the Enlightenment it is no longer possible to avoid the historical question of how this divinity is to be directly inferred from the history of Jesus of Nazareth and the tradition concerning him.

In effect, Barth gives every impression of being content to reinterpret the earlier 'classical' Christological tradition in the light of his 'theology of the Word', rather than establishing the foundations of that classical Christology in the first place. In this respect, as in so many others, Barth must be regarded as deliberately disengaging himself from what is widely regarded as one of the most crucial questions facing contemporary Christology in the post-Enlightenment period: the relation between faith and history. If the 'modern' period is characterized by its critical-historical attitudes (as Ernst Troeltsch suggested in his famous study of the Reformer Philip Melanchthon and the Lutheran scholastic Johann Gerhard), then Barth's Christology belongs to the pre-modern period. It is perhaps significant that Barth seems to be most at home in his dialogue with the Christology of the sixteenth and seventeenth centuries, rather than with that of the modern period.

Barth's attitude at this point may be contrasted with that of Brunner, whose concept of a Christologically concentrated 'historical dialogue' between God and humanity leads him to attempt a systematic engagement with the questions of faith and history. We shall explore this in the section which follows.

Emil Brunner

In his works prior to 1921, Brunner developed a Christology along fairly classical liberal lines; there is no trace of the concerns which characterize the writings of Karl Barth at this juncture. However, Barth was receiving considerable attention at this time, and Brunner could not remain isolated from the new currents sweeping through the German-speaking theological world.[23] His transition to a dialectical Christology may be detected in the 1921 work *Erlebnis, Erkenntnis und Glaube* ('Experience, Knowledge and Faith'), with its emphasis upon the objectivity of faith, and its clear move away from the liberal interest in the inner life of Jesus or the psychological phenomenon of his religious personality.[24] However, in this work a tendency can already be detected to construct Christology in terms of a dialogical analogy between God and humanity, with the move towards an anthropology which would ultimately lead to the rupture between Brunner and Barth in 1934.

The Critique of Ritschlianism: The Mediator

In *The Mediator* (1927), Brunner maintains that Christianity is essentially an incarnational-mediatorial phenomenon, deriving from and constituted by the person and work of Christ.[25] Arguing that this point had been ignored or distorted during the period of the nineteenth century, Brunner suggests that the Christological tradition from Schleiermacher to Harnack was essentially based upon a general conception of religion, of which Christianity was the highest and most developed manifestation. Thus he interprets Ritschl as having understood Christianity primarily as the introduction of an eternal divine idea into history in a definite historical event – the life of Jesus of Nazareth. As such, Ritschl's system does not make reference to a 'unique fact of history *(einmaliges Faktum der Geschichte)'*.[26] The fact that Ritschl chooses to express his Christology in personal and historical forms must not, in Brunner's view, be permitted to obscure the fact that it is essentially composed of rational and ethical ideas, with only the loosest of connections with history in general, and the person of Jesus Christ in particular.

Brunner notes that, of the possible Christological titles available to him from the Protestant tradition, Ritschl chooses that of 'royal prophet' rather than 'priestly mediator'. This, Brunner maintains, indicates that Ritschl understands Christ's relationship to Christianity to be essentially factual and causal rather than essential and necessary. In effect, Ritschl treats Jesus as nothing more than the historical point of departure for a self-sufficient idea. In other words, Ritschl affirms that Christ was the first to introduce the 'Christian idea' into history as a matter of historical fact, thus giving the impulse for the subsequent historical development of that idea in Christianity. For Brunner, this amounted to a mere matter of historical contingency, where what was required was a matter of historical necessity (in that it was Christ, and only Christ, who could do this).[27]

Brunner thus argues that a *theological* rather than an *historical* justification is required if the central significance of Jesus of Nazareth is to be upheld. This point is encapsulated in his choice of *Der Mittler* ('The Mediator') as the title for his book, as it indicates the need to ground the history of Jesus of Nazareth in the concept of special revelation and the absolute necessity of redemption, rather than the accidental truths of history. By doing so, he totally rejects such Jesuologies as the 'religious hero', the 'religious genius' or the 'moral personality': for Brunner, a Christ who is merely first among equals is not a Christ who can be preached. Brunner argues that modern theology, in its attempt to ground and interpret Christian faith in terms of human experience, has virtually removed from it any sense of sin or guilt, and thus rendered the idea of a 'Mediator' unnecessary.[28] It is for this reason that Brunner must be regarded as constructing his Christology 'from above', rather 'from below' (to use the later terms) at this stage.

However, Brunner insists that God must be conceived biblically rather than philosophically – in other words, as a person rather than as the originator or embodiment of a self-sufficient idea. Brunner is implacably opposed to the 'false (theological) objectivism' which he considers to have arisen through the intrusion of Greek philosophical thought into the theology of the early church (and his affinities with Harnack here are significant). He attempts to overcome it through a reinterpretation of the idea of the 'Word' of God. Although his initially resulting Christology, as found in *The Mediator*, is unquestionably docetic,[29] Brunner's developing theological personalism, evident in his rejection of idealism, contains the germs of his later solution to this deficiency.

Dialogue in History: A Personalist Christology

To understand this later development, it is necessary to appreciate the significance of the development of the concept of dialogical personalism in the early 1920s. The basic features of this philosophy were laid out in two major works to appear during this period: Ferdinand Ebner's (1882–1931) *Das Wort und die geistigen Realitaten* ('The Word and Spiritual Realities', 1921), and Martin Buber's (1878–1965) *Ich und Du* ('I and Thou'), which was published in 1923. Both works developed a powerful critique of contemporary idealism, and particularly of the concept of the isolation of the self. Instead, it is suggested that all human existential life should be analysed in *dialogical* terms. Buber analyses human experience as follows:

> The world is twofold for humanity according to our twofold attitude (*Haltung*).

The attitude of humanity is twofold according to the two basic
words we can utter.
The basic words are not single words, but pairs of words.
One basic word is the word pair I–You (*Ich–Du*).
The other basic word is the word pair I–It (*Ich–Es*).[30]

For Buber, the I–It relationship defines the world of experience
(*Erfahrung*), which may be regarded as the interaction of a subject and
object. The I–You relationship, however, establishes the world of
encounter (*Begegnung*), which must be regarded as the mutual interaction of two subjects. Whereas in the world of experience the subject
is active and the object passive, the world of encounter opens up the
possibility of both activity and passivity on the part of the subject as the
subject engages in a dynamic relationship with another subject. It is this
concept of the mutual interaction of two subjects which Buber attempts
to encapsulate in the untranslatable formula *Ich–wirkend–Du und
Du–wirkend–Ich*. Buber thus emphasizes the importance of the relationship (*das Zwischen*) between the 'I' and the 'You', which prevents the
improper reification or hypostasization of either. As Buber stresses,
'actuality' (*Wirklichkeit*) cannot be objectified. As we noted earlier, this
consideration is of importance in relation to Feuerbach's critique of the
notion of God, which he held to rest upon an illegitimate objectification
of human longings. Buber is able to place such longings within the
context of a contentless relationship.

While Buber locates the world of encounter primarily in human
relationships, he is clearly aware of its potential application to the
relationship between God and humanity. The development of Buber's
dialogical critique of the subject-object dichotomy was a major theme of
the theology of the second quarter of the twentieth century, and its most
significant Christological application may be found in Brunner's 1938
work on truth as 'encounter', *Die Wahrheit als Begegnung* ('Truth as
Encounter'), which had its origins as a series of lectures to theological
students in Sweden.

In this work, Brunner argues that faith is primarily a personal
encounter with the God who meets us personally in Jesus Christ. The
anti-intellectualism of this concept of divine revelation will be evident.
This reflects Brunner's conviction that the early church misunderstood
revelation as the divine impartation of doctrinal truth about God, rather
than self-revelation of God. For Brunner, 'truth' is itself a personal

concept, and the subject-object dichotomy a destructive element within Christian theology. The biblical revelation lies 'beyond objectivism and subjectivism', in that revelation is understood to be an event in history. This should not be interpreted to mean that history reveals God, but that God reveals himself within the historical process, and supremely in the work and person of Jesus Christ. By the phrase 'personal correspondence' (*personale Korrespondenz*, or, less frequently, *personhafte Korrespondenz*), employed extensively in this work, Brunner intends to convey the fact that revelation cannot be conceived propositionally or intellectually, but must be understood as an act of God, and supremely the act of Jesus Christ.

God reveals himself personally and historically, by communicating himself in Jesus Christ. The concept of 'truth as encounter' thus conveys the two elements of a correct understanding of revelation: it is *historical* and it is *personal*. By the former, Brunner wishes us to understand that truth is not something permanent within the eternal world of ideas which is disclosed or communicated to us but something which *happens* in space and time. Truth comes into being as the act of God in time and space. By the latter, Brunner intends to emphasize that the content of this act of God is none other than God himself, rather than a complex of ideas or doctrines concerning God:

> Truth as encounter is not truth about something, not even truth about something mental, about ideas. Rather it is that truth which breaks in pieces the impersonal concept of truth and mind, truth that can be adequately expressed *only* in the I–You form. All use of impersonal terms to describe it – the divine, the transcendent, the absolute – is indeed the inadequate way invented by the thinking of the solitary self to speak of it – or, more correctly, of Him.

The revelation of God is the 'imparting of himself' to us. For Brunner, divine revelation is necessarily Christocentric: he counters the false objectivism of Orthodoxy's doctrine of propositional revelation with Luther's dictum to the effect that Scripture is 'the manger in which Christ is laid'.

On the basis of this approach, Brunner develops a critique of any notion of revelation which represents itself as words or propositions about God. These objectify God, in the sense of reducing him to the status of an *object*, rather than of a *person*. 'No speech, no word, is adequate to the mystery of God as a Person.' Revelation cannot be understood as the impartation of data about God; 'it is never the mere communication of knowledge, but a life-giving and life-renewing fellowship'. In revelation, God communicates *himself*, not *ideas* about himself – and this communication is concentrated and focused in the person of Jesus Christ, as appropriated by the Holy Spirit. Although Brunner's rejection of any cognitive dimension to revelation seems seriously overstated, a significant point is being made, with important Christological implications.

The concept of our encounter with God necessarily implies that the person of God is historically and personally actualized in Jesus Christ. Jesus Christ establishes the 'point of contact (*Anknüpfungspunkt*)' between God and humanity through which this encounter takes place. It will therefore be clear that Brunner's understanding of the term 'Mediator' (*Mittler*) altered significantly from the 1927 work of that name, in that the original anti-intellectualist sense of the term was supplemented with the concept of Christ as the 'point of contact' between God and humanity.

The notion of the 'point of contact' proved to be the issue over which Barth and Brunner fell out. Although its Christological dimensions were fully explored only in 1938, the new trend within Brunner's thought was obvious by 1934. In this year, Brunner published a work entitled *Nature and Grace* in which he argues that 'the task of our theological generation is to find a way back to a legitimate natural theology'.[31] Brunner locates this approach in the doctrine of creation, specifically in the idea that human beings are created in the *imago Dei*, 'the image of God'. Human nature is constituted in such a way that there is an analogy with the being of God himself. Despite the sinfulness of human nature, the ability to discern God in nature remains. Sinful human beings remain able to recognize God in nature and the events of history, and to be aware of their guilt before God. There is thus a 'point of contact (*Anknüpfungspunkt*)' for divine revelation within human nature.

In effect, Brunner argues that human nature is constituted in such a way that there is a ready-made point of contact for divine revelation. Revelation addresses a human nature which already has some inkling of what that revelation is about. For example, take the idea of the gospel demand to 'repent of sin'. Brunner holds that this makes little sense unless human beings already have some idea of what 'sin' is. The gospel demand to repent is thus addressed to an audience which already has at least something of an idea of what 'sin' and 'repentance' might mean. Revelation brings with it a fuller understanding of what sin means – but in doing so, it builds upon an existing human awareness of sin.

Barth reacted with anger to this suggestion. His reply to Brunner – which brought their long-standing friendship to an abrupt end – has one of the shortest titles in the history of religious publishing: *Nein!* Barth was determined to say 'no!' to Brunner's positive evaluation of natural theology. It seemed to imply that God needed help to reveal himself, or that human beings somehow co-operated with God in the act of revelation. 'The Holy Spirit . . . needs no point of contact other than that which he himself establishes', was his angry retort. For Barth, there is no 'point of contact' inherent within human nature. Any such 'point of contact' is itself the result of divine revelation. It is something that is evoked by the Word of God, rather than something which is a permanent feature of human nature.

Underlying this debate is another matter, which is perhaps too easily overlooked. The Barth–Brunner debate took place in 1934, the year in which Hitler gained power in Germany. Underlying Brunner's appeal to nature is an idea, which can be traced back to Luther, known as 'the orders of creation'. According to Luther, God providentially established certain 'orders' within creation, in order to prevent it collapsing into chaos. Those orders included the family, the church and the state. (The close alliance between church and state in German Lutheran thought reflects this idea.) Nineteenth-century German liberal Protestantism had absorbed this idea, and developed a theology which allowed German culture, including a positive assessment of the state, to become of major importance theologically. Part of Barth's concern is that Brunner, perhaps unwittingly, has laid a theological foundation for allowing the state to become a model for God. And who wanted to model God on Adolf Hitler?

The transition from Brunner's early dialectical Christology to a 'historical-dialogical (*geschichtlich-dialogisch*)' Christology involved a major shift in his understanding of the manner in which God encounters humanity. For the later Brunner, that encounter does not take place in a vacuum (as he appeared to suggest in *The Mediator*), but in history itself, the sphere in which human beings are active interpreters rather than passive recipients of revelation. That encounter presupposes that humanity possesses a capability to respond to the personal, historical revelation of God in Christ, a capacity which Brunner terms *Angesproch-sein und Sichansprechenlassen*. This significant development inevitably meant that anthropological considerations came to exert an increasing influence over Brunner's Christology. From 1930 onwards, Brunner envisages a direct correlation between the person who hears the word of God and the appearance of the word of God in Christ, effectively treating humanity as God's 'conversation partner (*Gesprächspartner*)' in the continuum of history. It is this aspect of Brunner's 'historical-dialogical' Christology which distinguishes it so radically from the purely dialectical Christology of Karl Barth. The definitive statement of Brunner's 'historical-dialogical' Christology, found in the second volume of his *Dogmatics*, entitled *The Christian Doctrines of Creation and Redemption* (1950), indicates how closely his anthropology and Christology have become interrelated, without substantially developing any of the points noted above.[32]

Barth and Brunner on Dialogue in Christ

The development of the later Christology of Karl Barth is of consider-able interest, in that his earlier theology – especially as enunciated in the Romans commentary – appeared to leave no room for a 'Christology' in any meaningful sense of the term. Barth's move away from this earlier dialectical position is therefore of the greatest significance. In his earlier theology, Barth's thought is dominated by the 'diastasis' of God over and against humanity; in his later theology, 'diastasis' is replaced by 'dialogue'. How are we to account for this development?

A number of scholars, including Hans Urs von Balthasar, have argued that two critical turning points may be discerned in Barth's theological development:

1. A turning away from liberalism to Christian radicalism, which took place during the First World War, and received its expression in the Romans commentary;

2. The final liberation from the dross of philosophy, in order that an unadulterated and independent theology might result, which may be seen taking place around the year 1930.

The so-called 'Göttingen dogmatics', based on Barth's lectures at Göttingen (as a later successor to Albrecht Ritschl!), begin to explore more constructive approaches to Christology.

The early Barth can be regarded as a theological iconoclast, who was concerned to destroy theological and Christological 'towers of Babel' – human constructions erected in defiance of God. Yet Barth later appears to have realized that the decisive influence of Kierkegaard on his earlier dialectical theology represented the outcome of the hidden intrusion of philosophy and anthropology into theology, so that his dialectical theology, far from representing the *destruction* of anthropocentric theology, actually represented its *consolidation*. He had rejected Ritschl, only to adopt Kierkegaard. In this second phase, Barth may therefore be thought of as attempting to base his theology upon a *theological* rather than an *anthropological* foundation – and as identifying Jesus Christ, the Word of God, as that foundation.

This development may be seen in Barth's study of Anselm of Canterbury's theological method (1931), *Fides Quaerens Intellectum*. In this study, Barth argues that theology should be autonomous in relation to philosophy. At the heart of this work is the recognition of the importance of Anselm's insight that there is a 'ratio peculiar to the Word of God', a 'ratio of God', a 'Word spoken from God' which stands over and against human concepts of 'ratio' (that is, 'reason'). Truth is thus the consequence of God's own action, which Barth comes to identify with the event of God's own self-revelation in his Word in Jesus Christ, rather than a product of the autonomous human rational faculty. Whereas Barth once emphasized the enormity of the gulf fixed between God and humanity, he later came to emphasize the 'togetherness (*Zusammensein*)' or the 'dialogue (*Zwiesprach*)' between God and humanity in history itself. The introduction of this idea of a 'dialogue' between God and humanity clearly raises the question of the relation between Barth and Brunner on this point.

The liberal theology of the nineteenth century tended to treat God as an object, in the sense of his being at the disposal of human enquiry. Early dialectical theology insisted that God must be regarded as a subject, thus reversing his hitherto prevailing cognitive status. Indeed, Barth plays upon the two German terms usually employed to signify 'object' (*Objekt* and *Gegenstand*): God is not subject to the passive scrutiny of humanity as *Objekt*, but stands over and against us as *Gegen-stand*. Brunner adopted a similar attitude. The difference between Barth and Brunner lies in their understanding of our relation with respect to God as subject. The situation may be summarized as follows:

Liberal Theology: God as object, humanity as subject.

Brunner: God as subject, humanity as subject.
Barth: God as subject, humanity as object.

For the theologians of the nineteenth century in general, particularly those associated with the Ritschl–Herrman–Harnack tradition, humanity was the active partner in discovering the nature, identity and character of God. As we saw above, Brunner insists upon the mutual activity of God and humanity within the sphere of history, in order that the insights of dialogical personalism may by exploited theologically. Humanity is thus the reciprocating *Gesprachspartner* of God. It is therefore inevitable, as we noted above, that Brunner's theology in general, and particularly his Christology, is heavily dependent upon his anthropological presuppositions.

Barth, however, totally inverts the liberal understanding of the relation between God and humanity, insisting that humanity must be regarded as an object to whom the divine subject addresses his Word. By emphasizing humanity's passivity and God's activity in the process of revelation, Barth believes it is possible to exclude anthropological considerations altogether from theology. Just as he believes that the theologians of the nineteenth century had been forced to reduce theology to anthropology by their insistence that humanity was the active questing subject and God the passive and sought object, so Barth believes that theology may maintain an intellectual autonomy if it is God who is treated as the active questing subject, and humanity as the passive sought object, in the process of revelation. The crucial anthropological question arising from the liberal theology concerns the *possibility* of revelation: for Barth, the proper question concerns the *reality* of revelation. It is pointless to argue about whether revelation can take place, when it has already done so. Revelation is a divinely initiated and actuated event, in which it is God (rather than humanity) who responds to God in faith. This point is embodied in Barth's distinctive doctrine of the Trinity, in which the Holy Spirit plays a crucial hermeneutical role which might otherwise be assigned to a human interpretative agency. Barth thus effectively reduces the 'dialogue' between God and humanity to a 'monologue'.

Dialectical theology may be regarded as of decisive importance in restoring Christology to a central position in modern theology. The centrality of Christ is theologically linked with the necessity of revelation in the first place, and Christ as the bearer of that revelation in the second. Dialetical theology also points to the importance of the role of history, although Brunner and Barth have distinctive conceptions of the nature of that role. For Brunner, history is the arena within which the Christologically centred dialogue between God and humanity takes place; for Barth, it is the *theatrum gloriae Dei*, in which God graciously makes himself known as Lord through his self-revelation in Christ. Although in its initial phases (prior to 1925), dialectical theology appeared to have no interest in matters of history, a growing recognition of the importance of the issues can be discerned as the movement matured.

Yet there were those who were convinced that a retreat from the historical was both inevitable and theologically necessary. To understand how this development came about, and the problems which it raised in its wake, we must turn to consider the kerygmatic theology of Rudolf Bultmann.

A Disengagement from History: Bultmann and Tillich

Dialectical theology was unquestionably the dominant theological force within the Germany of the Weimar Republic. The disagreements within the movement would not become serious until the late 1930s, by which time the practical and ethical problems posed for the German churches initially by the Third Reich, and subsequently by the Second World War, served to inhibit the development of any serious alternative to the 'theology of the Word of God'. Although it is possible to argue that, considered as a theological force, dialectical theology was on the wane by the year 1935, its moral intensity in the face of National Socialism earned it a legitimate and continuing place in the religious consciousness of Germany both in the Nazi and the immediate post-war periods. Nevertheless, a new theological force had developed within Germany in the pre-war period, although it came to public attention only during the war itself. Its leading figure was the Marburg New Testament scholar, Rudolf Bultmann (1884–1976).

In understanding the importance of the approaches developed by Bultmann (and subsequently by Paul Tillich), it is necessary to return to the three aspects of the 'faith and history' problem originally identified by G. E. Lessing (see pp. 28–33). The third of those difficulties is existential in character. How can someone who lived two thousand years ago be of continuing relevance to modern humanity? The rise of existentialism allowed this question to be answered. Although the precise responses associated with Bultmann and Tillich are quite different in tone, as will become clear, they share a common assumption (inherited from Martin Kähler) that belief in Christ cannot ultimately be grounded purely in the provisional results of historical research.

Rudolf Bultmann

On 4 June 1941, Rudolf Bultmann delivered a lecture at the Alpirsbach conference of the *Gesellschaft für Evangelische Theologie* entitled 'Neues Testament und Mythologie'. The same work was published later the same year as a pamphlet, less than fifty pages in length. The lecture introduced a phrase into the German theological vocabulary which summarizes the Christological programme with which we are concerned in the present chapter – *die Entmythologisierung des Neuen Testaments* ('the demythologization of the New Testament') – as well as occasioning a crisis within popular German Protestantism.[1]

In view of the considerable degree of misunderstanding still surrounding Bultmann's theology in English-speaking circles, we propose to introduce it at greater length than usual. Bultmann's Christology is of importance in that it arises from a major new development in contemporary understandings of the nature of the New Testament documents, which sees the *kerygma* as the unifying principle between the Jesus of history and the Christ of faith. In the present chapter, we shall consider Bultmann's approach to Christology, as well as the developments and criticisms of this approach associated with Paul Tillich and Gerhard Ebeling.

The fundamental contention of Bultmann's controversial lecture of 1941 was that the New Testament proclamation or *kerygma* concerning Christ is stated and understood in mythological terms (which Bultmann attempted to derive from existing Jewish apocalyptic and Gnostic redemption myths, borrowing ideas deriving from the 'history of religions school') which, although perfectly legitimate and intelligible in the first century, cannot be taken seriously today:

> It is impossible to use electric light and radio equipment and, when ill, to claim the assistance of modern medical and clinical discoveries, and at the same time believe in the New Testament world of spirits and miracles (*die Geister- und Wunderwelt des Neuen Testaments*). Anyone who thinks they can manage this must be clear that, by explaining the content of the Christian

faith in this manner, they are making the Christian proclamation unintelligible and impossible in the present day.

The human understanding of the world and of human existence has changed radically since the first century, with the result that modern humanity finds the mythological worldview of the New Testament unintelligible and unacceptable. A worldview is given to people with the age in which they live, and they are in no position to alter it. The modern scientific and existential worldview means that that of the New Testament is now discarded and unintelligible. Furthermore, taking up Schweitzer's point about the thorough-going nature of the eschatological conditioning of the preaching of Jesus, Bultmann insists that it is impossible to be selective in relation to the New Testament *kerygma*. He notes two approaches to this problem. Each of them was popular in its own day and age; yet both are now, in Bultmann's view, discredited beyond hope of salvage. These two approaches are:

1. The *liberal* approach, which aimed to eliminate embarrassing 'mythological' elements (such as apocalypticism) after the manner of Harnack, by distinguishing the mythological 'husk' from its religious or ethical 'kernel'.

2. The approach of the *religionsgeschichtliche Schule*, particularly that of Troeltsch, which interpreted Jesus as an eternal symbol for the cultus of the Christian church, thus bypassing the specific question of the nature of his preaching and its cultural context.

Bultmann declares this process of reduction to be illegitimate, in that it compromises the *kerygma* by failing to bring out clearly that the New Testament speaks of Jesus as an event (*Ereignis*) through which God has brought about the salvation of the world (even if it articulates this event in mythological terms).

Liberalism had responded to the recognition of mythological elements within the New Testament by attempting to discover the universal truths nestling within these myths. Bultmann rejects such a move, declaring that the fundamental task of theology is not to *remove*, but to *interpret*, such mythological components. By removing them, liberalism had converted Christianity into a non-historical religion, reducing the proclamation of Christ in the *kerygma* to a timeless set of culturally-acceptable principles of religion and ethics. Yet something *new* has happened in Jesus – a point to which Bultmann returns frequently in his castigation of liberal Jesuologies.

For Bultmann, there are two, and only two, possibilities for the contemporary theologian: either the mythical worldview is accepted in its totality, or it is rejected in its totality. Both liberalism and the 'history of religions' approach evade this dilemma, and as a result offer false solutions.

Demythologization and Christology

The resolution of the contradiction between the radically divergent worldviews of the first and twentieth centuries can be overcome, according to Bultmann, only by *demythologizing* the New Testament. It must be emphasized that Bultmann has no time for those who suggest that the gospel is concerned with timeless moral truths or the historical manifestation of a self-sufficient idea: the gospel is, and remains, gospel – the decisive intervention of God in history through Christ in the 'Christ-event' (*Christusereignis* – note the deliberate contrast with the static *Christusprinzip*). In Christ something has happened of relevance not merely to the New Testament writers of the first century, but to everyone to whom the Christian gospel is proclaimed. The difficulty lies in articulating precisely what it is that has happened.

The liberals had attempted to eliminate the mythological elements in the New Testament, and thus found themselves totally incapable of dealing with the consequences of Schweitzer's 'consistent eschatology', which demonstrated that the entire synoptic *Christusbild* was conditioned by eschatological considerations. Bultmann, recognizing the futility of half-measures, seeks to interpret the mythological framework of the New Testament, and thus confronts directly the problem which the liberals had unsuccessfully attempted to evade. It cannot be over-emphasized that Bultmann does not understand the purpose of his programme of *Entmythologisierung* to be the *elimination* of myth. Bultmann places far too high a value on 'myth' to adopt so simplistic a course of action. For Bultmann, 'myth' is a primitive means of objectifying the forces which impinge upon and determine human existence, and thus conveys insights concerning it. It is necessary, therefore, to *reinterpret* the mythology of the New Testament anthropologically, or existentially. Bultmann thus takes as his point of departure the understanding of existence found in the New Testament, and his theological programme may thus be defined as the existential demythologization of the New Testament. Bultmann thus substitutes a twentieth-century myth for its first-century equivalent.

In order to understand Bultmann's Christology fully, we must consider his understanding of the nature of the New Testament *kerygma*, and his concern for the existentialist aspects of the gospel. Before this is appropriate, however, it is necessary to consider Bultmann's relation to the liberal and *religionsgeschichtlich* schools. The rise of dialectical theology in the early 1920s provided one alternative to these traditions: how, then, does Bultmann relate to them, and, indeed, to dialectical theology itself? It may seem outrageous to some readers to suggest that Barth and Bultmann have anything in common: is not one the pillar of neo-orthodox dogmatic theology, and the other a radical New Testament critic? In fact, as we shall see, the two have much in common, arising from the cultural aftermath of the First World War.

The Critique of Liberal Jesuologies

In his important essay of 1924, *Die liberale Theologie und die jüngste theologische Bewegung* ('The Liberal Theology and the Latest Theological Movement'), Bultmann deals with the relationship between Barth and Gogarten (whom he treats as the leading figures of dialectical theology) and 'liberal theology' (which, significantly, he identifies with the positions of Herrmann and Troeltsch, apparently glossing over their manifest differences). Bultmann stresses the significance of two facts: first, that dialectical theology did not originate from within traditional Orthodoxy, but from within liberal theology itself (Barth was a student at Marburg, Gogarten at Heidelberg, and Thurneysen at both of these liberal strongholds); second, that dialectical theology was not a protest against any individual theologian, but against a specific theological trend. Dialectical theology could not be passed off as a reversion to conservatism; rather, it had to be seen as a reaction from within liberalism against its obvious weaknesses. Bultmann himself shared that liberal heritage, and emphasized its intellectual integrity, and its opposition towards compromise, whether intellectual or spiritual.

The distinctive character of the liberal school, according to Bultmann, was its use of the critical-historical method, which it believed would free scholarship from the burden of dogmatic theology and permit the real historical figure of Jesus to become the foundation of faith. For Bultmann, this very method, so characteristic of what he somewhat loosely terms 'liberal' theology, in fact contains the seeds of its own destruction: 'Historical research can never lead to any conclusion which can serve as the basis of faith, because all its results have only relative validity (*Geltung*)'. Bultmann cites two works originating from the 'liberal school' which identified and recognized this crucial point, and yet apparently failed to acknowledge its full implications. The first was Troeltsch's 1911 essay 'The Significance of the Historical Existence of Jesus for Faith' (see pp. 115–22), which, for Bultmann, made Christian faith dependent upon the research of 'scholars and professors'; the second was the fourteenth question which Harnack addressed to Barth in their exchanges of 1923 (see pp. 128–9). For Bultmann, Barth's response (see p. 129) to this was totally correct:

> Historical criticism cannot be set aside; we must, however, understand its true significance: it educates us in freedom and truth – not only by freeing us from a specific traditional understanding of history, but because it frees us from every understanding of history (*Geschichtsbild*) possible for scientific knowledge, and brings us to the realisation that the world which faith wishes to lay hold of is totally unattainable with the assistance of scientific knowledge.[2]

Developing this point further, Bultmann emphasizes that the results of the application of the critical-historical method possess a purely relative validity, in that the original historical phenomena, to which the method may be applied, are themselves relative entities existing within an immense nexus of interrelated entities, none of which may claim absolute validity. 'Even the historical Jesus himself is one phenomenon among others, not an absolute entity.' Furthermore, the liberal approach to history assumes that the historian may be treated as standing outside that history, apart from it, as an indifferent observer, similar to the observer of the world of nature. But – and here we may see Bultmann's distinctively existential understanding of history being employed as a theological weapon, effective even against the historicist theology of Troeltsch – the observer is, in fact, a part of that history, lacking any privileged or objective vantage point.

Barth and Bultmann alike constantly emphasize, particularly during the period 1921–27, that Christian theology is about God, rather than humanity, and that Christology necessarily cannot content itself with dealing with 'Christ according to the flesh'. (Indeed, the liberal concern for the historical figure of Jesus is, as we have seen, more appropriately termed a 'Jesuology' than a 'Christology', the latter being regarded within the liberal school as a later dogmatic imposition upon the portrait of Jesus' religious personality contained within the synoptic gospels.)

The critical study of the New Testament is therefore to be welcomed, Bultmann argues, as it simply destroys the foundations of the liberal 'Jesuologies', without calling into question the fact that God acted in Christ to redeem the world. Yet salvation cannot be mediated objectively or physically through the historical Jesus; it is mediated existentially by the proclaimed Christ. But how is that 'act' of God in Christ to be described? It is at this point that we must return to an analysis of Bultmann's programme of demythologization.

Demythologization and Existentialism

For Bultmann, the New Testament makes statements about God – and therefore about human existence. Bultmann follows the great Marburg liberal, Wilhelm Herrmann, in emphasizing that theological statements cannot, in principle, be made about God as he is in himself, but rather as he relates to us. Therefore, according to Bultmann, they must consist in statements concerning the human existential situation. As such, Bultmann argues that it is both possible and necessary to interpret the New Testament myths in existentialist terms. It must be emphasized, and indeed, cannot be emphasized too strongly, that the term 'myth' does not in any way imply that the 'religious story' is in any sense untrue. Indeed, Bultmann defines myth as a form of thought which seeks to represent a transcendent reality in this-worldly terms. The New Testament relates 'stories' concerning remote and inaccessible times and places (such as 'in the beginning' or 'in heaven'), and involving supernatural agents or events. Bultmann declares that these stories possess an underlying existential meaning, which can be perceived and appropriated by a suitable process of interpretation.

Perhaps the most important of these is the eschatological myth of the imminent end of the world through direct divine intervention, leading to judgment and subsequent reward or retribution. This insight is of central importance to our narrative, in that it allows Bultmann to deal with Schweitzer's demonstration of the 'thorough-going eschatological conditioning' of the New Testament by a comprehensive process of demythologization. For Bultmann, this 'myth', and others like it, may be reinterpreted existentially. Thus, in the case of the eschatological myth, the recognition that history has not, in fact, come to an end does not necessarily invalidate the myth: interpreted existentially, the 'myth' refers to the here and now of human existence – the fact that human beings must face the reality of their own death, and are thus forced to make existential decisions. The 'judgment' in question is not some future event of *divine* judgment, to take place at the end of the world, but the present event of *our own judgment of ourselves*, based upon our knowledge of what God has done in Christ.

Bultmann's theology may be regarded as an ellipse constructed around two foci: first, the programme of demythologization, or existential interpretation, of the New Testament; second, the idea of the *kerygma*, the proclamation of a divine word addressed to us, occasioning an existential crisis and demanding an existential decision on our part. Beneath the strange language of the New Testament lies the proclamation of a way of life which is a present possibility for us and which we may appropriate as our own. The 'husk' of the myth contains the 'kernel' of the kerygma: by translating the mythical 'husk' into contemporary existential terms, the heart of the Christian proclamation may be recovered and made intelligible to modern humanity.

Bultmann argues that precisely this sort of demythologizing may be found in the Fourth Gospel, which was written towards the end of the first century, when the early eschatological expectations of the Christian community were fading. The *eschaton* is interpreted by Bultmann to refer to the moment of existential crisis, as human beings are confronted with the divine *kerygma* addressed to them. In a manner similar to Brunner, Bultmann develops the concept of *Angesprochensein* – the idea that we are addressed directly by the *kerygma* here and now. The 'realized eschatology' of the Fourth Gospel arises through the fact that the redactor of the gospel has realized that the *parousia* is not some future event, but one which has already taken place, in the confrontation of the believer with the existential *kerygma*:

To the 'Now' of the coming of the Revealer, there corresponds exactly the 'Now' of the proclamation of the word as an historical (*geschichtlich*) fact, the 'Now' of the present, of the moment. That is, Jesus is not the Revealer, since the 'Word became flesh', through his effect upon the history of the world, which obviously affects everyone, and is universally available for evaluation and decision, but through the preaching of the

word as a concrete event at a specified time . . . This 'Now' of
being addressed at a specific moment (*jeweiliges Jetzt des
Angesprochenseins*), this moment, is the eschatological 'Now',
because in it the decision is made between life and death. It is
the hour which is coming, and, in being addressed, now is . . .
Therefore it is not true that the *parousia*, expected by others as
an event occuring in time, is now denied or transformed by
John into a process within the soul, an experience. Rather, John
opens the reader's eyes: the *parousia* has already occurred![3]

Bultmann thus regards the Fourth Gospel as partially reinterpreting
the eschatological myth in terms of its significance for human existence.
Christ is not a past phenomenon, but the ever-present Word of God,
expressing not a general truth, but a concrete proclamation addressed to
us, demanding an existential decision on our part. For Bultmann, the
eschatological process became an event in the history of the world, and
becomes an event once more in contemporary Christian proclamation.
Thus Bultmann is able to argue that Christian theology, while speaking
of faith in 'objective' terms, must realize that it must go beyond
'objective' formulations in order to maintain its existential character. But
what understanding of human existence is appropriate for this programme of demythologization (which, once more, we wish to emphasize
does not concern the total or – still worse! – the partial elimination of
myth, but its interpretation and the restatement of its content)?

Existentialism and Christology

'Existentialism' denotes a class of philosophy concerned with human
existence, which attempts to understand this existence in terms of the
concrete experience of existing individuals. As such, it is primarily a
philosophical method rather that a specific body of doctrines, a type of
philosophy of such flexibility that it can embrace the nihilism of
Jean-Paul Sartre (1905–80) or the Catholicism of Gabriel Marcel
(1889–1973). Although it is particularly associated with the modern era,
it appears to make spasmodic appearances throughout history, whenever
humans have wished to distinguish between two fundamentally different
modes of existence: the individual being of humans, and the being of
objects in nature. This distinction is expressed by existentialist thinkers
in different manners: for Martin Buber, the former is expressed in terms

of the world of *Du* and the latter in terms of the world of *Es*: for Martin Heidegger (1889–1976), the former is expressed in terms of *Existenz* (existence in the full sense of the word) and the latter in terms of *Vorhandenheit* (a 'being to hand').

As the Oxford scholar John Macquarrie has perceptively pointed out, there are important parallels between Bultmann and Heidegger.[4] This must not be understood to mean that Bultmann is simply a religious acolyte of the philosopher Heidegger.[5] Rather, the two thinkers were concerned to explore similar questions by related routes, with the result that there are obvious convergences in their thinking, most notably in connection with the idea of a bipolarity within existence. It is an over-simplification to suggest that Bultmann merely adopts Heidegger's ideas, and puts them to use in an explicitly theological context. It is probably more helpful to think of the two writers as pursuing parallel trajectories, rather than of Bultmann simply 'baptizing' Heidegger.

Heidegger's distinction between *Existenz* and *Vorhandenheit* is of crucial importance in this respect. An inanimate object, such as a stone, clearly 'exists' in some sense of the word ('being extant') which is quite distinct from the existence of a conscious thinking and reflecting individual (which Heidegger broadly intends to convey by the use of the term *Dasein*). It is through the reflection of this existing individual upon his or her own existence that the distinctive characteristics of existence may be established. The four main characteristics of human existence, as established by Heidegger, are the following:

1. An individual human being (that is, to use Heidegger's terms, *Dasein*) has a relation to himself or herself, in that he or she may legitimately be said to be 'at one with himself' or 'at odds with herself'. In other words, a human being is not simply an object (whereas a stone unquestionably is), but is actually both subject and object, transcending the subject-object dichotomy in his or her inner relations.

2. A human being is a possibility, rather than a predetermined actuality. He or she is never complete or fixed in his or her being, but is open to various possibilities of existence, which may be chosen.

3. Every human being's existence is individual, unique to him or her, and defying precise classification (Heidegger coins the term *Jemeinigkeit* to refer to this characteristic of *Existenz*).

4. Human beings exist in the world (a characteristic which Heidegger rather awkwardly designates as *In-der-Welt-sein*), and as such are caught up with it, conditioned by it, limited by it, and concerned with it. This

is not merely a statement about the physical location of human existence: it is an existential statement concerning the way in which human *Existenz* is inextricably linked with the world itself. We are in the world, and yet not of it; our ways of being are distinctive – this, after all, is the essential distinction between *Existenz* and *Vorhandenheit*, which is of seminal importance to any existentialist theology.

Yet there is the possibility that our *Existenz* will be compromised by the world, and that it will, in effect, be reduced to the level of *Vorhandenheit*. There is every possibility that we will come to regard ourselves as objects extant, but not existing, in the world. There is thus an important ambiguity in the existential significance of the 'world'. It may be conceived neutrally, as the arena of our activity, our *Spielraum*; it may also be considered negatively, as a threat to authentic existence, in that we may lose ourselves in it, losing sight of our own *Existenz* as we 'fall' into the world. It is this possibility which underlies the important distinction between authentic (*eigentlich*) and inauthentic (*uneigentlich*) existence – a crucial distinction which underlies Bultmann's soteriology, and hence his Christology.

For Heidegger, 'inauthentic existence' arises from our absorption in this excessive concern with the world. This form of existence is directed towards the world, dehumanized, and is ultimately based upon misunderstanding and delusion. We delude ourselves that we are masters of our own destiny and world. Such a life is both meaningless and worthless. The final demonstration of the illusion of inauthentic existence is provided by death itself, which finally exposes the transience of this self-deception. Heidegger regards the concept of *Angst* ('anxiety') as a catalyst in the transition from inauthentic to authentic existence, revealing to us the fact that we have been 'thrown' into a world in which we are not at home. We may be said to have 'fallen' from existence (and here Heidegger's seminary background seems to bring his thought and terms close to those of Christianity). Our 'fallenness (*Verfallenheit*)' has several characteristics, of which the following are the most important:

1. We have fallen into the world, which may absorb us into the impersonal mass of collective existence.
2. We have fallen away from our own true selves. We may thus exist in a state of 'alienation' (*Entfremdung*) from our own true self and our true existence.

It is therefore necessary for 'fallen' human beings to recover their true way of being, recognizing their illusions of security as ontological anxiety discloses to them that they are 'not at home' in the world (and, once more, Heidegger's seminary background equipped him to note the importance of ontological anxiety for Christian theologians such as Augustine and Luther). For Heidegger, in fact, 'authentic' existence is an existence of recognized despair, free from illusion, as human beings live in the anticipation of their own death: however, it is important to appreciate that Bultmann will follow Heidegger only in his descriptions of the structures of existence (and particularly the important distinction between 'authentic' and 'inauthentic' existence), and does not commit himself to following Heidegger's prescriptions concerning them. Furthermore – and it is vitally important that this point be appreciated – Heidegger treats 'fallenness' as an existential possibility open to humanity, whereas Bultmann treats it as a present existential actuality. With Heidegger's analysis of existence in mind, we may turn to consider similar ideas as they are expressed in the work of Bultmann.

According to Bultmann, the New Testament recognizes two modes of human existence: unbelieving and unredeemed existence (that is, inauthentic existence); and believing and redeemed existence (that is, authentic existence). The former is characterized by the delusion of self-sufficiency, and by the adhesion to (and hence the dependence upon) the visible and transitory world. Although the goal of human endeavours (to attain our essential and authentic existence) is appropriate, the means which human beings adopt towards this end are inappropriate and, ultimately, self-defeating: they attempt to find themselves through their own unaided efforts, and, by doing so, merely become more and more deeply embedded in the transitory world of death and despair.

Believing and redeemed existence, however, arises through our abandoning every hope that we may attain this authentic existence through our own efforts or on the basis of the visible and transitory world in which we exist: we recognize that our life is given to us as a gift, and in an act of 'desecularization (*Entweltlichung*)', choose to base our existence upon what is invisible and intangible. Although we continue to exist in the world, our attitude to it is now one of freedom from it. Although we are in the world, we are no longer of the world (John 17:15-16). This approach to the New Testament may be illustrated from Bultmann's 1928 essay on the eschatology of the Fourth Gospel.

In this essay, Bultmann identifies existentialist categories as underlying what he terms the 'Johannine dualism' in which concepts such as light and darkness, truth and falsehood, life and death, are set in permanent antithesis. These antitheses serve to express the double possibility in human existence, and derive their meaning both from the threat which is perceived to be posed to human existence by the world, and the means by which the threat may be overcome. Thus we find Bultmann interpreting the key Johannine term *kosmos* ('world') in the twofold manner indicated by Heidegger – the world as the sphere of existence, and the world as the threat to existence:

> Through the event of revelation, two possibilities are actualized for the world: 1. 'To be world' (*Weltsein*) in the new sense of 'remaining world' (*Weltbleiben*) – to set the seal on one's fallenness (*Verfallenheit*), to hold fast to it, to hold fast to one's self. 2. 'Not to be world' (*Nicht-Welt-sein*), not to be 'of the world', and thus to be 'of the world' in the new sense of being 'out of' the world, namely, 'outside' it, no longer belonging to it.[6]

Bultmann is also able to apply an existential analysis to the Pauline soteriology (and particularly to the Pauline anthropological terms: his analysis of the Pauline term 'body' is particularly important in this respect).

It is significant that Bultmann regards Paul and the Fourth Gospel as being of greater value for Christology than the synoptic gospels, on account of their kerygmatic foundations. Thus for Bultmann, the fact that the Fourth Gospel is a source for the *kerygma* of the early church, rather than the historical Jesus, merely serves to increase, rather than (as with the liberal school) to diminish, its Christological importance. For Bultmann, the New Testament in general asserts that our true nature is no longer to be attained by our own efforts, which merely serve further to enmesh and embed us in our existential alienation. We cannot liberate ourselves from this existential alienation by our own effort: such liberation must come from without. The most fundamental difference between Heidegger and Bultmann is that the latter regards authentic existence as a possibility which we may achieve for ourselves, whereas the latter regards it as a possibility which comes about only by a gratuitous act of God:

So here is the crucial distinction between the New Testament and existentialism, between the Christian faith and the natural understanding of being. The New Testament speaks, and faith knows, of an act of God (*Tat Gottes*), which first makes possible faith, love, and the authentic (*eigentlich*) life of a person.

It is here that Bultmann's soteriology demonstrates its distinctive Christological concentration, in that this act of God is identified with the 'Christ-event' (*Christusereignis*) – the cross and resurrection of Jesus Christ.

At this point, Bultmann makes use of the categories of *Historie* and *Geschichte*, as introduced and employed by Martin Kähler (see p. 111). Bultmann understands these two terms to correspond, not so much to two different *kinds* of history, as to two different methods of *approaching* history on the part of the observer. *Historie* refers to an attitude to detached and uninvolved observation, in which the past is treated as a sequence of events. *Geschichte* designates an attitude in which the past is approached as existentially relevant; past events are considered from the standpoint of the fundamental questions of human existence. Viewed in this light, they are no longer past occurences, but present events that can transform one's personal existence. The *kerygma* is concerned with the transformation of Jesus from a *historisch* to a *geschichtlich* figure, with identifying his relevance to modern questions of human existence.[7]

This distinction allows us to consider the manner in which the cross and resurrection of Christ are related, a matter of considerable importance to a right understanding of Bultmann's thought. Jesus' life and death are seen by Bultmann as belonging to the realm of publicly observable and objective history. The resurrection, however, is to be regarded as an experience in the life of the disciples, an element of their subjective experience. It is 'historical' in the sense that it is an intrinsic aspect of the personal experiential history (*Geschichte*) of the disciples; it was not, however, an element of publicly observable history (*Historie*).

This might suggest that the cross is to be interpreted purely as an event in public history. Yet Bultmann has an important qualification to add to this: objective historical inquiry cannot disclose that Jesus of Nazareth possesses eschatological and soteriological significance. Only faith can understand the cross as an event which brings salvation. The cross, understood as a salvation event, is thus grounded in, but not

167

limited to, the cross as an event in objective history.[8] Thus Bultmann can write:

> As the salvation-event, the cross of Christ is not a mythical event, but an historical (*geschichtlich*) event which springs from the historical (*historisch*) crucifixion of Jesus of Nazareth.

At this point, it is necessary to introduce formally the term *kerygma*, which has already been employed without adequate discussion. For Bultmann, the *kerygma* is the word of proclamation through which the Christ-event confronts the individual here and now. The Word of God becomes a personal word of God, addressed to the individual, striking his or her conscience and demanding a decision. It confronts us here and now, in a specific historical situation, with the necessity for a decision on our part, if our state of inauthentic existence and fallenness is to be replaced with that of authenticity. The *kerygma* concentrates and compresses the history of salvation into an eschatological demand. Good Friday and Easter Day become the 'Today' of proclamation, in that it is the proclamation of the saving event which occasions the transition from the state of inauthentic to that of authentic existence. The existential significance of the history of salvation, as it is concentrated and focused in the death and resurrection of Jesus Christ, is thus distilled into the *kerygma*.

Through his programme of demythologization, Bultmann is able to extract the existential significance of the history of Jesus of Nazareth by removing the mythical 'husk' from the cosmic apocalyptic drama culminating in the resurrection narrated by the New Testament, thus revealing the 'kernel' of the proclamation of the permanent significance of Jesus Christ for human existence throughout the ages. Although the New Testament writers such as Paul (or, to a significantly lesser extent, John) use the mythological thought-forms of their day, their fundamental intention was, according to Bultmann, to present their readers with a new possibility of existence. This approach to the relation between the historical Jesus and the *kerygma* is particularly well expressed in an essay of 1929 dealing with the relation between Jesus and Paul.[9]

For Bultmann, the significance of the historical person of Jesus for the theology of Paul may be expressed in a single sentence: it is the historical person of Jesus which makes Paul's proclamation the gospel. Paul does not proclaim any new ideas about God, but an act of God in human history in Jesus the Messiah. Similarly, the primitive Christian community itself proclaimed no new apocalyptic or messianic ideas, save that Jesus was the Messiah – and hence that the historical person of Jesus was the 'decisive saving act of God (*der entscheidende Heilstat Gottes*)'. The death of Christ on the cross was implicitly recognized by the primitive community, and explicitly so by Paul, as the judgment of God upon humanity's previous self-understanding. For Paul, the actual historical event of the cross – which was most emphatically not a symbol or image of an eternal divine idea – lays down a challenge to human beings to relinquish their former selves and way of being, in favour of the new way of being which is offered to them.

Questions such as whether Jesus understood himself to be the Messiah are thus of little significance. If Jesus did understand himself as *Messias designatus*, all that would be implied for Bultmann was that Jesus employed a contemporary Jewish conception in order to bring home to his hearers the need for a decision on their part. Bultmann thus excludes the three great and influential portraits of Christ drawn by the theologians of the Enlightenment and the liberal school (Christ as teacher; Christ as example; Christ as hero), in that they merely correspond to 'Christ according to the flesh', a secular phenomenon (*Weltphänomen*) to be treated like other such phenomena.

For Bultmann, the cross and the resurrection are indeed secular phenomena (in that they took place within human history) – but they must be discerned by faith as divine acts. The cross and the resurrection are linked in the *kerygma* as the divine act of judgment and the divine act of salvation. It is this divine act, pregnant with existential significance, which is of continuing significance, and not the historical phenomenon which acted as its bearer. The *kerygma* is thus not concerned with matters of historical fact, but with conveying the necessity of a decision on the part of its hearers, and thus transferring the eschatological moment from the past to the here and now of the proclamation itself:

> This means that Jesus Christ encounters (*begegnet*) us in the *kerygma* and nowhere else, just as he confronted Paul himself and forced him to a decision. The *kerygma* does not proclaim universal truths or a timeless idea – whether it is an idea of God or of the redeemer – but an historical fact (*ein geschichtliches Faktum*) . . . Therefore the *kerygma* is neither a vehicle for

timeless ideas nor the mediator of historical information: what is of decisive importance is that the *kerygma* is Christ's 'that' (*Dass*), his 'here and now', a 'here and now' which becomes present in the address itself.[10]

One cannot therefore go behind the *kerygma*, using it as a 'source' (*Quelle*) in order to reconstruct an 'historical Jesus' with his 'messianic consciousness', his 'inner life', or his 'heroism'. That would merely be 'Christ according to the flesh', who no longer exists. It is not the historical (*historisch*) Jesus, but Jesus Christ, the one who is preached, who is the Lord.

Bultmann may thus be regarded as developing the insights of Martin Kähler in relation to the correlation between the historical Jesus and the Christ of faith – or, as we might describe him in this context, the Christ of the *kerygma*. The existentially significant Christ is not 'Christ according to the flesh', but the 'preached Christ', the Christ who is present in the *kerygma*. Although Bultmann does not reduce the theological significance of the resurrection to a single point, it is certainly true to suggest that, in Bultmann's view, the theological significance of the resurrection relates primarily to the presence of Christ in the faith and preaching of his disciples – that is, in the *kerygma*. Thus Bultmann has no hesitation in asserting that the Easter faith consists of faith that 'Jesus Christ is present in the *kerygma*'. The contemporary experience of the truth of Christ may be regarded as identical with the confrontation by the *kerygma*, and the existential decision it occasions.

Faith comes into being through an encounter with an historical event – the 'event of Christ', as it is evoked by the *kerygma* itself. Although that *kerygma* is based upon the history of Jesus of Nazareth, it now transcends it. Bultmann thus has no time for critical questions concerning the nature of the historical Jesus, and his relation to the Christ of faith, insisting that it is, in principle, both impossible and illegitimate to go behind the Christ of the *kerygma* to its historical foundations. All that it is necessary to state about Jesus is that the fact he has come, and that he is present in the *kerygma*. The mere fact of Jesus' existence (*das Dass*), apart from any concrete historical characteristics or predicates, is all that need be presupposed in order to account for the transition from unbelief to faith, from inauthentic to authentic existence. The *kerygma* contains in itself an adequate account of Jesus,[11] even if this *kerygma* is not historically verifiable:

In the Christian proclamation, we are not presented with an historical report or a piece of the past, which we can inspect and critically verify or falsify; but we are told that God has acted in what happened then, whatever it might have been, and that through this act of God, the word of divine judgment and forgiveness which now confronts us is authenticated (*legitimiert*); that the meaning of that act of God is nothing other than the actual establishment of this word, the proclamation of this word itself. No historical science can affect or confirm or reject this affirmation. The fact that this word and this proclamation are the acts of God stands on the other side of historical observation.

It may therefore be stated that the German repudiation of the 'quest of the historical Jesus' reached its zenith in the theology of Rudolf Bultmann. On the basis of his form-critical research (a full discussion of which lies beyond the present study), he concluded that such a quest was impossible (thus confirming the general conclusions of Wrede and Schweitzer); and on the basis of his existential theology, he concluded that such a quest was in any case illegitimate and unnecessary for faith. The recognition that the *kerygma* was the centre, not only of the gospels, but also of primitive Christianity, must be regarded as Bultmann's most significant contribution to the making of modern German Christology, in that this insight resulted in a decisive shift of emphasis away from the nineteenth-century preoccupation with the historical foundations of Christology towards an apparently legitimate existential concern with the underlying meaning of history. It thus found a formal analogy with contemporary understandings of historiography as concerned with underlying 'meaning', rather than a mere record of the brute facts of the past *wie es eigentlich gewesen war* ('as it actually was'). For Bultmann, history only survives as *kerygma*, in both senses of the term (that is, as the content of the message, and the act of preaching itself): the tradition concerning Jesus survived only to the extent that it served some specific kerygmatic function in the life and worship of the primitive church.

The gospels are thus to be seen as kerygmatic documents, proclaiming a faith which the historical (*historisch*) Jesus and the facts concerning him have been transformed irreversibly into the mythological proclamation of a divine pre-existent being who became incarnate, died for the sins of humanity, was raised from the dead, and whose return in triumph was shortly expected. It is impossible to get behind these mythological and theological images to the bare historical facts, although it is possible to assert both the continuity of the *kerygma* with the historical Jesus, and the possibility of reinterpreting the mythical elements of the *kerygma* existentially to relate to the modern worldview. The *kerygma* thus serves the dual function of witnessing to past events and interpreting the experience of present events.

Bultmann may therefore be regarded as having completed the destruction of the original 'quest of the historical Jesus (*Leben-Jesu-Forschung*)' of the closing decade of the nineteenth century by establishing the kerygmatic foundations of the New Testament, primitive Christianity and contemporary proclamation, thus giving a remarkably unified structure to his Christology. The twentieth century recognized that the gospels are primary sources for the history of the early church (and only secondarily for the history of Jesus), whereas the nineteenth century tended to regard the gospels as primary sources for the history of Jesus. This scholarly development is of incalculable Christological significance, and underlies Bultmann's kerygmatic Christology. It would be inept to characterize his Christology as a 'Christology from below', despite its heavy anthropological conditioning, for the obvious reason that Bultmann does not begin from the historical figure of Jesus of Nazareth, but from 'above' and 'below' as they are simultaneously given in the *kerygma*. This observation not merely demonstrates the futility of the 'above-below' Christological dichotomy, but indicates how it is possible for a theology to be based upon anthropological considerations (in this case, the structures of human existence) without being reduced to anthropology.

The main line of criticism directed against Bultmann's kerygmatic Christology concerns the relation between *kerygma* and history, and will be discussed at greater length in the next chapter. A further point of criticism relates to Bultmann's programme of demythologization. It was pointed out that Bultmann's method was heavily dependent upon the earlier *religionsgeschichtliche Schule*, which argued strongly for the influence of Gnostic redeemer myths on the New Testament. However, it is now generally considered that Gnosticism was a post-Christian phenomenon, so that Bultmann's thesis requires substantial revision.

It will be clear that Bultmann's Christology marks a decisive turning point in the making of modern German Christology. The new emphasis upon the centrality of the *kerygma* established the school of Bultmann as the dominant theological force in Germany in the immediate post-war period. The theme of the 'kerygmatic Christ' was developed further, and incorporated into a philosophical theology by an emigré from National Socialist Germany, who also exploited existentialism theologically – Paul Tillich (1886–1965).

Paul Tillich

Tillich left Germany in 1933 as the first non-Semitic university teacher to be dismissed by Hitler, to settle in the United States and develop his existential theology unimpeded by political considerations. The result is clearly continuous with the general trend evident in German Christology over the period 1933–65, and must be considered as an aspect of that development, although Tillich's influence upon the German Christological tradition itself has not been significant, largely due to delays in translating his work into German.

From the outset, Tillich regarded one of the most important tasks of theology to be the relation of theological thought to non-religious situations. In this sense, his theology may be seen as apologetic, rather than dogmatic, primarily concerned with making Christianity both attractive and intelligible to twentieth-century secular culture. His 'method of correlation' between the situation and the Christian message reflects this concern to make the Christian proclamation relevant to a world come of age.[12] A fundamental criticism against Tillich here is that his emphasis upon the apologetic task of theology is not adequately grounded in a dogmatic substructure. In other words, Tillich's attempt to deal with the questions raised by a secular culture is not undergirded by a responsible exposition of the truth claims of Christian faith.

Tillich's concern, then, was to make Christianity meaningful in a period in which it seemed to be losing its public credibility. Like Schleiermacher before him, he was concerned to make Christianity acceptable to 'its cultured despisers'. The key to this task was existentialism, in the form associated with Martin Heidegger. For a short period in 1924–25, Tillich and Heidegger were colleagues at Marburg, and it is evident, both from Tillich's own personal reflections, as well as the substance of his ontology, that he was greatly influenced by the Marburg existentialist. The theological importance which Tillich attaches to existentialism may be judged from the following passage in his *Systematic Theology*:

Theology, when dealing with our ultimate concern, presupposes in every sentence the structure of being, its categories, laws and concepts. Theology, therefore, cannot escape the question of being any more easily than can philosophy. The attempt of biblicism to avoid non-biblical, ontological terms is doomed to failure as surely as are the corresponding philosophical attempts.[13]

Tillich therefore follows a programme similar, in some respects, to Bultmann's programme of demythologization, attempting to extract the existential significance of the New Testament soteriological and Christological statements (which Tillich understands to be expressed 'symbolically').[14] Thus Tillich refers to 'the Fall' as a symbol, where Bultmann designates it as a myth. The story of 'the Fall' should not be interpreted literally, as an account of an event which happened 'once upon a time', but as a symbol for the human situation universally. For Tillich, 'existence' is estrangement, characterized by existential *Angst*, unbelief and hubris (pride). Nothing that exists is 'as it ought to be'.

Tillich's somewhat confusing distinction between 'essence' and 'existence' is perhaps best understood as follows. Tillich's concept of 'essence' broadly corresponds to Heidegger's concept of 'authentic existence', and Tillich's 'existence' to Heidegger's 'inauthentic existence'. According to Tillich, we know of no other existence other than 'estranged' or 'inauthentic' existence. This raises the interesting question as to how our 'essence' became corrupted to 'existence', a question which Tillich answers in a manner which will satisfy only his least critical admirers. It is, however, evident that Tillich is chiefly concerned with the question as to how the gap between existence and essence may be overcome (rather than the more tantalizing question as to how it got there in the first place). It is in this context that we encounter the Christologically related concept of 'New Being', which is the 'restorative principle' of Tillich's theological system.

It will be helpful at this point to consider the overall structure of Tillich's *Systematic Theology*. The work is divided into five parts. The first deals with the human quest for knowledge, showing how this is 'correlated' with the religious idea of revelation. Tillich understands this to mean that the existential questions raised by modern cultural situations find their answers in the symbols of Christian theology. The second part deals with the concept of God. The third part is of vital importance to this study. In this section, entitled 'Existence and the Christ', Tillich explores the situation of human existential alienation and the quest for salvation. This quest finds its answer in Jesus Christ, who is the appearance or manifestation of New Being under the conditions of existential estrangement. Parts four and five move on from this point to deal with the reality of human life, making use of a humanist philosophy of Spirit (strikingly similar to that of German idealism) which seems to his critics to take leave of any notion of a personal God.

It is thus appropriate to explore the place of Jesus Chrst within Tillich's theology. For Tillich, the event upon which Christianity is based has two aspects: the fact which is called 'Jesus of Nazareth', and the reception of this fact by those who received him as the Christ. The factual, or objective-historical, Jesus is not the foundation of faith apart from his reception as the Christ; here, the influence of Martin Kähler may easily be discerned. Indeed, it is obvious that Tillich has no interest in the historical figure of Jesus of Nazareth: all that he is prepared to affirm about him (in so far as it relates to the foundation of faith) is that it was a 'personal life', analogous to the biblical picture, who might well have had another name other than 'Jesus'. 'Whatever his name, the New Being was and is active in this man.'[15] If historical criticism were ever to demonstrate that the man Jesus of Nazareth never actually existed, Tillich declares that his theology would not be affected.

The symbol 'Christ' or 'Messiah' means 'he who brings the new state of things, the New Being', and the significance of Jesus of Nazareth lies in his being the historical manifestation of the New Being, who subjects himself to the conditions of existence, and by doing so conquers existential estrangement. 'It is the Christ who brings the New Being, who saves men from the old being, that is from existential estrangement and its destructive consequences.' In one personal life, that of Jesus of Nazareth, 'essential manhood' has appeared under the conditions of existence without being conquered by them. In other words, the significance of Jesus of Nazareth resides in his being the historical manifestation of a self-sufficient existential principle, which may be discussed without any reference to that original manifestation, save that it actually took place. Thus Tillich is able to follow Bultmann in stating that 'Christology is a function of soteriology', in that it is the soteriological problem which creates the Christological question.[16] It is, however, very difficult to avoid the conclusion that the intense theological seriousness which characterizes Bultmann's discussion of the relation between faith and history is absent from Tillich.[17]

There thus appears to be a near-total divorce of faith and history in Tillich's thought, suggesting his Christology is actually fundamentally idealist in character. Tillich's 'theology' is actually a philosophy of existence which attaches itself to the existence of Jesus of Nazareth in the most tenuous of manners, and which is not significantly disadvantaged if the specific historical individual Jesus of Nazareth did not exist. Thus Tillich does not follow Bultmann in asserting that the revelation which makes possible the transition from inauthenticity to authenticity is to be sought only in Jesus of Nazareth, although he does make it clear that he considers this revelation to be perfect (and hence 'final'). The revelation in Jesus may be said to illuminate the mystery of being; other sources of illumination are, however, available. Tillich here appears to return to the discredited Jesuologies of the liberal school, which regarded Jesus of Nazareth as the supreme exemplar of a particular moral or religious principle, without – as Bultmann pointed out – being able to justify this assertion theologically in the first place.

For example, Tillich emphasizes that God himself cannot appear under the conditions of existence, in that he is the ground of being. The 'New Being' must therefore come from God, but cannot *be* God. This inevitably leads to the conclusion that Jesus was a human being who achieved a union with God open to every other human being – a degree Christology which retains the notion of *Urbildlichkeit*, yet appears to lack the stabilizing notion of *Vorbildlichkeit* which prevents Schleiermacher's from lapsing into the same inadequacy (see pp. 44–5).

In the present chapter, we have been concerned with Christologies based upon an existential analysis of the human predicament, which see in the *kerygma* the means by which this predicament may be resolved. The significance of Christ is developed in terms of his relation to the *kerygma*, with three important consequences:

1. A minimum of attention is paid to the historical figure of Jesus of Nazareth: for Bultmann, it is merely necessary that he existed (*das Dass*). In many respects, Jesus of Nazareth is treated as having been the historical occasion for the introduction of a self-sufficient existential principle, henceforth expressed and transmitted in the *kerygma*. The critical-historical method is thus seen as possessing an essentially negative function, in that it destroys the inadequate Jesuologies of the liberal and *religiongeschichtliche Schule*. While it may be suggested that

this approach to the theological significance of the historical Jesus is simply an attempt to make a virtue out of necessity (in that it appeared impossible to obtain reliable information concerning him in the first place), it must be emphasized that Bultmann and his circle were developing already-existing theological insights, associated especially with Martin Kähler, which they regarded to have been justified by the new insights of the first four decades of the twentieth century concerning the nature of the New Testament documents.

2. This retreat from the historical Jesus runs the risk of detaching the Christian proclamation from Jesus of Nazareth. While Bultmann insists that this is an historical and theological impossibility, others were not so sure. Tillich's Christology is an excellent example of how it is possible to drive a wedge between the Christian proclamation and the historical figure of Jesus. For Tillich, the gospel is not dependent upon the existence of Jesus of Nazareth. While Tillich has been severely criticized for this move, it must be pointed out that it is perhaps the inevitable outcome of the approaches to Christology documented in this chapter.

3. The emphasis on the existential impact of Jesus upon the believer leads to the 'effects of Christ upon human existence' becoming a controlling Christological principle. It is the impact of Christ which both prompts and informs the later question concerning the identity of Jesus. To use the traditional categories of dogmatic theology, the human experience of the *work* of Christ thus precedes and controls discussion of the *person* of Christ. Christology follows soteriology, in that the *kerygma* is concerned with articulating the existential significance of Christ *pro nobis*, his perceived significance for believers, rather than his identity *per se*. The *kerygma* does not merely rehearse a factual account of history, or a sequence of historical events – rather, it directs an interpretation of these events (now independent of them) to humanity in the form of an imperative. Faith recognizes in the history of Jesus of Nazareth the hand of God, and responds to the latter, rather than the former. Bultmann cites Philip Melanchthon's dictum 'to know Christ is to know his benefits (*Christum cognoscere, eius beneficia cognoscere*)' in justifying his assertion of the priority of soteriology over Christology. If Christology is based upon the *kerygma*, as Bultmann and his circle suggest, its foundations are necessarily soteriological, for the simple reason that the *kerygma* articulates the perceived significance of Christ for believers. The question of the identity of Jesus follows on from the recognition of his impact upon the lives of believers.

Yet at this point, the question raised a century earlier by Feuerbach becomes important. Have we really spoken about Christ here – or are we speaking about human needs and aspirations? The appeal to the human need for salvation, or the human sense of 'having been saved', threatens to raise the spectre of a Christology of pure subjectivism, similar to that developed by Schleiermacher. A human feeling of existential alienation could come to function as the foundation of our understanding of the identity of Jesus – yet without this feeling being subjected to critical examination. This is one of the considerations which have led to growing disquiet concerning Bultmann's approach, and an increasing concern to return to history. This concern is the subject of the next chapter.

8

The Return to History: from Ebeling to Pannenberg

The original 'quest of the historical Jesus', called into question by developments over the period 1890–1914, had seemed to run into the sands through the rise of the kerygmatic approach adopted by Bultmann and his followers. However, in the aftermath of the Second World War, growing anxieties concerning the reliability of Bultmann's approach were voiced. It seemed to an increasing number of writers, within the fields of both New Testament and dogmatic studies, that Bultmann had merely cut a Gordian knot, without resolving the serious historical issues at stake.

How may a theological account be given of the transition from the preaching of Jesus to the proclamation of Christ? How can it be shown that the *kerygma* is not simply a spurious self-legitimating product of early Christianity, but is grounded in and necessitated by the history of Jesus of Nazareth? The considerable emphasis given to the *kerygma* by the Bultmannian school served only to heighten, rather than to resolve, such questions. This concern lay behind the criticism of Bultmann by a cluster of writers, such as Herbert Braun (b. 1903), Hans Conzelmann (b. 1915), Gerhard Ebeling (b. 1912), Ernst Fuchs (1903–83), and Ernst Käsemann (b. 1906). We shall consider two such criticisms: Gerhard Ebeling's critique, mainly based upon explicitly theological considerations, and that of Ernst Käsemann, reflecting new trends in New Testament scholarship, focusing especially on the renewed interest in the 'historical Jesus question'.

179

Gerhard Ebeling

In turning to deal with Gerhard Ebeling, we encounter one of the most significant theologians of recent years. There is no doubt that he represents the most important and influential thinker in the tradition of Bultmann. The starting point of Ebeling's theological development was determined by his engagement in questions of historical theology (many English-speaking theologians still think of Ebeling only as a brilliant Luther scholar!) and particularly Luther's hermeneutics, in which he may be regarded as attempting to correlate the theology of the young Luther with the existential hermeneutics of Bultmann. This programme may be regarded as culminating in his *Wesen des christlichen Glaubens* ('Essence of the Christian Faith', 1959), in which his differences with Bultmann over the significance of the historical Jesus became clear. These differences were more substantially developed in the important work *Theologie und Verkündigung* ('Theology and Proclamation', 1962). The culmination of Ebeling's theological insights may be seen in his three-volume *Dogmatik des christlichen Glaubens* ('Dogmatics of the Christian Faith', 1979).[1]

The most appropriate point at which to begin an analysis of Ebeling's Christology is his understanding of faith.[2] For Ebeling, faith is to be interpreted existentially: 'faith concerns what gives existence stability (*was der Existenz Bestand gibt*)', and thus concerns Being or Non-Being (*Sein oder Nichtsein*). Faith is an existential attitude, and most emphatically does not have an object. To have faith is not to have faith *in* something or someone; it is simply to have an attitude of faith. Ebeling sets out a comprehensive programme of 'de-objectification (*Ent-objektiverung*)' which is parallel, at least in some respects, to Bultmann's programme of 'demythologization (*Entmythologisierung*)'. Ebeling's basic goal is to exclude any idea of Christian faith as a purely historical faith, *fides historica*, resting upon the naked facts of history.

The concept of non-intellectual experiential knowledge has, according to Ebeling, been legitimized by Luther and neo-Kantian epistemology. Ebeling argues – controversially, it has to be said – that the Reformers excluded all substantial and objectifying understandings of the relationship between humanity and God. Human beings are to be regarded as persons constituted and determined by the relations which they have with external reality. As such, Ebeling is able to insist that the 'ontology of relation' is a general method for analysing human experience which is significant theologically. The threat posed to human existence by death is for Ebeling, as for existentialism in general, a means by which the inauthenticity of our present existence (which Ebeling terms *Nichtsein*) is brought home to us. This inauthenticity may be overcome as we receive the foundation and meaning of our existence from outside our situation in a relation of faith. The parallels between Bultmann and Ebeling at this point will be evident.

Similarly, Ebeling employs the results of Bultmann's programme of demythologization to overcome the contradiction between 'biblical realism' and 'modern experiential knowledge' by arguing that the New Testament worldview arises from a 'deficient historical consciousness' (*mangelndes Geschichtsbewusstsein*) on the part of the New Testament writers, which the modern period has a duty to remedy.[3] For Ebeling, the only historical fact (*historisches Faktum*) on which Christology is based is the cross: the remainder of the New Testament account of the 'history' of Jesus (such as the virgin birth, the descent into hell and the resurrection) cannot be regarded as objective history (*Historie*).[4] The application of the critical-historical method thus serves to eliminate all mythological elements from the essence of the Christian faith: like Bultmann, Ebeling sees the method as purely negative, having a valuable purgative function in that it destroys false Christologies, although unable to erect anything in their place.

The differences between Bultmann and Ebeling emerge fully only in their assessment of the theological significance of the historical figure of Jesus of Nazareth. For Bultmann, all that could be, and could be required to be, known about the historical Jesus was the fact that (*das Dass*) he existed. For Ebeling, the person of the historical (*historisch*) Jesus is the fundamental basis (*das Grunddatum*) of Christology, and if it could be shown that Christology was a misinterpretation of the significance of the historical Jesus, Christology would be brought to an end. In this, Ebeling may be seen as expressing the concerns which underlie the 'new quest of the historical Jesus', to be discussed in the following section.

Ebeling here points to a fundamental deficiency in Bultmann's Christology: its total lack of openness to investigation (perhaps 'verification' is too strong a term) in the light of historical scholarship. Might not Christology rest upon a mistake? How can we rest assured that there is a justifiable transition from the preaching *of* Jesus to the preaching *about* Jesus? Ebeling develops criticisms which parallel those made elsewhere by Ernst Käsemann (see pp. 184–7), but with a theological, rather than a purely historical, focus.

Ebeling stresses that even Bultmann's minimal *das Dass* actually requires justification in terms of *das Was* or *das Wie* – that is, in terms of the implicit content of the *kerygma*. (The three German terms just used can be translated as 'the that', 'the what' and 'the how' respectively.) Ebeling argues that it is necessary to demonstrate the manner in which the historical Jesus and modern humanity are related – a manner which is necessarily independent of time and place. Ebeling locates this point of contact in the faith of Christ – the total dependence of Christ upon God, evident throughout his mission, and culminating in the historical event of the cross. Indeed, Ebeling is able to assert that the cross is the fulfilment of the proclamation of Jesus for this very reason.[5] The resurrection serves two functions in this context:

1. It denotes the end of the possibility of factual historical statements concerning Jesus.

2. It demonstrates that the faith of Jesus in God was not in vain, thus justifying his own faith, and the faith of those who followed him.

Ebeling also emphasizes that the resurrection does not amount to the communication of new or additional revelation to that given in Jesus, but the continued witness to the faith of Jesus. The post-Easter Christ is not distinct from the pre-Easter Jesus, but rather represents the 'right understanding' of Jesus himself; through the resurrection, Jesus is present in the *kerygma* as the basis of faith. The cross is thus a manifestation of the manner in which existential doubt may be replaced with certainty – a transition which underlies Ebeling's 'de-objectified' concept of 'pure faith'.

Das Was of Christology, according to Ebeling, is thus Christ as a prototype (*Vorbild*) and evoker of faith. The crucial transition from *Historie* (objective history) to *Geschichte* (experiential history) is thus effected through understanding the historical (*historisch*) Jesus as the example of the existential attitude which corresponds to and occasions an identical (or at least an analogous) attitude in the personal experiential history of the individual who responds to the *kerygma*. The faith of Jesus is hence the fundamental theological and historical (*historisch*) essence of the Christian faith, which may be transferred to the present day, and, upon doing so, proves to be relevant to the existential situation of contemporary humanity. Jesus is thus the 'pioneer and perfecter of faith' (Hebrews 12:2). Thus the *event* of the cross becomes the *word* of the cross, evoking belief even to this day.[6] This is, of course, perfectly consistent with Ebeling's de-objectified concept of faith: Jesus is not the content of faith, but merely its basis and its evoker, or cause. Jesus is a witness to the same faith shared by his followers; yet, Ebeling insists, he is also the ground of faith for those followers.

Nevertheless, it will be clear that Ebeling has not resolved the vexed problem of the relation of faith and history, even though he evidently attaches considerably more significance to *das Was* of the historical Jesus than Bultmann. Ebeling's positive approach to the question of the historical Jesus – seen, for example, in his assertion that the situation qualified by Jesus 'legitimizes' the *kerygma* – should be understood to refer to the demonstration of the relation of the *kerygma* to Jesus, rather than a demonstration of the truth of the *kerygma* itself. Of particular importance in this respect is Ebeling's observation that, whereas in other historical phenomena a complex relationship of diversity and discrepancy exists between an historical individual and his perceived significance, a remarkable exception must be conceded in the case of Jesus: in Jesus everything in his actions, attitudes and preaching is concentrated and focused upon the evoking of faith. Much the same idea underlies Ernst Fuchs' insistence that the *kerygma* is essentially the 'echo' of the existential decision which Jesus himself made.

For Ebeling, the crucial aspect of Christology is that the event of the cross has become the word of the cross. The existential certainty which Jesus demonstrated upon the cross is transmitted through the *kerygma*, the Christologically determined word-event which mediates the essence of the Christian faith in the historical process. The concepts of 'faith' and 'the cross' are correlated in a 'theology of the cross' which is both concentrated and constituted Christologically.[7] As the disciples acquired the existential certainty of faith, they transmitted the experience of this existential certainty in the 'word-event',[8] which presents contemporary humanity with the possibility of that certainty. It is this aspect of his theology (and, indeed, similar aspects of the theology of Fuchs) which has been criticized, in that Ebeling appears to be too heavily dependent upon actual linguistic affinities between Jesus and the early church – for example, in the case of the concept of 'faith'. Thus J. M. Robinson points out the necessity of demonstrating a continuity of intention, rather than mere linguistic affinities, between the teaching of Jesus and the *kerygma*.[9] It is considerations such as these which underlie the so-called 'new quest of the historical Jesus',[10] which we shall consider in the following section, with particular reference to the works of Ernst Käsemann.

Ernst Käsemann

Ernst Käsemann (b. 1906) is widely credited with reawakening interest in the historical dimensions of Christology, in response to Bultmann's programme of detachment from the issues of history. A 'new quest of the historical Jesus' is generally regarded as having been inaugurated with Käsemann's lecture of October 1953 on the problem of the historical Jesus. The lecture in question was delivered to a group of Bultmann's pupils (the *alte Marburger*).[11] The full importance of this lecture emerges only if it is viewed in the light of the presuppositions and methods of the Bultmannian school up to this point. Käsemann concedes that the synoptic gospels are primarily theological documents, and that their theological statements are often expressed under the form of the historical. In this, he endorses and recapitulates key axioms of the Bultmann school, here based upon insights of Kähler and Wrede.

Nevertheless, Käsemann immediately goes on to qualify these assertions in a significant manner. Despite their obviously theological concerns, the evangelists nevertheless believed that they had access to historical information concerning Jesus of Nazareth, and that this historical information is expressed and embodied in the text of the synoptic gospels. The gospels include both the *kerygma* and historical narrative.

Building on this insight, Käsemann points to the need to explore the continuity between the preaching *of* Jesus and the preaching *about* Jesus. There is an obvious discontinuity between the earthly (*irdisch*) Jesus and the exalted and proclaimed Christ; yet a thread of continuity links them, in that the proclaimed Christ is already present, in some sense, in the historical Jesus. It must be stressed that Käsemann is not suggesting that a new inquiry should be undertaken concerning the historical Jesus in order to provide historical legitimation for the *kergyma*;[12] still less is he suggesting that the discontinuity between the historical Jesus and the proclaimed Christ necessitates the deconstruction of the latter in terms of the former. Rather, Käsemann is pointing to the *theological* assertion of the identity of the earthly Jesus and the exalted Christ being *historically grounded* in the actions and preaching of Jesus of Nazareth.

The theological affirmation is, Käsemann argues, dependent upon the historical demonstration that the *kerygma* concerning Jesus is already contained in a nutshell or embryonic form in the ministry of Jesus. In that the *kerygma* contains historical elements, it is entirely proper and necessary to inquire concerning the relation of the Jesus of history and the Christ of faith.

It must be stressed that this does not in any sense represent a return to some form of liberal theology. Käsemann has no intention of travelling along this historically and theologically discredited route. He insists that our only access to the Jesus of history is through the proclamation of the community of faith. There is no possibility of reconstructing any other 'historical Jesus' than that which is presented to us by the *kerygma*. 'The historical Jesus meets us in the New Testament . . . *not* as he was in himself, *not* as an isolated individual, but as the Lord of the community which believes in him.' A return to history is theologically legitimate, on account of the continuity between the historical Jesus and the Christ of faith. 'The history of Jesus (*Historie Jesu*) was constitutive for faith, because the earthly and the exalted Lord are one and the same.'

It will be clear that the 'new quest of the historical Jesus' is qualitatively different from the discredited quest of the nineteenth century. Käsemann's argument rests upon the recognition that the discontinuity between the Jesus of history and the Christ of faith does not imply that they are unrelated entities, with the latter having no grounding or foundation in the former. Rather, the *kerygma* may be discerned in the actions and preaching of Jesus of Nazareth, so that there is a continuity between the preaching of Jesus and the preaching about Jesus. Where the older quest had assumed that the discontinuity between the historical Jesus and the Christ of faith implied that the latter was potentially a fiction, who required to be reconstructed in the light of objective historical investigation, Käsemann stresses that such reconstruction is neither necessary nor possible.

The growing realization of the importance of this point led to intense interest developing in the question of the historical foundations of the *kerygma*. Four positions of interest may be noted:
1. Joachim Jeremias (1900–79), perhaps representing an extreme element in this debate, seemed to suggest that the basis of the Christian faith lies in what Jesus actually said and did, in so far as this can be established by theological scholarship. The first part of his *New*

Testament Theology was thus devoted in its totality to the 'proclamation of Jesus' as a central element of New Testament theology.[13]

2. Käsemann himself identified the continuity between the historical Jesus and the kerygmatic Christ in their common declaration of the dawning of the eschatological kingdom of God. Both in the preaching of Jesus and the early Christian *kerygma*, the theme of the coming of the kingdom is of major importance. [14]

3. As we saw above, Gerhard Ebeling locates the continuity in the notion of the 'faith of Jesus', which he understands to be analogous to the 'faith of Abraham' (described in Romans 4) – a prototypal faith, historically exemplified and embodied in Jesus of Nazareth, and proclaimed to be a contemporary possibility for believers.

4. Günter Bornkamm (b. 1905) laid particular emphasis upon the note of authority evident in the ministry of Jesus. In Jesus, the actuality of God confronts humanity, and calls men and women to a radical decision. Whereas Bultmann located the essence of Jesus' preaching in the future coming of the kingdom of God, Bornkamm shifted the emphasis from the future to the present confrontation of individuals with God through the person of Jesus. This theme of 'confrontation with God' is evident in both the ministry of Jesus and the proclamation about Jesus, providing a major theological and historical link between the earthly Jesus and the proclaimed Christ.[15]

By 1960, there was thus a new interest in the historical Jesus. The Bultmannian detachment from history had been reversed, with a new concern for the historical foundation of the proclamation of Christ. It must be stressed that there was no significant alteration in the sources or methods to be employed in the Christological debate: the new developments related to the extent to which historical elements could be discerned within the New Testament documents, especially the synoptic gospels. Whereas Bultmann regarded it as pointless and impossible to explore the relation between the Jesus of history and the proclaimed Christ, his later followers (as exemplified by Käsemann) thought otherwise.

Reinhard Slenckza has summarized the growing consensus within the 'new quest' as follows.[16] In the first place, there was general agreement that it was both possible and necessary to go behind the *kerygma* to its historical foundations. In the second, the task of Christology was agreed to be not merely the 'unfolding (*Entfaltung*)' of the New Testament Christological statements, but their 'establishment

(*Begründung*)' in the first place. On the basis of these presuppositions, the 'new quest' was able to demonstrate that the *kerygma* has its *origins* in Jesus of Nazareth himself, rather than in the needs of the early Christian church, and that it has its *foundations* in the history of Jesus himself. (It must be stressed that this does not mean that the *kerygma* is understood to be *purely* historical in nature.)

In addition to this new confidence in the historical elements of the *kerygma*, a new pressure to take history seriously must be noted. Marxism was becoming of major significance in German academic life, especially in relation to its philosophy of history. With the benefit of hindsight, Marxism may be seen to have reached the height of its influence and plausibility in the late 1960s and early 1970s, coinciding with some of the Christological developments noted in this chapter. To many of its adherents, the attractiveness of Marxism lay in its ability to engage directly with the historical process, interpret its flux, and provide a means of changing the way things are as a result. There was a new cultural respectability towards a direct engagement with history, which had hitherto been lacking.

The scene was thus set for an informed return to history as the ultimate foundation of Christology. The first major steps in this direction were taken in 1959, with the publication of an essay by Wolfhart Pannenberg (b. 1928), entitled 'Redemptive Event and History'.[17]

Wolfhart Pannenberg

Pannenberg's early views on the theological role of history emerged within the context of what eventually came to be known as the 'Pannenberg Circle', an interdisciplinary group of graduate students at Heidelberg, who met weekly during the 1950s in an attempt to forge an integrated theological programme which would overcome the radical separation of biblical studies and systematic theology, which was seen to be the inevitable outcome of the approach of Barth and Bultmann. Initially, the group consisted of Klaus Koch (b. 1926, Old Testament), Pannenberg himself (systematic theology), Rolf Rendtorff (b. 1925, Old Testament), Dietrich Rössler (b. 1927, New Testament) and Ulrich Wilckens (b. 1928, New Testament). As we shall see below, Rössler's contribution to this group appears to have been of some considerable significance to the evolution of Pannenberg's understanding of the potential of history as a theological resource.

Pannenberg's essay opens with an appeal to universal history:

> History (*Geschichte*) is the most comprehensive horizon of
> Christian theology. All theological questions and answers have
> meaning only within the framework of the history which God
> has with humanity, and through humanity with the whole
> creation, directed towards a future which is hidden to the world,
> but which has already been revealed in Jesus Christ.[18]

These crucially important opening sentences sum up the distinctive
features of Pannenberg's theological programme at this stage in his
career. They immediately distinguish him from both the a-historical
theology of Bultmann and his school and the suprahistorical approach of
Kähler. Christian theology is based upon an analysis of universal and
publicly accessible history, rather than the inward subjectivity of
personal human existence or a special interpretation of history, mediated
through the *kerygma*. For Pannenberg, revelation is essentially a public
and universal historical event which is recognized and *interpreted* as an
'act of God'. To his critics, this seemed to reduce faith to insight, and
deny any role to the Holy Spirit in the event of revelation.[19]

Pannenberg's argument takes the following form. History, in all its
totality, can only be understood when it is viewed from its endpoint.
This point alone provides the perspective from which the historical
process can be seen as a whole, and thus be properly understood.
However, where Marx argued that the social sciences, by predicting the
goal of history to be the hegemony of socialism, provided the key to the
interpretation of history, Pannenberg declared that this was provided only
in Jesus Christ.

The end of history is *disclosed proleptically* in the history of Jesus
Christ. The end of history, which has yet to take place, has been made
known in advance of the event through the resurrection. Although the
end of history has yet to happen, its outcome has been revealed within
history itself. This tells us much about the end of history – yet even
more about the one through whom that end is revealed: Jesus Christ.

The Apocalyptic Context of Christology

But how is this idea of a 'proleptic disclosure of the end of history' to be justified? Pannenberg argues that the apocalyptic worldview provides the key to understanding the New Testament interpretation of the significance and function of Jesus. Whereas Bultmann chose to demythologize the apocalyptic elements of the New Testament, Pannenberg treats them as a hermeneutical grid or framework by which the life, death and – above all – *resurrection* of Christ may be interpreted. Such views are developed and justified in the volume *Offenbarung als Geschichte* ('Revelation as History'), edited by Pannenberg, in which these ideas are explored at some length by members of his circle.

In view of the importance of the apocalyptic understanding of history to Pannenberg's early work, we may consider it in more detail. The 'new quest of the historical Jesus' demonstrated a new willingness to come to terms with the apocalyptic character of Jesus' preaching – a willingness perhaps most powerfully stated in Käsemann's famous affirmation, 'Apocalyptic is the mother of Christian theology.'[20] This new interest in apocalyptic heightened the need for a clearer definition of the precise nature of this hitherto ill-defined notion. For example, the fourth German edition of Gerhard von Rad's *Theology of the Old Testament* (1965) included a completely revised section on apocalyptic, which concluded with the statement that the 'concept of apocalyptic urgently requires critical revision'.

Käsemann himself believed that the pre-understanding (*Vorverständnis*) essential to a correct reading of the New Testament was not a Bultmannian existentialism, characteristic of twentieth-century humanity, but an apocalyptic outlook, characteristic of the first century. This insight was picked up and developed by the Pannenberg circle. Ulrich Wilckens contributed an essay on the understanding of revelation within early Christianity, which demonstrated an awareness of the importance of apocalyptic elements in its formation.[21] Most important of all, however, was a monograph by Dietrich Rössler on the history of Jewish apocalyptic, which argued for the centrality of salvation-history within the movement.[22] This monograph circulated in unpublished form in 1957, and was published three years later. It seems to have served as a foundation for Pannenberg's distinctive approach to universal history.

According to Rössler, the basic theme of Jewish apocalyptic is 'history in its totality': the apocalyptic visionary sees history as a unified process which is directed towards a goal, determined by the will of God.[23] The apocalyptic seer was granted a vision of the end of history, which allowed him to understand his own situation, without necessitating his dislocation from that point in the historical process. The visionary gains an understanding of the *end* of history from *within* history. History is a process which can be understood only from the standpoint of its final goal; the visionary, granted a 'preview' of that final goal, is able to understand his own situation in its light.

In his essay on the nature of revelation in early Christianity, Wilckens insists that Jesus was an apocalypticist rather than a rabbi (thus building upon, rather than bypassing, the insights associated with Schweitzer). Wilckens interprets Jesus' message and claims in terms of 'proleptic anticipation', aligning himself with Rössler's approach. Pannenberg himself, as we shall indicate, is also indebted to it. It is therefore somewhat disconcerting to observe that Rössler's work has been the subject of intense and hostile criticism within the scholarly community, raising the most serious doubts concerning its credibility.[24]

The point just made becomes clearer if Pannenberg's 'Dogmatic Theses on the Doctrine of Revelation' are considered.[25] The first five of these seven theses are of especial importance for our purposes here:
1.   The self-revelation of God in Scripture did not take place directly, after the fashion of a theophany, but indirectly, in the acts of God in history.
2.   Revelation is not completely apprehended at the beginning, but at the end of revelatory history (*am Ende der offenbarenden Geschichte*).
3.   In contrast to special divine manifestations, the revelation of God in history is publicly and universally accessible, and open to anyone who has eyes to see it.
4.   The universal revelation of God is not fully realized in the history of Israel; it was first realized in the destiny of Jesus of Nazareth, in so far as the end of history is anticipated in that destiny.
5.   The Christ-event cannot be regarded as revealing God in isolation; it is set in the context of the history of God's deaings with Israel.

It will be clear that Pannenberg insists that meaning is inherent to events. It is impossible to draw an absolute distinction between an event and its interpretation, in that the meaning of an event is part of that event; it is only in the subsequent process of reflection that a distinction between 'event' and 'meaning' arises. The idea of 'meaning-free' events is a nonsense:

It is simply not the case that one can take uninterpreted

(*deutungsfrei*) established facts and then subsequently ascribe to them this or that meaning as one wishes, so that one could, for instance, also place a revelatory meaning on the list next to other equally possible meanings. On the contrary, events always bring their original meaning along with them from the context to which they have been assigned by their having happened.[26]

Pannenberg makes this point especially forcefully in relation to the meaning of the resurrection of Christ:

> [The] splitting up of historical consciousness into a detection of facts and an evaluation of them . . . is intolerable to Christian faith, not only because the message of the resurrection of Jesus and of God's revelation in him necessarily becomes merely subjective interpretation, but also because it is the reflection of an outmoded and questionable historical method . . . We must reinstate today the original unity of facts and their meaning.[27]

Events and their interpretations can be considered only in the unitary totality of their original historical context (*Geschehenzusammenhang*).

This is an important point. If we may digress from Pannenberg's argument for one moment to consider the application of his ideas, it will be clear that his approach has devastatingly negative implications for the Enlightenment approach to Christology. In effect, this approach involves the imposition of an alien interpretative framework (Enlightenment rationalism) upon the history of Jesus of Nazareth. For Pannenberg, the only interpretative framework which has any legitimacy or propriety in this respect is that given with that history in the first place – that is to say, the apocalyptic context against which the life, death and resurrection of Jesus take place.

Pannenberg argues that it is possible to identify three pervasive and characteristic features of apocalypticism:

1. The full revelation of God is to be found only at the end of history. God discloses himself in the history of Israel; this, however, does not amount to a *full* disclosure.

2. The end of history is of universal significance. It embraces both Jew and Gentile, and discloses that God is the God of all peoples and all of creation.

3. The end of history entails a general resurrection of the dead.

The third of these three features is of especial importance, in that it relates directly to Pannenberg's methodological appeal to the resurrection of Christ as a theological principle.

It is therefore, according to Pannenberg, necessary to undertake an historical investigation of the 'history and destiny (*Geschichte und Geschick*)' of Jesus, in order to demonstrate the legitimacy of interpreting this event as divine revelation. This is the task which Pannenberg sets himself in his early Christological *Hauptwerk*, known in English as *Jesus – God and Man*. Sadly, this title does little to prepare the reader for the nature of the work in question, which is primarily a study in Christological *method*, rather than the development of a specific Christology. (The German title *Grundzüge der Christologie* conveys the methodological slant of the work, and could easily have been translated as the more illuminating 'Foundations of Christology'.) It is to this major work that we now turn.

Christological Method: Jesus – God and Man

Perhaps the most distinctive, and certainly the most commented upon, aspect of this work is Pannenberg's insistence that the resurrection of Jesus is an objective historical event, witnessed by all who had access to the evidence. Whereas Bultmann treated the resurrection as an event within the experiential world of the disciples, Pannenberg declares that it belongs to the world of universal public history.

This immediately raises the question of the historicity of the resurrection. A group of Enlightenment writers, including Diderot, Hume and Lessing, had argued that our only knowledge of the alleged resurrection of Jesus was contained in the New Testament. In that there were no contemporary analogues for such a resurrection, the credibility of those reports had to be seriously questioned. In a similar vein, Ernst Troeltsch had argued for the homogeneity (*Gleichartigkeit*) of history; in that the resurrection of Jesus appeared radically to disrupt that homogeneity, it was to be regarded as of dubious historicity. The general point raised by such suggestions had been noted earlier by Martin Kähler: the explicit or implicit appeal to the principle of analogy inevitably undermined in advance any claims to uniqueness on the part of Jesus. As one modern scholar noted, 'without the principle of analogy, it seems impossible to understand the past; if, however, one employs the principle of analogy, it seems impossible to do justice to the alleged uniqueness of Christ'.[28] So how were these issues to be met?

Pannenberg initially responded to these difficulties in his essay 'Redemptive Event and History', and subsequently in *Jesus – God and Man*.[29] Pannenberg suggests that the principle of analogy can be used in two different manners. In its *positive* sense, the principle allows certain events associated with the history of Jesus of Nazareth to be regarded as inherently plausible. For example, take the crucifixion of Jesus. This event has ample analogues to allow it to be regarded as historically plausible. This does not, it must be stressed, allow anyone to conclude that it *did* take place, on the basis of this consideration alone; it merely indicates that it conforms to a well-documented type of event. In its *negative* sense, the principle appeals to David Hume's argument that if an event which is alleged to have happened in history is totally without modern-day analogues, its veracity is to be doubted. Pannenberg notes that there are no contemporary analogues of any kind for the resurrection of Jesus, and that this has driven some commentators – such as Troeltsch – to conclude that it is 'non-historical (*unhistorisch*)'.

Pannenberg's basic argument against this position can be set out as follows. According to Pannenberg, Troeltsch has a narrow view of history, which rules out certain events in advance, on the basis of a set of provisional judgments which have improperly come to have the status of absolute laws. Troeltsch's unwarranted 'constriction of historico-critical inquiry' is 'biased' and 'anthropocentric'. It presupposes that the human viewpoint is the only acceptable and normative standpoint within history. Analogies, Pannenberg stresses, are always analogies *viewed from the standpoint of the human observer*; that standpoint is radically restricted in its scope, and cannot be allowed to function as the absolutely certain basis of critical inquiry. Pannenberg is too good a historian to suggest that the principle of analogy should be abandoned; it is, after all, a proven and useful tool of historical research. Yet, Pannenberg insists, that is *all* that it is: it is a working tool, and cannot be allowed to define a fixed view of reality.

If the historian sets out to investigate the New Testament already precommitted to the belief 'dead people do not rise again', that conclusion will merely be read back into the New Testament material. The judgment 'Jesus did not rise from the dead' will be the presupposition, not the conclusion, of such an investigation. As Pannenberg puts it:

Historical inquiry always takes place within a predetermined context of meaning (*Bedeutungszusammenhang*), from a preunderstanding (*Vorverständnis*) of the object of inquiry, which is, however, modified and corrected in the process of investigation on the basis of the phenomenon. If history (*Historie*) does not begin in a dogmatic manner with a restricted concept of reality according to which 'dead people do not rise', it is not clear why history could not fundamentally be in a position to speak about the resurrection of Jesus as the best-established explanation of events such as the experiences of the disciples and the discovery of the empty tomb.[30]

Pannenberg's discussion of this question represents an impassioned and impressive plea for a *neutral* approach to the resurrection. The historical evidence pointing to the resurrection of Jesus must be investigated without the prior dogmatic presupposition that such a resurrection could not have happened.

This approach does leave some loose ends lying around, which Pannenberg's critics in North America were quick to seize upon. For example, some have argued that Pannenberg's use of the ill-defined category of 'metaphor' to speak of the resurrection places his position uncomfortably close to that of Bultmann.[31] Others suggest that he appears to place the resurrection in an historical category of its own, outside the scope of universal history.[32] Nevertheless, many observers sense that Pannenberg has made it theologically respectable to speak once more of the resurrection of Jesus of Nazareth as an historical event.

Having argued for the historicity of the resurrection, Pannenberg turns to deal with its interpretation within the context of the apocalyptic framework of meaning. Pannenberg explores the immediate significance of the resurrection in six theses, of which the first four are of major importance to our theme:[33]

1. If Jesus has been raised, then the end of the world has begun.
2. If Jesus has been raised, a Jew could only interpret this as God himself confirming the pre-Easter activity of Jesus.
3. Through his resurrection, Jesus moved so close to the apocalyptic figure of the Son of Man that the only possible conclusion is that this Son of Man is none other than the man Jesus, who will come again.
4. If Jesus, having been raised from the dead, is ascended to God, and if the end of the world has dawned as a result, then God is ultimately revealed in Jesus.

It may be helpful to unpack the dense material of these theses, and explore their Christological implications. The end of history has taken place *proleptically* in the resurrection of Jesus from the dead. This assumption dominates Pannenberg's interpretation of the resurrection of Christ. The resurrection of Jesus anticipates the general resurrection at the end of time, and brings forward into history both that resurrection and the full and final revelation of God. The resurrection of Jesus is thus organically linked with the self-revelation of God in Christ:

> Only at the end of all events can God be revealed in his divinity, that is, as the one who works all things, who has power over everything. Only because in Jesus' resurrection the end of all things, which for us has not yet happened, has already occurred can it be said of Jesus that the ultimate already is present in him, and so also that God himself, his glory, has made its appearance in Jesus in a way that cannot be surpassed. Only because the end of the world is already present in Jesus' resurrection is God himself revealed in him.[34]

The resurrection thus establishes Jesus' identity with God, and allows this identity with God to be read back into his pre-Easter ministry.

Pannenberg's Christology seems to have been the subject of excitement and criticism in about equal measure. The idea of establishing the gospel on the basis of universal history seemed a daring and creative gesture, allowing theology to reclaim the intellectual high ground that many had thought had long since been forfeited to Marxism. A Christology 'from below' seemed to offer new possibilities to Christian apologetics, apparently bypassing the trap laid by Feuerbach, who had argued that the Schleiermachian type of Christology from below (beginning from human experience) was little more than a Christology constructed through the objectification of human feelings, and their projection on to the figure of Jesus. Pannenberg, by his appeal to history, is able to avoid this impasse by insisting that Christology arises out of history, not merely out of human feelings of redemption or of the presence of God.[35] An objective historical criterion prevents a degeneration into a vulnerable Jesuology of personal experience. However, *Jesus – God and Man* did not mark the end of Pannenberg's Christological reflections; these have now been stated definitively in the mature work to which we now turn.

The Christology of the Systematic Theology

The first two volumes of his *Systematische Theologie* ('Systematic Theology', 1990–91) afford Pannenberg the opportunity to develop further the basic Christological approach set out in *Jesus – God and Man*, while at the same time responding to its critics.[36] Some of those developments are hinted at in the afterword to the second English edition of the work (1977), in which Pannenberg, acknowledging weaknesses of this work, provides a thumbnail sketch of the improvements he would wish to make in a future treatment of the topic.[37] A full discussion of the theological position advocated in this major work must await the appearance of its third and final volume. However, two major elements of this new work may be explored here, in that they are not substantially dependnent upon the material to be included in the final volume – the apocalypic context of the resurrection, and the place of the cross.

1. *The apocalyptic context of the resurrection.* Earlier, we noted the importance of apocalyptic to the Pannenberg circle, and the crucial hermeneutical role which Pannenberg accords it in *Jesus – God and Man*. We also hinted at the less than favourable critical reception given to such views, which were widely regarded as at best an optimistic overinterpretation by the movement, and at worst a serious misrepresentation of its objectives and concerns. Pannenberg modifies his views on this matter, with important ramifications for his understanding of the meaning of the resurrection of Jesus.

In his discussion of the nature of revelation, Pannenberg adopts an approach to revelation which is sensitive both to the complexity of the notion, and to the development of the concept within Scripture.[38] Pannenberg argues that a cluster of apocalyptic understandings of revelation had gained the ascendency by the time of the New Testament. He describes these ideas of revelation as follows:

> Apocalyptic texts speak of revelation in two ways. First there is the disclosure of the eschatological future (and the way to it) by the vision which is communicated to the seer. This aspect corresponds to the experience of revelation in intuitive manticism, and also to the prophetic reception of the word. On the other hand, there is the future occurrence of what is seen, the final bringing to appearance (*endzeitliche In-Erscheinung-Treten*) as revelation of what is now still hidden in God.[39]

196

This approach is of major importance in dealing with the objection to an incarnational Christology laid down by Ernst Troeltsch. As we noted earlier (pp. 115–22), Troeltsch's precommitment to relativism leads him to reject the idea of an 'absolute' revelation of God in history: 'the Absolute lies beyond history and is a truth that in many respects remains veiled . . . It belongs to the future, and will appear in the judgment of God and the cessation of earthly history'. Pannenberg's understanding of revelation cuts the ground from under this criticism, by allowing us to understand how Christ can be the revelation of God within history. The 'cessation of earthly history' has taken place proleptically in the resurrection of Christ – an event within human history.

The continuing crucial role accorded by Pannenberg to the apocalyptic tradition in relation to the correct interpretation of the resurrection becomes clear from the substantial discussion of 'the justification of Jesus by the Father in his resurrection (*Auferweckung*) from the dead'.[40] In a series of seven theses, Pannenberg demonstrates how 'Jewish eschatological expectations' (the word 'apocalyptic' is studiously avoided) provide the context for interpreting the resurrection. The basic approach remains the same as that employed in *Jesus – God and Man*:

> The Jewish expectation of an eschatological resurrection – whether this is to judgment or to eternal life – does not deal with the resurrection of an individual prior to the end of this age. Primitive Christianity appears to have interpreted this event (in close connection with the identification of the appearances of Jesus as eschatological resurrection from the dead) as the beginning of the end-events.

2. *The place of the cross.* One of the most puzzling and heavily criticized features of *Jesus – God and Man* was its marginalization of the cross. Pannenberg's methodological concerns lead to a preoccupation with the resurrection, and a neglect of the cross – a development which stands sharply in tension with the emphasis observed within the New Testament. In part, Pannenberg's defence rests upon the nature of this early work: *Jesus – God and Man* is, as we stressed above, best seen as an essay in Christological *method*, rather than a substantive work of Christology. In the *Systematic Theology*, Pannenberg has the opportunity

to devote more attention to the place and role of the cross in Christian theology.

In practice, however, the cross continues to be relegated to a discussion of the doctrine of redemption found in this later work.[42] Although its discussion of the cross is of considerable importance, especially Pannenberg's emphasis upon the importance of the notion of 'substitution (*Stellvertretung*)' in interpreting the cross, it represents a detached discussion of the role of the cross. The cross is here treated as possessing a purely soteriological function, without any significant epistemological dimension. In other words, the cross does not appear to be able to disclose God, even though we are reconciled to him on its basis. Pannenberg can expect to continue to attract considerable continuing criticism for this reason. Whereas the resurrection continues to be of foundational significance to his doctrine of God (playing a central theological role within the context of the concerns of the first volume of the *Systematic Theology*, which deals primarily with the doctrine of God), the cross plays no such role.

This highlights the contrast between Pannenberg and Jürgen Moltmann and Eberhard Jüngel, to whom we will now turn.

The End of the Enlightenment: Moltmann and Jüngel

It is now clear that influence of the Enlightenment upon Western culture is in a state of permanent decline. One important cultural reaction, with important implications for theology, against the central Enlightenment presupposition of the universal authority of human reason, is post-modernism – a vague and ill-defined notion, which perhaps could be described as the general intellectual outlook arising after the collapse of modernity. Since the 1960s, there has been growing evidence of a lack of confidence in the basic assumptions of the Enlightenment, especially its somewhat uncritical reliance upon the power of reason to provide foundations for a universally valid knowledge of the world, including God. Reason fails to deliver a morality suited to the real world in which we live. And with this collapse in confidence in universal and necessary criteria of truth, relativism and pluralism have come to flourish on Western college campuses. The Enlightenment vision of a single rational worldview has, quite simply, perished.

Yet much modern Christological debate continues to be conducted within a context which has been determined by the presuppositions of the Enlightenment. G. E. Lessing's formulation of the problem of 'faith and history' (see pp. 28–33) clearly rests upon rationalist assumptions, grounded in the philosophical writings of René Descartes. The growing disenchantment with these rationalist presuppositions is evident at every point in modern theology, and is perhaps most notably seen in the rise of 'narrative theology' in the United States and elsewhere.

A further feature of importance within the German theological context has been the rise of secularism in the post-war era, with the erosion of the cultural stability upon which liberal Protestantism depended so heavily. *Kulturprotestantismus* found itself increasingly unable to ground itself in a self-evidently Christian culture, as the process of religious erosion within Germany took place around it. Perhaps the Nazi era may serve as a symbol of this new godlessness; certainly, the writings of Dietrich Bonhoeffer (1906–45) suggest that the rise of Nazism within Germany symbolizes a 'world come of age', which feels that it can dispense with God.

Bonhoeffer contributed significantly to the debate on Christology within German Protestantism during the 1930s. His lectures on Christology, delivered at the faculty of theology of the University of Berlin during the academic year 1932–33, developed the thesis that Christology is prior to soteriology, in that it is the identity of the person which determines the significance of his or her actions. Yet it is perhaps fair to suggest that Bonhoeffer's importance to the modern German Christological tradition lies not so much in his Christological views in the narrow sense of the term, as in his analysis of the cultural situation within which Christ is to be proclaimed in the modern world.[1]

On 5 April 1945, Bonhoeffer was arrested by the Gestapo for his alleged involvement in a plot against Adolf Hitler. During the eighteen months of his imprisonment at Berlin's Tegel prison, he wrote his celebrated *Letters and Papers from Prison*, in which he reflected on the question of the identity of Jesus Christ in a 'world come of age', a time of 'no religion at all'. He argued passionately for a 'religionless Christianity'.

This powerful phrase has often been misunderstood. Bonhoeffer directs his criticisms against forms of Christianity based on the assumption that human beings were naturally religious – an assumption that Bonhoeffer regarded as untenable, given the new godless situation. A 'religionless Christianity' is a faith which is not based upon the outdated and discredited notion of 'natural human religiosity', but upon God's self-revelation in Christ. An appeal to culture, metaphysics, or religion was thus to be avoided, in that they are inherently implausible in the new secular world, and inevitably lead to distorted understandings of God (there are strong affinities between Barth and Bonhoeffer here). The crucified Christ provides us with a model of God for the modern world – a God who 'allows himself to be pushed out of the world and on to the cross'.[2] These ideas, especially as they related to the new secularism and the need to ground theology elsewhere than in religion or metaphysics, were to prove seminal to post-war German Christology.

The Christologies of Jürgen Moltmann (b. 1926) and Eberhard Jüngel (b. 1934) may be regarded as a decisive attack on the remaining Cartesian influences in the modern Christological debate, linked with a willingness to make the cross of Christ – rather than human culture, religiosity or metaphysics – the foundation of authentically Christian theology. For these writers, three central Cartesian assumptions are called into question, on the basis of the history of Jesus of Nazareth.

1. The belief that history is incapable of disclosing information, upon which any kind of theological system may be built. This assumption, central to the theology of rationalist writers such as Lessing, had already been severely undermined by the Pannenberg circle in the 1950s and 1960s; it now received further criticism at the hands of both Moltmann and Jüngel, who demonstrated how the narrative of Jesus of Nazareth, culminating in his death and resurrection, could function as a critical foundation for Christian theology. To pick up the subtitle of *The Crucified God*, one of Moltmann's most notable writings developing this theme, the cross of Christ is 'the foundation and criterion of Christian theology'.

2. The belief in the competence of reason to lay down in advance what God is like. For both Moltmann and Jüngel, we need to be *told* who God is, and what he is like. The idea of revelation – and, more specifically, a revelation concentrated in the person of Jesus Christ – has come to be of increasing significance. In this respect, both writers may be said to build upon Barthian foundations. This insistence that we must attend to God as he has made himself known is of particular importance in relation to the idea of the 'impassibility of God'.

3. The belief that God, being perfect, is incapable of suffering. This central Cartesian belief, grounded in an abstract philosophical notion of 'perfection' rather than in the self-revelation of God, had a deep impact upon Western theology, especially in relation to the problem of suffering. Indeed, it may be argued that this Cartesian assumption lies at the root of much of modern atheism, in that it makes the existence of suffering a disconfirmation of the goodness of God. Moltmann and Jüngel demonstrated the inadequacy of this notion, and supplanted it with a doctrine of a 'suffering God', rooted in the self-revelation of God upon the cross.

This final point is of especial importance. The criticism of alien philosophical elements in Christology, the inclusion of which in theological reflection is ultimately due to the continuing influence of Enlightenment rationalism, is proving to be a model case for the elimination of rationalist ideas in theology in general. The work of Jüngel opens the way to the final purging of Christian theology from the influence of the Enlightenment, and a return to more authentically Christian concepts of divinity and humanity. Indeed, Jüngel argues that the doctrine of the Trinity, which the Enlightenment ridiculed as little more than an outdated absurdity, contains the key to the fully Christian understanding of God. In that this doctrine is Christologically grounded in the death and resurrection of Jesus Christ, it can be seen that Christological considerations are of decisive importance in the rediscovery of the *Christian* doctrine of God.

Jürgen Moltmann

Moltmann's first major piece of theological writing represented an engagement with the new interest in apocalyptic. His *Theologie der Hoffnung* ('Theology of Hope') (1964) developed the idea of taking eschatology as the 'universal horizon of all theology in general'. Moltmann, drawing on some of Barth's more radical eschatological statements in his Romans commentary, insisted that Christianity is *totally* eschatological in character. By thus transferring eschatology from the appendices to the introductory sections of works of Christian dogmatics, Moltmann was able to characterize Christianity as a 'religion of expectation' orientated towards the future and the promised fulfilment of the promises of God. All theological statements are thus 'statements of hope', and theological concepts are 'anticipations (*Vorgriffe*)' of the future with God.

The strong parallels with Marxism (which many commentators were coming to see as a form of Christian messianism or apocalyptic, stripped of its belief in God) were obvious. Just as Pannenberg's appeal to history lent his approach added credibility in the German academic atmosphere of the 1960s (younger academics were generally sympathetic to Marxism at this stage), so Moltmann's emphasis upon the theme of liberation was well received at this juncture. Indeed, his programmatic statement has obvious parallels with Marx's critique of Feuerbach: 'The theologian is not concerned with *interpreting* the world, history and human nature, but with their *transformation*, in the expectation of a divine transformation.'[3]

But how does this theology of hope relate to Christ? What is its Christological foundation? It will be obvious that the resurrection is of central importance to Moltmann's emphasis upon hope; but what of the crucifixion? In what manner does Moltmann relate the cross and resurrection of Christ? The Christological grounding of the 'theology of hope' was made clear in what is regarded as one of the finest of Moltmann's writings, *Der gekreuzigte Gott* ('The Crucified God'). This is clear from its opening assertion that

> The theology of the cross is nothing other than the reverse side of the Christian theology of hope, if this has its point of departure in the resurrection of *the one who was crucified*. The 'theology of hope' itself was, as may be seen therein, already being developed into an *eschatologia crucis* . . . The 'theology of hope' is set up by the *resurrection* of the one who was crucified, and I am now turning to examine the *cross* of the one who is risen. I was then concerned with the remembrance of Christ in the form of the *hope* of his future, and I am now concerned with hope in the form of the remembrance of his death.[4]

This important and explicit statement makes it clear that Moltmann's *Crucified God* is both a continuation and a qualification of the 'theology of hope'.

It should be noted that *The Crucified God* derived both its title and a substantial part of its substance from the celebrated 'theology of the cross' forged by the German reformer Martin Luther (1483–1546) over the period 1515–20.[5] In the preface to the work, Moltmann indicates the high importance which he came to attach to Luther's theology of the cross, particularly on account of its emphasis upon the notion of abandonment by God. This resonated with the experience of a generation of German theologians, as they emerged from the ruins of Nazi Germany to face the unknown future. For Luther, everything in Christian theology was established by, and was subject to criticism on the basis of, the cross of Christ. *Crux probat omnia! Crux sola nostra theologia!* ('The cross tests everything! The cross alone is our theology!') For Moltmann, the cross of Christ represents either the end of all theology, or the beginning of all specifically *Christian* theology. While God can be known to a limited extent through nature, the definitive revelation of God is to be found only in the cross:

> The crucified Christ alone is 'humanity's true theology and knowledge of God'. This presupposes that while an indirect knowledge of God is possible through his works, the being of God can be seen and known directly only in the cross of Christ.[6]

If there is no more to the end of Jesus than his death and abandonment by God, then atheism is the only acceptable and proper response to the suffering of the world. The connection between the person and preaching of Jesus is so intimate that the message of Jesus would have to die with the person of Jesus.

Central to Moltmann's argument is the affirmation that the 'death of Jesus' is a statement about God. He notes the tendency of liberal Protestantism to speak somewhat blandly of the death of Jesus as faithfulness to his calling, and an example of obedience in suffering. But this has nothing to do with *God*. He also faults classical Protestantism for its obsession with the question of what the death of Christ meant for us (traditionally explored in doctrines of the atonement), while failing to ask what it means for God. Moltmann insists that the death of Jesus gives us insights into the nature and purposes of God himself.

How, then, does Moltmann begin to explore the Christological implications of the cross? To understand his full significance, we must turn to consider the idea of the 'impassibility of God' – the notion that God cannot experience or be affected by suffering. Moltmann's decisive contribution to modern theology lies in his persuasive argument that the cross of Christ opens the way to the rediscovery of the notion of 'the crucified God', thus bringing a new depth of meaning to the concept of 'God' and the suffering of Christ, as well as offering new hope to a humanity experiencing suffering.

The Impassibility of God?

To appreciate Moltmann's contribution at this point, we must consider how the Christian tradition came to be dominated by the idea of an 'impassible God'.[7] The notion of perfection dominates the classical understanding of God, as it is expressed in the Platonic dialogues, such as *The Republic*. The perfect is the unchanging and self-sufficient. It is impossible for such a perfect being to be affected by or be changed by anything outside itself. Furthermore, perfection was understood in very static terms. If God is perfect, he cannot change in any way. If he changes, he moves either *away from* perfection (in which case he is no longer perfect), or *towards* perfection (in which case, he was not perfect in the past). Aristotle, echoing such ideas, declared that 'change would be change for the worse', and thus excluded God's divine being from change and suffering.

This understanding passed into Christian theology at an early stage. Philo (*c.* 20 BC – AD 50), a Hellenistic Jew whose writings were much admired by early Christian writers, wrote a treatise entitled *Quod Deus immutabilis sit*, 'That God is unchangeable', which vigorously defended the impassibility of God. Biblical passages which seemed to speak of God suffering were to be treated as metaphors, and not to be allowed their full literal weight. To allow that God changes was to deny his perfection. 'What greater impiety could there be than to suppose that the Unchangeable changes?'

Within this classical tradition, God thus could not be thought of as suffering, or undergoing anything which could be spoken of as 'passion'. Anselm of Canterbury (*c.* 1033–1109), influenced by this idea, argued that God was compassionate in terms of our experience, but not in terms of his own being. The language of love and compassion is treated as purely figurative. Compassion implies suffering; therefore, God cannot be compassionate in himself, even if we experience him as compassionate. Anselm meditates along these lines in his *Proslogion*:

> You are compassionate in terms of our experience, but not in terms of your being . . . For when you see us in our wretchedness, we experience the effect of compassion, but you do not experience that feeling. So you are compassionate, in that you save the wretched and spare those who sin against you; and yet you are not compassionate, in that you are affected by no sympathy for wretchedness.

Thomas Aquinas develops this approach, especially when reflecting on the love of God for sinners. Love implies vulnerability and, potentially, that God could be affected by our sorrows, or moved by our misery. Aquinas dismissed this possibility: 'Mercy is especially to be attributed to God, provided that it is considered as an effect, not as a feeling of suffering . . . It does not belong to God to sorrow over the misery of others.' The new emphasis placed upon the perfection of God by Descartes at the dawn of the modern period led to an increased conviction that God could not change, or be affected by suffering. This was, in effect, the theological orthodoxy of the eighteenth and nineteenth centuries.

Now an obvious difficulty arises here. Jesus Christ suffered and died on the cross. And traditional Christian theology declared that Jesus was God incarnate. It therefore followed (or so it seemed) that God suffered in Christ. Not so, declared most of the patristic writers, deeply influenced by the pagan idea of the impassibility of God. Christ suffered in his human nature, not his divine nature. God thus did not experience human suffering, and remained unaffected by this aspect of the world.

Moltmann poses a fundamental challenge to this outlook. He does so, however, within a cultural and theological context which, it can be argued, was more than ready for this development. Three pressures can be identified, all focusing on the period immediately after the First World War, which seem to have prepared the ground for the rediscovery of a suffering God. These three factors, taken together, gave rise to widespread scepticism concerning traditional ideas about the impassibility of God.

1. *The rise of protest atheism.* The sheer horror of the First World War made a deep impact upon Western theological reflection. The suffering of the period led to a widespread perception that liberal Protestantism was fatally compromised by its optimistic views of human nature. It is no accident that dialectical theology arose in the aftermath of this trauma. Another significant response was the movement known as 'protest atheism', which raised a serious moral protest against belief in God. How could anyone believe in a God who was above such suffering and pain in the world?

Traces of such ideas can be found in Fyodor Dostoyevsky's (1821–81) novel *The Brothers Karamazov* (1880). The ideas were developed more fully in the twentieth century, often using Dostoyevsky's character Ivan Karamazov as a model. Karamazov's rebellion against God (or, perhaps more accurately, against a particular *idea* of God) has its origins in his refusal to accept that the suffering of an innocent child could ever be justified. The French existentialist writer Albert Camus

(1930–60) developed such ideas in *L'homme révolté*, ('The Rebel', 1951), which expressed Karamazov's protest in terms of a 'metaphysical rebellion'. Moltmann saw in this protest against an invulnerable God 'the only serious atheism'. This serious, and intensely moral, form of atheism demanded an equally serious theological response – which was provided by a theology of a suffering God.

2. *The rediscovery of Luther*. In 1883, as part of the celebration of the 400th anniversary of Luther's birth, the Weimar Edition of Luther's complete works was launched. The resulting availability of Luther's works (many of which were hitherto unpublished) led to a renaissance in Luther studies, especially within German theological circles. Scholars such as Karl Holl (1866–1926) opened the way for a new interest in the reformer during the 1920s. The result was a perceptible quickening in interest in many of Luther's ideas, especially the 'theology of the cross'. Luther's ideas about the 'God who is hidden in suffering' became available at almost exactly the moment when they were needed.

3. *The growing impact of the 'history of dogma' movement*. Earlier, we noted the origins of this movement within the *Aufklärung* (pp. 25–6), and its development in the writings of Adolf von Harnack (see pp. 89–98). Although this movement reached its climax in the closing days of the nineteenth century, it took some while for the implications of its programme to percolate into Christian theology as a whole. As noted earlier, Harnack himself had suggested that the idea of 'incarnation' was the unacceptable result of Hellenistic influence upon Christian theology. In practice, this specific criticism proved to be misguided. However, by the time the First World War had ended, there was a general awareness within German theology of the possibility that a number of Greek ideas might well have found their way into Christian theology. Sustained attention was given to eliminating these ideas. The idea of an 'impassible' God turned out to be one of them.

Protest atheism created a climate in which it was apologetically necessary to speak of a suffering God. The 'history of dogma' approach declared that Christian thinking had taken a wrong turn in the patristic period, and that this could be successfully reversed. Christian declarations that God was above suffering, or invulnerable, were now realized to be inauthentic. It was time to recover the authentically Christian idea of the suffering of God in Christ.

Two additional considerations may also be noted. Fresh studies of the Old Testament – such as Abraham Heschel's (b. 1907) *God of the*

Prophets (1930) – drew attention to the manner in which the Old Testament often portrayed God as sharing in the *pathos* of his people. God is hurt and moved by the suffering of his people. If classical theism was incapable of accommodating that insight, it was argued, then so much the worse for it.

Second, the notion of 'love' itself became the subject of considerable discussion in the twentieth century. Theologians rooted in the classical tradition – such as Anselm and Aquinas – had defined love in terms of expressions and demonstrations of care and goodwill towards others. It was thus perfectly possible, as we noted above, to speak of God 'loving impassibly' – that is, loving someone without being emotionally affected by that person's situation. Yet the new interest in the psychology of human emotions has raised questions over this notion of love. Can one really speak of 'love', unless there is some mutual sharing of suffering and feelings? Surely 'love' implies the lover's intense awareness of the suffering of the beloved, and thus some form of sharing in his or her distress? Such considerations undermined the intuitive plausibility (yet not, interestingly, the intellectual credibility) of an impassible God.

In *The Crucified God*, Moltmann argues that the cross is both the foundation and criterion of true Christian theology. The passion of Christ, and especially his cry of God-forsakenness – 'My God, my God, why have you forsaken me?' (Mark 15:34) – stands at the centre of Christian thinking:

> 'My God, why have you forsaken me?' Every Christian theology and every Christian existence fundamentally respond to this question of the dying Jesus. Both protest atheism and the metaphysical revolt against God also respond to this question. Either the Jesus who was abandoned by God is the end of all theology, or the beginning of a specifically Christian, and therefore critical and liberating, theology and existence.[8]

The cross must be seen as an event between the Father and the Son, in which the Father suffers the death of his Son in order to redeem sinful humanity:

> God was not reduced to silence, nor was he inactive in the cross of Jesus. Nor was he absent in the God-forsakenness of Jesus.

He acted in Jesus, the Son of God. In that human beings betrayed him, handed him over, and delivered him up to death, God himself delivered him up. In the passion of the Son, the Father himself suffers the pain of abandonment. In the death of the Son, death comes upon God himself, and the Father suffers the death of the Son in his love for sinful humanity.[9]

The idea of a suffering God might at first sight seem to be heretical in the eyes of Christian orthodoxy. The patristic period identified two unacceptable views relating to the suffering of God – patripassianism and theopaschitism. The former was regarded as a heresy, and the latter as a potentially misleading doctrine. They merit brief discussion before proceeding further.

Patripassianism arose during the third century, and was associated with writers such as Noetus, Praxeas and Sabellius. It centred on the belief that the Father suffered as the Son. In other words, the suffering of Christ on the cross is to be regarded as the suffering of the Father. According to these writers, the only distinction within the Godhead was a succession of modes or operations. In other words, Father, Son and Spirit were just different modes of being, or expressions, of the same basic divine entity – a form of modalism, often known as Sabellianism.

Theopaschitism arose during the sixth century, and was linked with writers such as John Maxentius. The basic slogan associated with the movement was that 'one of the Trinity was crucified'. This formula is perfectly orthodox (it reappears as Martin Luther's celebrated formula, picked up by Moltmann, 'the crucified God'), and was defended as such by Leontius of Byzantium. However, it was regarded as potentially misleading and confusing by more cautious writers, including Pope Hormisdas (d. 523), and fell into disuse.

The doctrine of a suffering God rehabilitates theopaschitism, and interprets the relation of the suffering of God and of Christ in such a way that it avoids the patripassian difficulty. Moltmann's *Crucified God* develops the following position: the Father and the Son suffer, but they experience that suffering in different manners. The Son suffers the pain and death of the cross; the Father gives up his Son, and suffers his loss. Although both Father and Son are thus involved in the cross, their involvement is not *identical* (the patripassian position), but *distinct*. In the passion of the Son, the Father himself suffers the pain of abandonment. In the death of the Son, death comes upon God himself, and the

Father suffers the death of the Son in his love for sinful humanity.

Moltmann also poses a powerful challenge to the rational or Cartesian view of the perfection of God – a view which had passed into the general Enlightenment worldview, and created such difficulties for Christian apologetics in the face of atheist criticism. He argues that a God who cannot suffer is a *deficient*, not a perfect, God. Stressing that God cannot be subjected to change or suffering against his will, Moltmann declares that God willed to undergo suffering. In his freedom, God willed that he would suffer.

> A God who cannot suffer is poorer than any human being. For a God who is incapable of suffering is a being who cannot be involved. Suffering and injustice do not affect him. And because he is so completely insensitive, he cannot be affected or shaken by anything. He cannot weep, for he has no tears. But the one who cannot suffer cannot love either. So he is also a loveless being.

Moltmann here brings together a number of the considerations we noted earlier, including the idea that love involves the lover participating in the sufferings of the beloved.

Some fifteen years after the publication of *The Crucified God*, Moltmann returned to explore central Christological themes in his *Der Weg Jesu Christi: Christologie in messianischen Dimensionen* ('The Way of Jesus Christ: Christology in Messianic Dimensions'). This volume, which first appeared in German in 1989, is the third (and hence central) volume of a projected five-volume systematic theology. Although restating many of the insights of *The Crucified God*, this work represents a move away from the views developed in earlier writings. Among the major new trends, the following may be noted.

1. This work unquestionably represents a consciously *post-Enlightenment* Christology. The Enlightenment is over; no longer need Christology be unduly preoccupied with an alien agenda, but may revert to its proper task of exploring the identity and significance of Jesus Christ on its own terms. Moltmann is especially critical of the impact of the anthropocentric worldview of the Enlightenment within Christian theology, and argues that it is no longer credible. The Christological effect of this anthropocentrism, according to Moltmann, has been the creation of a series of Jesuologies which project the ideals of their

culturally conditioned creators on to the figure of Jesus.

2. Moltmann identifies two Christological paradigms which have exercised major influence in the past – the *cosmological* paradigm of the patristic era, and the *anthropocentric* paradigm of the Enlightenment (which has, in effect, been the subject of the present study of modern German Christology). Although critical of both, Moltmann shows an ecologically grounded sympathy for the patristic view: its emphasis upon the importance of the physical aspects of humanity and the creation has much to offer the church as it faces a crisis in the environment. This crisis, interestingly, Moltmann partly attributes to the dominance of the Enlightenment worldview, which neglected the environment through its emphasis upon human domination. Both these paradigms require to be transcended, through a return to the biblical foundations of Christianity on the one hand, and by an appropriate engagement with and interpretation of the human situation on the other.

It remains to be seen what the impact of these ideas will be; our attention now turns to the related theology associated with Eberhard Jüngel.

Eberhard Jüngel

Jüngel's theological programme relates fundamentally to the question of how it is possible to speak of God in a responsible manner in a world in which people live, to use Dietrich Bonhoeffer's phrase, *etsi Deus non daretur* ('as if God were not given'). In an age still influenced by the characteristic Enlightenment anthropocentrism (which occasionally verges on a Feuerbachian-legitimated anthropotheism), Jüngel may be regarded as having developed a theological programme whose chief concern is to distinguish between God and humanity.

In his doctoral dissertation on the relation between Jesus of Nazareth and the primitive Christian proclamation, Jüngel developed Ernst Fuchs' contribution to the 'new quest of the historical Jesus' by emphasizing the unity of the person and proclamation of Jesus in the parables of the synoptic gospels. However, while Fuchs and the existentially orientated 'new hermeneutics' regarded eschatology as an essentially anthropological concept, Jüngel had no hesitation in asserting that it was an authentically theological concept.[11] In doing this, he placed himself close to the views then becoming associated with the Pannenberg circle, especially in relation to the manner in which New Testament apocalyptic was to be interpreted. Like Pannenberg, Jüngel insisted that 'fact' and 'meaning' were inextricably connected within their historical context,[12] thus moving decisively away from the older rationalist imposition of meaning upon events from a standpoint determined by the anthropological concerns of the Enlightenment.

Jüngel's distinctive approach to the historical aspects of Christology are set out clearly in his *Thesen zur Grundlegung der Christologie* ('Theses on the Foundation of Christology'), given in the course of his Christology lectures at Tübingen during the academic year 1969–70. We may begin by considering his attitude to the resurrection. For Jüngel, the proclamation of the resurrection of Jesus (which is unique to the Christian faith) must be investigated in two manners:

1. on the basis of the historical (*historisch*) origins of the tradition concerning the resurrection;
2. on the basis of the way in which the resurrection was portrayed, within the context of the 'history of religions' (*Religionsgeschichte*).[13]

This is a vitally important distinction: the resurrection *event* cannot be explained away within the context of the 'history of religions'; it does not conform to some general pattern of belief within world religions at the time. However, the manner in which the resurrection is to be *interpreted* is conditioned by the network of religious expectations at the time, which can be investigated by 'history of religions' approaches. The 'history of religions' is not competent to pass judgment on the historicity of the resurrection; it does, however, cast light on the interpretative framework.

So what was that framework? Jüngel suggests that the apocalyptic tradition was of suggestive, but not of *decisive*, importance in interpreting the meaning of the resurrection. For example, Jüngel insists that this apocalyptic framework allowed the appearances of Jesus after his death to be interpreted in terms of his *resurrection from the dead*.[14] The apocalyptic worldview could not accommodate the resurrection of a single individual; the movement looks ahead to the general resurrection of the dead at the end of history. Furthermore, the Messiah or Son of Man was not visible to the world at large; yet an integral aspect of the apocalyptic expectation concerned the *visible* appearance of the Messiah or Son of Man. It was only through the proclamation of the resurrection of Christ that faith was generated. Jüngel thus argues that the resurrection of Jesus was *sui generis*, in a category of its own, possessing a 'once-for-all character (*Eingmaligkeit*)' which cannot be verified by analogy. There is an obvious parallel with Pannenberg at this point, in that the resurrection is, in effect, declared to be a unique historical category, and not amenable to the normal methods and assumptions – such as Troeltsch's affirmation of the 'homogeneity' of history.

Jüngel develops this point by reiterating his emphasis upon the unity of event and interpretation. Indeed, the resurrection is treated as a case-study of the manner in which the narrative of Jesus intermingles event and interpretation, in such a manner that they cannot be had in isolation from one another. Christological language in general, and language about the resurrection in particular, refuses to separate an event from its interpretation;[15] the New Testament accounts of the resurrection in particular represent a complex and irreducible mixture of historical and dogmatic truth-affirmations (*eine Verwechslung und Vermischung historischer und dogmatischer Wahrnehmung*).[16]

Why is the resurrection important? For Pannenberg, as we noted earlier, its significance lies in its proleptic disclosure of the end events, and the consequences of this for the identity of Jesus and his relation to God. Jüngel, however, develops a position closer to that of Moltmann: God identifies himself with the crucified Christ,[17] so that faith recognizes the crucified human being Jesus of Nazareth as identical to God. This insight becomes of central importance in his 1977 work *Gott als Geheimnis der Welt* ('God as the Mystery of the World'), in which he addresses the question of how it is meaningful to speak of God in a world from which he has been displaced. Like Moltmann, Jüngel firmly anchors the Christian understanding of God – which he sharply distinguishes from that of theism – in the crucified Christ:

> The Christian tradition of speaking (*die christliche Sprach-überlieferung*) insists that we *must be told* what we are to *think* of the word 'God'. It is thus presupposed that only the God who speaks can himself finally tell us what we are to understand by the word 'God'. Theology expresses this fact with the category of revelation . . . When we attempt to think of God as the one who communicates and expresses himself in the human being Jesus, it must be remembered that, in fact, this human being was *crucified*, that he was killed in the name of the law of God. The one who was crucified is thus precisely the concrete definition (*Realdefinition*) of what is meant by the word 'God',

for responsible Christian use of the word. Christianity is thus fundamentally a 'theology of the one who was crucified (*Theologie der Gekreuzigten*)'.[18]

The basis of all heresy, according to Jüngel, is to be located in the refusal or reluctance to recognize God in Jesus Christ.[19] Like Schleiermacher (see pp. 45–7), Jüngel treats heresy as possessing a strongly *Christological* dimension.

Jüngel then moves on to make the cross the centre of the trinitarian history of God. A proper interpretation of the crucifixion of Christ leads decisively away from the undifferentiated monotheism of classical theism, towards the distinctively and authentically *Christian* doctrine of the Trinity. The cross reveals a differentiation between Father and Son. (A similar point had been made by Moltmann, who points out the different manners in which Father and Son experience suffering, as we noted above.) The resurrection, however, affirms the unity of Father and Son, God and Jesus. How is this to be interpreted? Jüngel maps out a road which leads to the doctrine of the Trinity with his declaration that 'the knowledge of the identification of God with Jesus necessitates the distinction of God from God'.[20] The New Testament itself makes such a distinction, when it distinguishes God the Son (the crucified Jesus) from God the Father (who raised him from the dead).[21]

This 'self-differentiation (*Selbstdifferenzierung* or *Selbstunterscheidung*)' within God, recognized on the basis of the relation between the resurrection and crucifixion of Christ, constitutes the basis of the doctrine of the Trinity. It also forms the basis of the Christian critique of both monotheism and metaphysical theism, as well as the types of atheism which correspond to these forms of theism.[22] The Father and Son are held together by the bond of unity, the Holy Spirit. As with Moltmann, the Spirit is seen as the ground of the unity between Father and Son, allowing their inherent unity to be maintained in spite of the self-differentiation evident in the cross. If Jüngel seems to repeat themes already associated with Moltmann, he develops his insights in a vigorously polemical manner, demonstrating their destructive impact upon the whole Cartesian theological enterprise upon which the Enlightenment was ultimately grounded.

Yet to discuss the *suffering* of God in Christ is to lead on to the question of whether it is meaningful and proper to speak of the *death* of God in Christ – an issue which we shall now address.

The Death of God?

Hymns, as much as theology textbooks, bear witness to the beliefs of Christianity. A number of significant hymns of the Christian church make reference to the death of God, exulting in the paradox that the immortal God should die on the cross. Perhaps the most celebrated example is Charles Wesley's eighteenth-century hymn *And can it be?*, which includes the following lines:

> Amazing love! how can it be
> That thou, my God, shouldst die for me?

The notion of the immortal God giving himself up to death on behalf of the people whom he loves thus found its expression in English piety long before the new interest in the question during the twentieth century. To return to Wesley's hymn:

> 'Tis mystery all! the immortal dies!
> Who can explore his strange design?

This raises a fundamental question: how can one speak of God 'dying'? Here, an English-language influence upon the development of German Christology may be noted.

For a few weeks in 1965, theology hit the national headlines in the United States. *Time* magazine ran an edition declaring that God was dead. Slogans such as 'God is dead' and 'the death of God' became of national interest. In its issue of 16 February 1966, the leading theological journal *Christian Century* provided a satirical application form for its readers to join the 'God-Is-Dead-Club'. New words began to appear in the learned journals: 'theothanasia', 'theothanatology' and 'theothanatopsis' became buzz words, before happily lapsing into fully merited obscurity.

Two quite distinct interpretations may be discerned behind the slogan 'the death of God':
1. The belief, especially linked with the German philosopher Friedrich Nietzsche (1844–1900), that human civilization has reached the stage at which it may dispense with the notion of God. The crisis of faith in the West, especially Western Europe, which developed during the nineteenth century, finally matured. Nietzsche's declaration (*The Happy Science*,

1882) that 'God is dead! God remains dead! And we have killed him!' expresses a general cultural atmosphere which finds no place for God. This secular outlook is well explored in Gabriel Vahanian's (b. 1927) *Death of God: The Culture of our Post-Christian Era* (1961). William Hamilton (b. 1924), widely regarded as the third member of the triumvirate of the 'death of God' school – the other two members being Thomas J. J. Altizer (b. 1927) and Paul van Buren (b. 1924) – expressed this feeling well:

> We are not talking about the absence of the experience of God, but about the experience of the absence of God . . . The death of God must be affirmed; the confidence with which we thought we could speak of God is gone . . . There remains a sense of not having, of not believing, of having lost, not just the idols or the gods of religion, but God himself. And this is an experience that is not peculiar to a neurotic few, nor is it private or inward. The death of God is a public event in our history.[23]

Subsequent predictions of the total secularization of Western society remain conspicuously unfulfilled, with a new public interest in religion embarrassing those who predicted its demise. Nevertheless, the 'death of God' motif seems to capture the atmosphere of an important moment in Western cultural history, perhaps culminating in the late 1960s. As noted earlier, it finds earlier expression in Dietrich Bonhoeffer's writings from prison, which speak of God having been pushed out of the world (p. 200), or of modern humanity living *etsi Deus non daretur*, 'as if God were not given', before reaching its mature development in the intellectual tumult of the 1960s.

This development had important implications for those Christian theologians who took their lead from cultural developments in North America. In his *Secular Meaning of the Gospel* (1963), Paul van Buren, arguing that the word 'God' has ceased to have any meaning, sought to restate the gospel in purely a-theological terms. Belief in a transcendent God was replaced by commitment to a 'Jesus-ethic', centred on respect for the lifestyle of Jesus. Thomas J. J. Altizer's *Gospel of Christian Atheism* (1966) refocused the question, by suggesting that, while it was no longer acceptable to talk about Jesus being God, one could still talk about God being Jesus – thus giving a moral authority to Jesus' words and deeds, even if belief in a God was no longer to be retained.

2. The totally distinct belief that Jesus Christ has such a high profile of identification with God that one can speak of God 'dying' in Christ. Just as God suffers in Christ, so one can speak of God experiencing death or 'perishability' (Eberhard Jüngel: see below) in the same manner. It is this approach which is developed by both Moltmann and Jüngel, and which merits further discussion. Nevertheless, it is clear that Jüngel's discussion of this question takes place against an informed awareness of the importance of the question within the American culture of the 1960s – an observation which allows the growing importance of American theology within the West, and its increasing impact upon the German situation, to be understood.

We may take up the theme of the 'death of God' in German theology, and especially Christology, by considering a German Lutheran hymn, composed by Johann Rist (1607–67) at some point around 1641, and which appeared in the *Hohensteinisches Gesangbuch* shortly afterwards. Its second verse opens as follows:

> O grosse Not! Gott selbst liegt tot,
> am Kreuz ist er gestorben.

> O greatest distress! God himself lies dead,
> he died upon the cross.

The words 'God himself lies dead' caused quite a rumpus at the time. Indeed in 1917 a nervous hymnal revision committee altered the closing words of the first line to read '*Gotts Sohn liegt tod* (God's Son lies dead)'. However, the hymn in its unexpurgated form came to the attention of Hegel, who saw in these words an opportunity to develop a speculative theology of 'the death of God' without being classed as an atheist at a moment in German cultural history when this was not such a good idea.

Hegel is thus able to speak of the 'feeling that God himself is dead (*das Gefühl: Gott selbst ist tot*)' – note the exact correspondence with the words of Rist. Informing his audience that he was simply quoting a 'Lutheran hymn', he transforms this theological affirmation into the philosophical idea of a 'speculative Good Friday', the 'truth and harshness of God-forsakenness' – that is, the basic atheistic feeling of the modern period, to which Hegel's philosophy of the Absolute was addressed.[24] In many ways, the 'death of God' movement can be seen as the outcome of this cultural shift, noted by Hegel, accelerated by Nietzsche, and addressed from prison by Bonhoeffer.

Jüngel argues for the need for Christian theology to reclaim the idea of the 'death of God', and to insist that it be interpreted in a responsible and Christian manner. Rightly understood, it encapsulates the Christian understanding of the nature of God. Yet it is only the Christian faith itself which allows the 'dark word of the death of God' to have its full meaning, as Jüngel demonstrates during the course of a sustained engagement with Hegel and Bonhoeffer.[25] The origins of the phrase are Christological; it must therefore be expounded in a Christological context. Outside this context, it can only bear the reduced and theologically illegitimate sense of a diminished cultural awareness of the divine.

With this point in mind, Jüngel traces the 'dark word of the death of God' back to its origins, which he identifies as lying in part in the writings of Martin Luther. Drawing extensively on Luther's 'theology of the cross', especially its crucial distinction between the 'revealed God (*deus revelatus*)' and the 'hidden God (*deus absconditus*)', Jüngel argues for the need to interpret experience within this framework. God is *present in a hidden manner* to faith. God acts in such a way that he appears to be hidden to those who expect him to behave in a preconceived and different manner. Faith, however, learns to recognize the presence of God in the apparent God-forsakenness of the death of Jesus on the cross.

In this way, Jüngel transforms the cross of Christ from a purely soteriological to an epistemological resource. Christology discloses patterns of divine activity and presence within the world, which can be discerned only through a framework of interpretation which is securely grounded in Christology. This framework entails the rejection of 'the metaphysical conception of God (*das metaphysische Gottesgedank*)', which, Jüngel argues, underlies both classical theism and its antithetical atheisms. For Jüngel, *atheism is antitheism*. The Trinity expresses the characteristically Christian conception of God, which is not vulnerable to the critique of atheism in the manner of the Cartesian notion of 'a perfect being'.

Jüngel argues that the atheisms of both Feuerbach and Nietzsche appear to be based upon exactly such a 'metaphysically conceived God'.[26] Their critiques of Christianity are therefore to be dismissed as abortive, in that those critiques are actually directed against a concept of God which does not correspond to that of Christianity. Jüngel argues that the slogan 'the death of God' must therefore be understood to mean 'the death of the *metaphysical* God', which is discredited both by the critiques of atheism and by a trinitarian conception of God:

> The dark word of the death of God, at any rate by forcing theology to make an unequivocal decision, achieves the clarity of an alternative: *either* the unity of God with temporality (*Vergänglichkeit*) is conceived in such a way that God and faith are things of the past, and atheism is the destiny of the spirit; *or* the unity of God with temporality is conceived in such a way that previous conceptions of both God and temporality are recognized to have been inadequate, and the way of the spirit can be opened up through the (dubious) alternative of theism and atheism into a situation in which God may once more be conceived in the presence of the spirit.[27]

Here, as with Moltmann, the cross is allowed to act as both the foundation and criterion of faith, subjecting existing notions of divinity to criticism in the light of the God who makes himself known through the cross. *Crux probat omnia!* As Jüngel stresses, we need to be told who God is, and what he is like; that disclosure takes place fully through the cross, and nowhere else. That self-revelation obliges us to speak of a God who 'suffers', or a God who 'dies', thus setting responsible Christian theology on a collision course with its metaphysical rivals. For Jüngel, this is to be welcomed. At long last, Christian theology can liberate itself from its self-imposed bondage to a Cartesian idea of God, and rediscover the God who revealed himself in and through Christ.

Conclusion

Our survey of the development of Christology within German-speaking Protestantism is now complete. The Christological implications of the agenda of the Enlightenment have been explored with great care and thoroughness by theologians within the German tradition, with each assumption and approach being subjected to critical examination as one generation gave way to the next. Standing back from this development, and surveying it from a distance, three factors may be noted.

    1. The vulnerability of Christology to cultural accommodationism. Jesus has often been cast in the role of one who endorses the accepted

cultural outlook of a specific peer group (unsurprisingly, usually that to which the theologian in question belongs). This is most obviously the case with liberal Protestantism, which tended to portray Christ as one who echoed the settled cultural values of middle-class mid-nineteenth-century Germany. The plausibility of this approach, as well as its intellectual credentials, have been seriously undermined by scholarship since 1890.

2. The role of Jesus Christ within Christian theology. The period covered within this work has witnessed an intense debate over the importance of Jesus Christ for Christian theology. The Enlightenment treated Jesus as important where he happened to endorse its moralist agenda; at other times, it marginalized him, relegating him to a secondary place. Reason was capable of disclosing and establishing all that needed to be known; there was no revelational role to be ascribed to Jesus Christ. A related approach is adopted more recently by Tillich, whose theology is, as he himself makes clear, unaffected by the historicity of Jesus: if Jesus did not exist, Tillich's theology would not, by his own admission, be significantly altered (p. 175).

Such outlooks were subjected to criticism within the liberal tradition during the nineteenth century, which argued that Jesus did indeed make something *new* available, in the form of his religious personality. In the twentieth century, the Barthian tradition – here represented, in various forms and to various degrees, by Barth, Brunner, Bonhoeffer, Moltmann and Jüngel – has argued that Jesus Christ is theologically and historically constitutive for Christian theology. However, as we noted in relation to Barth, there is a question about what is *new* about Christ. Kähler's question remains of decisive importance: 'Has Christ merely provided us with insights concerning an existing state of affairs, or is he the founder of a new state of affairs?' (see p. 136). The issues raised by Kähler remain central to modern Christology. Barth, as we have suggested, tends to regard Christ as providing insights or assurance concerning our knowledge of the human situation – but does not fundamentally alter that situation himself.

3. The impact of the prevailing philosophical consensus upon Christology. Especially during the late eighteenth and nineteenth centuries, Christology has been deeply influenced by the prevailing outlooks of philosophy. The Enlightenment regarded it as self-evidently true that history could not give rise to significant truths, which reason alone could provide. This assumption automatically denied any

constitutive theological role to Jesus Christ. In the last decade, especially in the writings of Jüngel, there has been a marked attempt to liberate Christian theology from its self-incurred tutelage to prevailing philosophical currents, which – like cultural values and norms – are increasingly being recognized as matters of historical contingency, rather than theological necessity.

We have thus come full circle. The Enlightenment believed that it did not need to be told what God was like. It already knew, through the critical exercise of the faculty of human reason. As a result, it was able to subject the traditional Christian understandings of God and the person and work of Christ to critical rationalist examination, leading to an anthropologically conceived and anthropocentric conception of God and the 'word of the cross'. The fact that Moltmann and Jüngel deemed the moment to be right to overturn this order of priority, and that their approach has been so influential in recent theology, signals a major shift within Western theology in general, with Christology coming to the fore.

More generally, there has been an increased willingness to recognize the limitations placed upon historical knowledge. The Enlightenment assumption that it could determine precisely what did – or did not – happen in history has been set to one side as imperialist. New Testament scholar Walter Wink points out how, in the past, people have been notoriously dogmatic about what could *not* have happened in the New Testament:

> Historians still can demand that adequate warrants or evidence be produced for believing that something unusual has happened . . . They can provide invaluable checks on superstition by casting a critical eye on extraordinary claims that have a tendentious bent. But to go beyond this to dogmatic assertions that faith healing, or clairvoyance, or resuscitation of the dead is impossible, is to go beyond one's competence as a historian to the faith assertions of a person caught in the narrow confines of a particular worldview – or what Paul Ricoeur has called 'the available believable' . . . What seemed 'impossible' only five years ago is now regarded by increasing numbers of competent researchers as within the realms of possibility. What has happened here? We have received not one shred of new evidence from the first century. What has changed is our conception of what is possible, on analogy with contemporary

experience. The 'available believable' has shifted, and with it, historians' judgments. We cannot but be children of our age. For this reason it would be far more honest for historians (and we are all historians when we approach these texts) to suspend judgment about what is possible, and speak only within their competence.[28]

This is precisely what happened to Christology at the time of the Enlightenment: it became trapped within the rigid and narrow worldview of rationalism, which refused to contemplate that anything beyond its own limited experience of the world could ever have taken place, or that such an event – if it ever happened – could be of any permanent significance. Such characterisic ideas, found in the writings of individuals such as G. E. Lessing and Ernst Troeltsch, have made a major impact upon German Christology; they are now being eliminated, partly through the force of arguments and approaches such as those documented in the final two chapters of this volume, but more generally through the abandoning of the Enlightenment axiom of universal rationality. There has been a major change in cultural mood, similar to that which led to the rise of the Enlightenment in the first place.

So where will Christology go next? It is too soon to say. But what can be said is this: in a postmodern world in which all the old certainties of liberalism and rationalism have evaporated, Christianity can and must continue to seek and find its point of reference in Jesus Christ. Here is its central legitimating and defining resource. The tasks of theology may change; but he is the same, yesterday, today, and for ever.

Suggestions for Further Reading in English

The notes to this study identify many works, whether books or articles, of direct relevance to its themes. The following section notes books in English which will of be of use to interested readers.

For an excellent survey of many of the nineteenth-century writers noted in this work, see:

Ninian Smart, John Clayton, Patrick Sherry and Steven T. Katz (eds.), *Nineteenth-Century Religious Thought in the West*, 3 vols. (Cambridge: Cambridge University Press, 1985).

Claude Welch, *Protestant Thought in the Nineteenth Century*, 2 vols. (New Haven: Yale University Press, 1972–85).

For a valuable survey of several of the twentieth-century writers noted in this work , see:

David F. Ford (ed.), *The Modern Theologians*, 2 vols. (Oxford/Cambridge, MA: Blackwell Publishing, 1990).

Stanley J. Grenz and Roger E. Olson, *Twentieth-Century Theology: God and the World in a Transitional Age* (Downers Grove, Ill.: InterVarsity Press, 1992).

For excellent surveys of developments within modern Christology, including the German tradition, see:

Colin Brown, *Jesus in European Thought 1778–1860* (Durham, NC: Labyrinth Press, 1985).

John Macquarrie, *Jesus Christ in Modern Thought* (London: SCM Press/Philadelphia: Trinity Press International, 1990).

For individual writers and themes, see the following studies:

Bauckham, Richard, *Moltmann: Messianic Theology in the Making* (Basingstoke: Marshall Pickering, 1987).

Coakley, Sarah, *Christ without Absolutes: A Study of the Christology of Ernst Troeltsch* (Oxford: Clarendon Press, 1988).

Grenz, Stanley J., *Reason for Hope: The Systematic Theology of Wolfhart Pannenberg* (New York: Oxford University Press, 1990).

Harvey, Van A., *The Historian and the Believer* (London: SCM Press, 1967).

Küng, Hans, *The Incarnation of God: An Introduction to Hegel's Theological Thought as Prolegomena to a Future Christology* (Edinburgh: T. & T. Clark, 1987).

Mackintosh, Hugh R., *Types of Modern Theology: Schleiermacher to Barth* (London: Nisbet, and New York: Charles Scribner's Sons, 1937).

Reardon, B. M. G., *Liberal Protestantism* (Stanford: Stanford University Press, and London: A. & C. Black, 1968).

Richmond, James, *Ritschl: A Reappraisal* (London: Collins, 1978).

Robinson, J. M., *A New Quest of the Historical Jesus* (London: SCM Press, 1959).

Schweitzer, Albert, *The Quest of the Historical Jesus* (London: A. & C. Black, 3rd edn, 1954).

Taylor, Mark Kline, *Paul Tillich, Theologian of the Boundaries* (San Francisco: Collins, 1987).

Thompson, John, *Christ in Perspective: Christological Perspectives in the Theology of Karl Barth* (Edinburgh: St Andrew Press, 1978).

Way, David V., *The Lordship of Christ: Ernst Käsemann's Interpretation of Paul's Theology* (Oxford: Clarendon Press, 1991).

Webster, J. E., *Eberhard Jüngel: An Introduction to his Theology* (Cambridge: Cambridge University Press, 1986).

Yerkes, James, *The Christology of Hegel* (Albany, NY: State University of New York Press, 1983).

Suggestions for Further Reading in German

Many readers of this work will be competent in German, and may well find the following suggestions for further reading of value. All have been consulted during the writing of this work; those marked with an asterisk (*) are of especial value as introductions to the field.

Althaus, Paul, 'Theologie und Geschichte: Zur Auseinandersetzung mit der dialektischen Theologie', *Zeitschrift für systematische Theologie* 1 (1923), pp. 763–76.

Amberg, E.-H., *Christologie und Dogmatik: Untersuchung ihres Verhältnisses in der evangelischen Theologie der Gegenwart* (Tübingen: Mohr, 1966).

Baur, F. Ch., *Lehrbuch der christlichen Dogmengeschichte* (Darmstadt: Wissenschaftliche Buchgesellschaft, 3rd edn, 1968).

Baur, Joerg, *Salus Christiana: Die Rechtfertigungslehre in der Geschichte des christlichen Heilsverständnisses* (Gütersloh: Mohn, 1968).

Betz, H.-D., 'Zur Problem des religionsgeschichtlichen Verständnisses der Apokalyptik', *Zeitschrift für Theologie und Kirche* 63 (1966), pp. 391–409.

Bohlin, T., 'Die Reich-Gottes-Ideen im letzten halben Jahrhundert', *Zeitschrift für Theologie und Kirche* 10 (1929), pp. 1–27.

Fuchs, Ernst, *Zur Frage nach dem historischen Jesus* (Tübingen: Mohr, 1960).

*Graf, F. W. (ed.), *Profile des neuzeitlichen Protestantismus*, vol. 1

(Gütersloh: Mohn, 1990).

*Greschat, Martin (ed.), *Theologen des Protestantismus im 19. und 20. Jahrhundert*, 2 vols. (Stuttgart: Kohlhammer, 1978).

Greive, Wolfgang, 'Jesus und Glaube: Das Problem der Christologie Gerhard Ebelings', *Kerygma und Dogma* 22 (1976), pp. 163–80.

Günther, Ernst, *Die Entwicklung der Lehre von der Person Christi im 19. Jahrhundert* (Tübingen: Siebeck, 1911).

*Härle, W., and Herms, E., 'Deutschsprachige Protestantische Dogmatik nach 1945', *Verkündigung und Forschung* 27 (1982), pp. 2–100; 28 (1983), pp. 1–91.

*Hirsch, E., *Geschichte der neueren evangelischen Theologie* (Gütersloh: Mohn, 4th edn, 1968).

Klappert, Berthold, *Die Auferweckung des Gekreuzigten: Der Ansatz der Christologie Karl Barths im Zusammenhang der Christologie der Gegenwart* (Neukirchen: Neukirchener Verlag, 1971).

Link, H.-G., *Geschichte Jesu und Bild Christi: Die Entwicklung der Christologie Martin Kählers* (Neukirchen: Neukirchener Verlag, 1975).

*Mildenberger, F., *Geschichte der deutschen evangelischen Theologie im 19. und 20. Jahrhundert* (Stuttgart: Kohlhammer, 1981).

Müller, H. M., *Kulturprotestantismus: Beiträge zu einer Gestalt des modernen Christentums* (Gütersloh: Mohn, 1991).

Prenter, Regin, 'Karl Barths Umbildung der traditionellen Zweinatur-lehre in lutherischen Beleuchtung', *Studia Theologica* 11 (1957), pp. 1–88.

*Sauter, Gerhard, 'Fragestellungen der Christologie', *Verkündigung und Forschung* 11 (1966), pp. 37–68.

*—, 'Christologie in geschichtlicher Perspektive', *Verkündigung und Forschung* 21 (1976), pp. 2–31.

*—, 'Fragestellungen der Christologie II', *Verkündigung und Forschung* 23 (1978), pp. 21–41.

Slenczka, Reinhard, *Geschichtlichkeit und Personsein Jesu Christi: Studien zur christologischen Problematik der historischen-Jesu-Frage* (Göttingen: Vandenhoeck & Ruprecht, 1967).

A Glossary of German
Christological Terms

The following terms are often encountered in German Christological discussions, and are often associated with specific writers. The following brief explanations may be helpful.

Aukflärung. Literally, 'a clearing up'. The German term which was used extensively during the eighteenth century to refer to what is now known as 'the Enlightenment'. Related terms to be noted include '*Aufklärungszeit* (period of the Enlightenment)' and '*Aufklärer* (a representative of the Enlightenment)'.

Christusbild. 'A portrait of Christ'. The term is used frequently to refer to the 'understanding of Christ' associated with a given thinker or school of thought, especially where extensive historical reconstruction of the personality of Jesus is involved, as with liberal Protestantism.

das Gefühl. 'Feeling' or 'sentiment', especially as employed by writers sympathetic to Romanticism, such as Novalis or Schleiermacher. The term denotes a deep sense of inner awareness of the infinite, rather than a sensation or experience of the external world. See pp. 39–40.

Geschichte. One of two German terms which can be translated as 'history' (the other being *Historie*). As developed by writers such as

Martin Kähler and Rudolf Bultmann, the term has the meaning 'events which transform personal existence or *make* history', as opposed to 'events which take place in history'. Related terms include '*geschlichtlich* (historical)' and '*Geschichtlichkeit* (historicity)'.

geschlichtliche Christus, der. A term used in the writings of Martin Kähler to refer to the historic figure of Jesus Christ, as he transcends the limitations of any one period in history. For Kähler, this suprahistorical Christ is to be contrasted with the 'historical Jesus (*der historische Jesus*)', who is both limited in his historical impact and is in any case the artificial construction of the scholarly community.

Historie. One of two German terms which can be translated as 'history' (the other being *Geschichte*). As developed by writers such as Martin Kähler and Rudolf Bultmann, the term has the meaning 'events which take place in history', as opposed to 'events which transform personal existence or *make* history'. Related terms include '*historisch* (historical)' and '*Historismus* (historicism)'.

historische Jesus, der. 'The historical Jesus', often used in a sense best rendered as 'Jesus, as he can be reconstructed on the basis of speculative historical investigation'. The implication in many writings of the late eighteenth century is that the historical Jesus is Jesus as he actually was, as opposed to the mythical or fictional construction of 'the dogmatic Christ'. The latter was regarded as the invention of the church; the former can be rediscovered by historical investigation. For Kähler, *der historische Jesus* was itself an idealized and artificial construction, having little relation to the real Christ of faith.

irdische Jesus, der. 'The earthly Jesus', a term often used to refer to 'Jesus during his earthly period', embracing the period from his birth to crucifixion, as opposed to 'the exalted Jesus'. Although the term can be regarded as synonymous with 'the historical Jesus', it avoids the negatively reductionist associations which have come to be linked to the latter.

Kulturprotestantismus. A term of disparagement, used to refer to liberal Protestantism (especially as associated with A. B. Ritschl) by its opponents. The term reflects the general conviction that liberalism was culturally and morally derivative, gleaning its theological intuitions from contemporary cultural norms, rather than from the resources of the Christian tradition.

Leben–Jesu–Forschung. Often translated as 'the quest of the historical Jesus', although a more prosaic translation would be 'research into the life of Jesus'. The term denotes the general scholarly attempt to clarify the historical figure of Jesus, including the more ambitious reconstructions of his personality associated with liberal Protestantism.

Menschwerdung. A term normally translated as 'incarnation', which possesses important overtones within Hegel's philosophical system. It is also used extensively by Karl Barth.

Religionsgeschichte. Literally, 'the history of religions'. The approach to religious history, and Christian origins in particular, which treats Old and New Testament developments as responses to encounters with other religions, such as Gnosticism. Of particular importance was the *religionsgeschichtlich* suggestion that the idea of the resurrection of Christ was the result of encounters with the Gnostic redeemer and resurrection myths. 'Die religionsgeschichtliche Schule' was the school of thought, especially associated with the faculty of theology of the University of Göttingen in the period 1890–1920, which adopted this approach. Its leading representatives included such writers as Hermann Gunkel, Wilhelm Bossuet and Ernst Troeltsch.

Urbildlichkeit. 'The quality of being an ideal', an idea especially associated with Schleiermacher, for whom Jesus of Nazareth was the ideal of human God-consciousness. The close affinities with the Enlightenment notion of Christ as a moral example are modified by Schleiermacher's notion of *Vorbildlichkeit*.

Vergegenständlichung. The idea of 'projection' or 'objectification', especially associated with the left-wing Hegelian writer Ludwig Feuerbach. On the basis of his analysis of how human experience is interpreted, Feuerbach argues that the notion of God arises through the improper 'objectification' of human self-experience (*das selbstfühlende Gefühl*), which is then incorrectly interpreted as experience of God. Knowledge of oneself is thus misunderstood as knowledge of God.

Versöhnung. A term posing some difficulties for translators, in that it can be rendered equally as 'atonement' or 'reconciliation'. The term is of particular importance within the Hegelian system, in which it comes to signify the reconciliation of God and humanity within the context of the idea of incarnation.

Vorbildlichkeit. 'The quality of being able to evoke an ideal in others'. For Schleiermacher, Jesus of Nazareth is not simply the instantiation of an ideal, but one who possesses an ability to evoke or arouse this quality in others.

Vorstellung. A Hegelian term, best translated as 'representation', which refers to the religious representation or pictorializing of concepts. The most important such representation is that of incarnation, in which the Christian representation of this idea, in the person of Jesus Christ, is regarded as the most significant and well-developed religious expression of the philosophical idea of *Menschwerdung.* Although this idea finds its expressions in other religions, Hegel regarded the Christian representation of the idea as supreme.

Weltanschauung. A term used frequently in the literature to refer to the 'worldview' or cultural mood of a particular period in history. The term *Zeitgeist,* often translated as 'spirit of the age', expresses a similar notion.

Wie es eigentlich gewesen war. A slogan, usually translated 'as it actually was' or 'as it actually happened', used to designate a form of historical positivism which gained credibility in nineteenth-century German historiography. It was asserted that it was possible to uncover the past reliably and accurately. This belief had a considerable impact on the 'quest of the historical Jesus', which largely rested on the assumption that historical research was capable of accurately reconstructing the 'historical Jesus'. More recent historical writing has tended to dismiss the 'as it actually was' approach as hopelessly naive and idealistic.

Notes

Chapter 1: The Enlightenment

1. See A. O. Dyson, 'Theological Legacies of the Enlightenment: England and Germany', in S. W. Sykes (ed.), *England and Germany: Studies in Theological Diplomacy* (Peter Lang: Frankfurt/Berne, 1982), pp. 45-62.

2. For useful introductions, see Peter Gay, *The Enlightenment: An Interpretation* 2 vols (Wildwood House: London, 1973); G. R. Cragg, *Reason and Authority in the Eighteenth Century* (Cambridge: Cambridge University Press, 1964). See also the recent overview to be found in John W. Yolton (ed.), *The Blackwell Companion to the Enlightenment* (Oxford/Cambridge, Mass.: Blackwell Publishing, 1992).

3. See Ernst Cassirer, *The Philosophy of the Enlightenment* (Princeton, NJ: Princeton University Press, 1951); Roger Scruton, *Kant* (Oxford: Oxford University Press, 1982).

4. The case of Italy is fascinating. See F. Venturi, *Settecento Riformatore* (Turin: Einaudi, 1969); D. Carpanetto and G. Ricuperah, *Italy in the Age of Reason* (London: Longman, 1987).

5. David Hume, *Dialogues Concerning Natural Religion*, ed. Norman Kemp Smith (Edinburgh: Nelson, 2nd edn, 1947).

6. Immanuel Kant, *Grundlegung zur Metaphysik der Sitten*; in *Werke*, ed. G. Hartenstein (Leipzig, 1867-9), vol. 5, p. 34.

7. Iris Murdoch, *The Sovereignty of the Good* (London: Macmillan, 1970), p. 80.

8. See Alister E. McGrath, 'The Moral Theory of the Atonement. An Historical and Theological Critique', *Scottish Journal of Theology* 38 (1985), pp. 205-20.

9. For what follows, see Gordon E. Michalson, *Lessing's Ugly Ditch: A Study of Theology and History* (University Park: Pennsylvania State University Press, 1985). On Lessing in general, see Henry Allison, *Lessing and the Enlightenment* (Ann Arbor, MI: University of Michigan, 1966).

10. Lessing, 'On the Proof of the Spirit and Power', in H. Chadwick (ed.), *Lessing's Theological Writings* (Stanford: Stanford University Press, and London: A. & C. Black, 1956), pp. 53-5.

11. Lessing, 'On the Proof of the Spirit and Power', pp. 53-5.

12. Lessing, 'On the Proof of the Spirit and Power', p. 53.

13. Lessing, 'On the Proof of the Spirit and Power', p. 54.

14. Albert Schweitzer, *The Quest of the Historical Jesus* (London: A. & C. Black, 3rd edn, 1954), p. 17.

Chapter 2: F. D. E. Schleiermacher

1. John W. Yolton, *Perceptual Acquaintance from Descartes to Reid* (Oxford: Basil Blackwell, 1984).

2. See John P. Wright, *The Sceptical Realism of David Hume* (Manchester: Manchester University Press, 1983).

3. B. M. G. Reardon, *Religion in the Age of Romanticism* (Cambridge: Cambridge University Press, 1985); René Wellek, 'The Concept of Romanticism in Literary History', in *Concepts of Criticism* (New Haven/London: Yale University Press, 1963), pp. 128-221.

4. For excellent introductions see Brian A. Gerrish, *A Prince of the Church: Schleiermacher and the Beginnings of Modern Theology* (London: SCM Press, 1984). See also his brief introduction 'F. D. E. Schleiermacher', in N. Smart *et al.* (eds.), *Nineteenth-Century Religious Thought*, 3 vols (Cambridge: Cambridge University Press, 1985), vol. 1, pp. 123-56; Martin Redeker, *Schleiermacher* (Philadelphia: Fortress Press, 1973); R. R. Williams, *Schleiermacher the Theologian* (Philadelphia: Fortress Press, 1978).

5. For the role of feeling in Schleiermacher's thought, see W. Schulze, 'Schleiermachers Theorie des Gefühls und ihre religiöse Bedeutung', *Zeitschrift für Theologie und Kirche* 53 (1956), pp. 75-103; F. W. Graf, 'Ursprüngliches Gefühl unmittelbarer Koinzidenz des

Differenzen: Zur Modifikation des Religionsbegriffs in der verschiedenen Auflagen von Schleiermachers Reden über die Religion', *Zeitschrift für Theologie und Kirche* 75 (1978), pp. 147–86. On the role of experience in theology in general, see Alister E. McGrath, 'Theology and Experience: Reflections on Cognitive and Experiential Approaches to Theology', *European Journal of Theology* 2 (1993), 65–74.

6. F. D. E. Schleiermacher, *The Christian Faith* (Edinburgh: T. & T. Clark, 2nd edn, 1928), p. 52.

7. Schleiermacher, *The Christian Faith*, p. 375.

8. Schleiermacher, *The Christian Faith*, p. 429.

9. Schleiermacher, *The Christian Faith*, p. 430.

10. Schleiermacher, *The Christian Faith*, p. 98.

11. For a detailed analysis of Schleiermacher's notion of heresy, see K. M. Beckmann, *Der Begriff der Häresie bei Schleiermacher* (Munich: Kaiser Verlag, 1959), pp. 36–62.

Chapter 3: The Hegelian School

1. See Peter C. Hodgson, 'Hegel' in N. Smart *et al.* (eds.), *Nineteenth-Century Religious Thought in the West*, 3 vols. (Cambridge: Cambridge University Press, 1985), vol. 1, pp. 81–121; Hans Küng, *The Incarnation of God: An Introduction to Hegel's Theological Thought as Prolegomena to a Future Christology* (Edinburgh: T. & T. Clark, 1987); James Yerkes, *The Christology of Hegel* (Albany, NY: State University of New York Press, 1983). For a helpful review of Küng's work, see Joseph Fitzer, 'Hegel and the Incarnation: A Response to Hans Küng', *Journal of Religion* 52 (1972), pp. 240–67. On Hegelianism in general, see John E. Toews, *Hegelianism: The Path Towards Dialectical Humanism* (Cambridge: Cambridge University Press, 1985), pp. 71–369.

2. For helpful explorations of the ideas included in this section, see Michael Rosen, *Hegel's Dialectic and Its Criticism* (Cambridge: Cambridge University Press, 1985), pp. 55–91; Malcolm Clark, *Logic and System: A Study of the Transition from Vorstellung to Thought in the Philosophy of Hegel* (The Hague: Nijhoff, 1970).

3. G. W. F. Hegel, *Vorlesungen über die Philosophie der Religion*; in *Werke*, vol. 12, pp. 320–1.

4. Hans Frei, 'David Friedrich Strauss', in N. Smart *et al.* (eds.), *Nineteenth-Century Religious Thought in the West*, 3 vols. (Cambridge: Cambridge University Press, 1985), vol. 1, pp. 215–60; M. C. Massey,

'The Literature of Young Germany and D. F. Strauss' *Life of Jesus*', *Journal of Religion* 59 (1979), pp. 298–323.

5. D. F. Strauss, *The Life of Jesus* (Philadelphia: Fortress Press, 1972), pp. 86–7.

6. Strauss, *Life of Jesus*, p. 758.

7. Strauss, *Life of Jesus*, p. 768.

8. Strauss, *Life of Jesus*, p. 772.

9. Strauss, *Life of Jesus*, pp. 783–4.

10. Adolf von Harnack, *What is Christianity?* (New York: Harper, 1957), p. 20.

11. See Peter C. Hodgson, *The Formation of Historical Theology: A Study of Ferdinand Christian Baur* (New York: Charles Scribner's Sons, 1966); Robert Morgan, 'Ferdinand Christian Baur', in N. Smart *et al.* (eds.), *Nineteenth-Century Religious Thought in the West,* 3 vols. (Cambridge: Cambridge University Press, 1985), vol. 1, pp. 261–89. On the critical question of Baur's attitude to Schleiermacher, see Heinz Liebing, 'Ferdinand Christian Baurs Kritik an Schleiermachers Glaubenslehre', *Zeitschrift für Theologie und Kirche* 54 (1957), pp. 225–43.

12. F. C. Baur, 'Das christlich des Platonismus oder Sokrates und Christus', *Tübinger Zeitschrift für Theologie* 10 (1837), pp. 1–154.

13. On this, see F. C. Baur, 'Über die Composition und den Charakter des johanneïschen Evangeliums', *Theologische Jahrbücher* 3 (1844), pp. 1–191; 397–475; 615–700.

14. See Max Wartofsky, *Feuerbach* (Cambridge: Cambridge University Press, 1982); W. I. Brazall, *The Young Hegelians* (New Haven/London: Yale University Press, 1970); James Bradley, 'Across the River and Beyond the Trees: Feuerbach's Relevance to Modern Theology', in S. W. Sykes and D. Holmes (eds.), *New Studies in Theology* (London: Duckworth, 1980), pp. 139–61.

15. Ludwig Feuerbach, *Das Wesen des Christentums*, 2 vols. (Berlin: Akademie Verlag, 1956), vol. 1, pp. 51–2. For a detailed account of Feuerbach at this point, see Wartofsky, *Feuerbach*, pp. 220–6.

16. For a helpful introduction, see Martin Redeker, *Schleiermacher: Life and Thought* (Philadelphia: Fortress Press, 1973).

17. See John Glasse, 'Barth on Feuerbach', *Harvard Theological Review* 57 (1964), pp. 69–96; M. H. Vogel, 'The Barth–Feuerbach Confrontation', *Harvard Theological Review* 59 (1966), pp. 27–52.

18. Karl Marx, *Das Kapital*, 3 vols. (Moscow: Progress Publishers, 1958–9), vol. 1, p. 79.

19. Karl Marx, 'Zur Kritik der hegelschen Rechtsphilosophie', in *Werke*, 4 vols. (Berlin, 1959–61), vol. 1, p. 379.

20. Marx, 'Zur Kritik der hegelschen Rechtsphilosophie', in *Werke*, vol. 1, p. 488.

21. This is an extremely difficult notion to analyse in English, not least on account of the subtle interaction between the two German words Marx uses (*Entäusserung* and *Entfremdung*) to describe the phenomenon. Readers are referred to Bertell Ollman, *Alienation: Marx's Conception of Man in Capitalist Society* (Cambridge: Cambridge University Press, 1977) for a full analysis.

22. Karl Marx, 'Kritik der hegelschen Rechtsphilosophie', in *Werke*, vol. 1, p. 488.

23. Marx, 'Kritik der hegelschen Rechtsphilosophie', in *Werke*, vol. 1, p. 488.

24. Marx, *Das Kapital*, vol. 1, p. 79.

25. Marx, 'Thesen über Feuerbach', in *Werke*, vol. 2, p. 4.

26. For a biography, see Ernest Jones, *Sigmund Freud: Life and Work*, 3 vols. (London: Hogarth Press, 1953–7).

27. See the helpful study of Fraser Watts and Mark Williams, *The Psychology of Religious Knowing* (Cambridge: Cambridge University Press, 1988), pp. 24–37.

28. Sigmund Freud, *The Future of an Illusion*, in *Complete Psychological Works*, 24 vols. (London: Hogarth Press, 1953–), vol. 21, p. 30.

Chapter 4: The Liberal Picture of Christ

1. I. A. Dorner, 'Über die richtige Fassung des dogmatischen Begriffs der Unveränderlichkeit Gottes', in *Gesammelte Schriften aus dem Gebiet der systematischen Theologie* (Berlin, 1883), pp. 188–377.

2. I. A. Dorner, 'Die deutsche Theologie und ihre dogmatischen und ethischen Aufgaben in der Gegenwart', in *Gesammelte Schriften aus dem Gebiet der systematischen Theologie* (Berlin, 1883), pp. 1–47.

3. For an excellent study, see D. L. Mueller, *An Introduction to the Theology of Albrecht Ritschl* (Philadelphia: Fortress Press, 1959). See also James Richmond, *Ritschl: A Reappraisal* (London: Collins, 1978); D. L. Deegan, 'Critical Empiricism in the Theology of Albrecht Ritschl', *Scottish Journal of Theology* 18 (1965), pp. 40–56.

4. A. B. Ritschl, *The Christian Doctrine of Justification and*

Reconciliation (Edinburgh: T. & T. Clark, 1900), vol. 3, p. 386 (my emphasis).

5. Ritschl, *Justification and Reconciliation*, p. 3.

6. Ritschl, *Justification and Reconciliation*, p. 591.

7. Ritschl, *Justification and Reconciliation*, p. 465.

8. A. B. Ritschl, 'Theology and Metaphysics', in *Three Essays*, ed. P. Hefner (Philadelphia: Fortress Press, 1972), p. 178. See the related comments in *Justification and Reconciliation*, pp. 451–2.

9. For an excellent study, see H. Timm, *Theorie und Praxis in der Theologie Albrecht Ritschls und Wilhelm Hermanns: Ein Beitrag zur Entwicklungsgeschichte des Kulturprotestantismus* (Tübingen: Mohr, 1967).

10. See Karl Barth, 'Die dogmatische Prinzipienlehre bei Wilhelm Herrmann', in *Die Theologie und die Kirche* (Munich: Kaiser Verlag, 1928), pp. 240–80; quote at p. 252.

11. This point is brought out in T. Mahlmann, 'Das Axiom des Erlebnisses bei Wilhelm Herrmann', *Neue Zeitschrift für systematische Theologie und Religionsphilosophie* 4 (1962), p. 74.

12. See Wilhelm Herrmann, 'Der geschichtlichen Christus, der Grund unseres Glaubens', *Zeitschrift für Theologie und Kirche* 2 (1892), pp. 232–73.

13. Adolf von Harnack, *History of Dogma*, 7 vols. (Edinburgh, 1894–9), vol. 7, p. 272.

14. Harnack, *History of Dogma*, vol. 1, pp. 14–15.

15. See E. J. Meijering, *Theologische Urteile über die Dogmengeschichte: Ritschls Einfluss auf von Harnack* (Leiden: Brill, 1978).

16. E. J. Meijering, *Die Hellenisierung des Christentums im Urteil Adolf von Harnack* (Amsterdam: Kampen, 1985), pp. 19–48.

17. Ritschl, 'Theology and Metaphysics', pp. 195, 204.

18. Adolf von Harnack, *What is Christianity?* (New York: Harper, 1957), p. 144. (Emphasis in the original).

19. For documentation and critical assessment, see Aloys Grillmeier, 'Hellenisierung-Judaisierung des Christentums als Deuteprinzipien der Geschichte des kirchlichen Dogmas', *Scholastik* 33 (1958), pp. 321–55; 528–55.

20. Harnack, *History of Dogma*, vol. 7, p. 75.

21. Harnack, *What is Christianity?*, p. 173.

22. Harnack, *What is Christianity?*. p. 217.

23. Harnack, *What is Christianity?*, pp. 13–14.
24. Harnack, *What is Christianity?*, pp. 202–5; 232–3.
25. Harnack, *What is Christianity?*, p. 31.
26. Harnack, *What is Christianity?*, p. 145.
27. Harnack, *What is Christianity?*, p. 146.
28. See the useful collection of material in H. M. Rumschiedt, *Revelation and History: An Analysis of the Barth–Harnack Correspondence of 1923* (Cambridge: Cambridge University Press, 1972), especially pp. 68–119.
29. George Tyrrell, *Christianity at the Cross-Roads* (1909; repr. London: Faber, 1963), p. 49.

Chapter 5: The Collapse of the Liberal Christology

1. Albert Schweitzer, *The Quest of the Historical Jesus* (London: A. & C. Black, 3rd edn, 1954), p. 242.
2. George Tyrrell, *Christianity at the Cross-Roads* (1909; repr. London: Faber, 1963), p. 47. Note also the citation at p. 49, quoted on p. 98 of the present volume.
3. See James M. Robinson, *A New Quest of the Historical Jesus* (London: SCM Press, 1959), pp. 26–31.
4. On this, see G. W. Ittel, 'Die Hauptgedanken der religionsgeschichtlichen Schule', *Zeitschrift für Religions- und Geistesgeschichte* 10 (1958), pp. 61–78. For the general outlook of the school, especially in relation to its understanding of history, see Robert Morgan, *The Nature of New Testament Theology: The Contribution of William Wrede and Adolf Schlatter* (London: SCM Press, 1973), pp. 1–67.
5. See R. Schäfer, 'Das Reich Gottes bei Albrecht Ritschl und Johannes Weiss', *Zeitschrift für Theologie und Kirche* 61 (1964), pp. 68–88.
6. Johannes Weiss, *Jesus' Proclamation of the Kingdom of God* (London: SCM Press, 1971), p. 133. Cf. pp. 84–96; 129–31. For useful comments, see D. L. Holland, 'History, Theology and the Kingdom of God: A Contribution of Johannes Weiss to Twentieth Century Theology', *Biblical Research* 13 (1968), pp. 54–66.
7. Weiss, *Kingdom of God*, p. 114.
8. See Schweitzer, *Quest of the Historical Jesus*, pp. 328–95.
9. Schweitzer, *Quest of the Historical Jesus*, p. 401.
10. See W. C. Robinson Jr, 'The Quest for Wrede's Secret Messiah',

Interpretation 27 (1973), pp. 10–30.

11. What follows is a précis of William Wrede, *The Messianic Secret* (Cambridge/London: Mowbrays, 1971), pp. 5–7.

12. See Schweitzer, *Quest of the Historical Jesus*, pp. 328–95.

13. John Macquarrie, *An Existentialist Theology: A Comparison of Heidegger and Bultmann* (London: Collins, 1973), pp. 159–62.

14. Carl E. Braaten, in his translation of Martin Kähler, *The So-Called Historical Jesus and the Historic, Biblical Christ* (Philadelphia: Fortress Press, 1964), p. 21. The translator's introduction to this work will be found very helpful to students beginning the study of Kähler, and is strongly recommended. Readers should note that the German term *sogenannte* does not necessarily possess the pejorative overtones associated with the English term 'so-called', which is the most natural English translation of the term.

15. Kähler, *So-Called Historical Jesus*, p. 43.

16. For the details, see Wilhelm Herrmann, 'Der geschichtliche Christus der Grund unseres Glaubens', *Zeitschrift für Theologie und Kirche* 2 (1892), pp. 232–73.

17. Otto Ritschl, 'Der historische Christus, der christliche Glaube und die theologische Wissenschaft', *Zeitschrift für Theologie und Kirche* 3 (1893), pp. 371–426.

18. There is a substantial literature, of which the following works are of especial interest to our theme: Sarah Coakley, *Christ without Absolutes: A Study of the Christology of Ernst Troeltsch* (Oxford: Clarendon Press, 1988); L. Allen, 'From Dogmatik to Glaubenslehre: Ernst Troeltsch and the Task of Theology', *Fides et Historica* 12 (1980), pp. 37–60; J. P. Clayton (ed.), *Ernst Troeltsch and the Future of Theology* (Cambridge: Cambridge University Press, 1976).

19. On this, see Ernst Troeltsch, 'Die christliche Weltanschauung und die wissenschaftlichen Gegenströmen', *Zeitschrift für Theologie und Kirche* 3 (1893), pp. 493–528; 4 (1894), pp. 164–231.

20. Ernst Troeltsch, 'Über historische und dogmatische Methode der Theologie', *Theologische Arbeiten aus dem rheinischen wissenschaftlichen Predigerverein* 4 (1900), pp. 81–108.

21. This is made especially clear in his destructive remarks concerning the credibility of Herrmann's *Christusbild*: see the 1909 essay 'Half a Century of Theology: A Review', in *Ernst Troeltsch: Writings on Theology and Religion*, ed. R. Morgan and M. Pye (London: Duckworth, 1977), pp. 53–81 (note that this translation is of the second

edition of the essay, which dates from 1913).

22. The exceptionally sympathetic efforts of Sarah Coakley to bring order, coherence and credibility to Troeltsch's inconsistencies deserve full recognition: *Christ without Absolutes*, pp. 136–63.

23. Coakley, *Christ without Absolutes*, pp. 103–35.

24. For an excellent analysis, see Brian A. Gerrish, 'Jesus, Myth and History: Troeltsch's Stand in the "Christ-Myth" Debate', *Journal of Religion* 55 (1975), pp. 13–35.

25. On this, see Ernst Troeltsch, 'On the Significance of the Historical Existence for Faith', in *Ernst Troeltsch*, ed. Morgan and Pye, pp. 182–207.

26. Note the important additions to the second (1911) edition of the work, noted in *Ernst Troeltsch: The Absoluteness of Christianity* (Richmond, VA: John Knox, 1968), p. 148.

27. For the argument and texts, see Coakley, *Christ without Absolutes*, pp. 160–2.

28. Ernst Troeltsch, 'On the Possibility of a Liberal Christianity', reprinted and translated in the appropriately entitled *Unitarian Universalist Christian* 29 (1974), pp. 27–38.

Chapter 6: The Dialectical Christologies

1. See Wolfgang Huber, 'Evangelische Theologie und Kirche beim Ausbruch des Ersten Weltkriegs', *Studien zur Friedensforschung* 4 (1970), pp. 148–215.

2. Karl Barth, *Evangelische Theologie im 19. Jahrhundert* (Zurich: Zollikon, 1957), p. 6. See further Wilfried Härle, 'Der Aufruf der 93 Intellektuellen und Karl Barths Bruch mit der liberalen Theologie', *Zeitschrift für Theologie und Kirche* 72 (1975), pp. 207–24.

3. *Briefwechsel Karl Barth–Eduard Thurneysen, 1913–1921*, 2 vols. (Zurich: Zollikon, 1973–4), vol. 1, p. 121.

4. There is an enormous literature, of which the following are illustrative: K. Budde, 'Die Theologie von Krisis und der Weltkrieg', *Christliche Welt* 41 (1927), pp. 1104–5; Peter Lange, *Konkrete Theologie: Karl Barth und Friedrich Gogarten 'Zwischen den Zeiten' (1922–1933)* (Zurich: Zollikon, 1972).

5. Karl Barth, *Römerbrief* (Zurich: Zollikon, 8th edn, 1947), p. xiii. The term *Kreuzweg* can mean 'crossroads' or 'way of the cross'.

6. Barth, *Römerbrief*, pp. 5–6; 72–4. There is much useful material

relating to these points in F. Stevens, *Die Ewigkeit Gottes und die Zeitlichkeit des Menschen* (Göttingen: Vandenhoeck & Ruprecht, 1979), which explores Barth's conception of time in some depth, comparing it with that of Martin Heidegger.

7. See H. M. Rumscheidt, *Revelation and Theology: An Analysis of the Barth–Harnack Correspondence of 1923* (Cambridge: Cambridge University Press, 1972).

8. See Karl Barth, 'Die dogmatische Prinzipienlehre bei Wilhelm Herrmann', in *Die Theologie und die Kirche* (Munich: Kaiser Verlag, 1928), pp. 240–80.

9. For details of this important controversy, see Hans-Georg Drescher, 'Entwicklungsdenken und Glaubensentscheidung: Troeltschs Kierkegaardsverständnis und die Kontroverse Troeltsch–Gogarten', *Zeitschrift für Theologie und Kirche* 79 (1982), pp. 80–106.

10. Karl Barth, *Church Dogmatics*, 13 vols (Edinburgh: T. & T. Clark, 1933–75), II/2, pp. 52–4. Useful studies of Barth's later Christology include Charles Waldorp, *Karl Barth's Christology* (Berlin: de Gruyter, 1984); John Thompson, *Christ in Perspective: Christological Perspectives in the Theology of Karl Barth* (Edinburgh: St Andrew Press, 1978). A valuable study of the role of Jesus Christ in Barth's theology as a whole may be found in S. W. Sykes, 'Barth on the Centre of Theology', in *Karl Barth – Studies of His Theological Methods*, ed. S. W. Sykes (Oxford: Oxford University Press, 1979), pp. 17–54.

11. Eric Peterson, 'Was ist Theologie?', reprinted in *Theologie als Wissenschaft: Aufsätze und Thesen*, ed. Gerhard Sauter (Munich: Kaiser Verlag, 1971), pp. 132–51; quote at p. 137. For an excellent analysis, see Eberhard Jüngel, 'Von der Dialektik zu Analogie: Die Schule Kierkegaards und der Einspruch Petersons', in *Barth Studien* (Zurich: Benziger Verlag, 1982), pp. 127–79.

12. See the classic study of H. G. Pöhlmann, *Analogia entis oder analogia fidei? Die Frage nach Analogie bei Karl Barth* (Göttingen: Vandenhoeck & Ruprecht, 1965).

13. For what follows, see Alister E. McGrath, 'Karl Barth als Aukklärer? Der Zusammenhang seiner Lehre vom Werke Christi mit der Erwählungslehre', *Kerygma und Dogma* 30 (1984), pp. 273–83.

14. A classic study of this point is to be found in Jacques de Senarclens, 'La concentration christologique', in *Antwort: Karl Barth zum siebzigsten Geburtstag* (Zurich: Zollikon, 1956), pp. 190–207, especially p. 202: 'Jésus Christ récapitule en lui-même toute la réalité.'

15. What follows is a very brief précis of *Church Dogmatics* II/2, pp. 94–194. For further details, see McGrath, 'Barth als Aufklärer?'. There is useful material also in Karl Stock, *Anthropologie der Verheissung: Karl Barths Lehre vom Menschen als dogmatisches Problem* (Munich: Kaiser Verlag, 1980), pp. 44–61.

16. Emil Brunner, *The Christian Doctrine of God* (London: Lutterworth Press, 1949), pp. 348–51.

17. Barth, *Church Dogmatics* IV/1, p. 515–16; 518.

18. Alister E. McGrath, 'Karl Barth and the *Articulus Iustificationis*: The Significance of His Critique of Ernst Wolf within the Context of His Theological Method', *Theologische Zeitschrift* 39 (1983), pp. 349–61.

19. Barth, *Church Dogmatics* IV/1, p. 288.

20. Barth, *Church Dogmatics* IV/2, p. 92. *Cf.* D. M. Baillie, *God was in Christ* (2nd edn, 1955; repr. London: Faber, 1973), pp. 61–2.

21. Barth, *Church Dogmatics* IV/2, p. 51.

22. Barth, *Church Dogmatics* IV/2, pp. 88–9.

23. Note especially his suggestive review of the first edition of Barth's Romans commentary in *Kirchenblatt für die reformierte Schweiz* 34 (1919), pp. 29–32.

24. See Heinrich Leopold, *Missionarische Theologie: Emil Brunners Weg zur theologischen Anthropologie* (Gütersloh: Mohn, 1974); Roman Roessler, *Person und Glaube: Der Personalismus der Gottesbeziehung bei Emil Brunner* (Munich: Kaiser Verlag, 1965), pp. 19–20; Stephan Scheld, *Die Christologie Emil Brunners* (Wiesbaden: Franz Steinbeck, 1981), pp. 48–92.

25. Emil Brunner, *The Mediator* (London: Lutterworth, 1934), p. 56; Scheld, *Christologie*, pp. 103–99.

26. See Brunner's essay 'Das Einmalige und der Existenz', *Blätter für deutsche Philosophie* 3 (1929), pp. 265–82.

27. Brunner, *The Mediator*, p. 97.

28. Brunner, *The Mediator*, pp. 21–41. See also Scheld, *Christologie*, pp. 104–28. For an excellent account of Brunner's Anselmian theory of redemption, see Scheld, pp. 162–75.

29. As demonstrated by Paul Althaus, 'Brunner's Mittler: Zur Aufgabe der Christologie', *Theologische Aufsätze*, 2 vols. (Gütersloh: Mohn, 1935), vol. 2, pp. 174–7.

30. Martin Buber, *I and Thou* (Edinburgh: T. & T. Clark, and New York: Charles Scribner's Sons, 3rd edn, 1970), p. 53. For an excellent study, see Steven T. Katz, 'Dialogue and Revelation in the Thought of

Martin Buber', *Religious Studies* 14 (1978), pp. 57–68.

31. For excellent studies of this debate, see P. Lehmann, 'Barth and Brunner: The Dilemma of the Protestant Mind', *Journal of Religion* 20 (1940), pp. 124–40; J. E. O'Donovan, 'Man in the Image of God: The Disagreement between Barth and Brunner Reconsidered', *Scottish Journal of Theology* 39 (1986), pp. 433–59; D. D. Williams, 'Brunner and Barth on Philosophy', *Journal of Religion* 27 (1947), pp. 241–54.

32. See Scheld, *Christologie*, pp. 221–316.

Chapter 7: A Disengagement from History

1. See the survey of Eduard Lohse, 'Die evangelische Kirche von der Theologie Rudolf Bultmanns', *Zeitschrift für Theologie und Kirche* 82 (1985), pp. 173–91.

2. Rudolf Bultmann, 'Liberal Theology', in *Faith and Understanding*, ed. R. W. Funk (London: SCM Press, 1966), pp. 28–52; quote at p. 31.

3. Rudolf Bultmann, 'The Eschatology of the Gospel of John', in *Faith and Understanding*, pp. 165–83; quote at p. 175.

4. See John Macquarrie, *An Existentialist Theology: A Comparison of Heidegger and Bultmann* (London: Collins, 1973).

5. See the careful analysis provided recently by Gareth Jones, 'Phenomenology and Theology: A Note on Bultmann and Heidegger', *Modern Theology* 5 (1989), pp. 161–80.

6. Bultmann, 'Eschatology of the Gospel of John', p. 170.

7. See Rudolf Bultmann, *The Presence of Eternity: History and Eschatology* (New York: Harper & Row, 1957), pp. 117–22. See further Norman J. Young, *History and Existential Theology* (Philadelphia: Westminster Press, 1969), pp. 23–4.

8. Rudolf Bultmann, 'New Testament and Mythology', in *Kerygma and Myth* (New York: Harper & Row, 1961), pp. 37–42.

9. Rudolf Bultmann, 'The Significance of the Historical Jesus for the Theology of Paul', in *Faith and Understanding*, pp. 220–46.

10. Bultmann, 'Significance of the Historical Jesus', p. 241.

11. Bultmann, 'New Testament and Mythology', pp. 37–42.

12. See John Clayton, *The Concept of Correlation* (Berlin/New York: de Gruyter, 1980).

13. Paul Tillich, *Systematic Theology*, 3 vols. (Chicago: University of Chicago Press, 1978), vol. 1, p. 21. For a useful discussion of some

of these issues, see Adrian Thatcher, *The Ontology of Paul Tillich* (Oxford: Oxford University Press, 1978), pp. 2–7, and references therein.
14. Tillich's idea of 'symbol' is confusing: see H. McDonald, 'The Symbolic Theology of Paul Tillich', *Scottish Journal of Theology* 17 (1964), pp. 414–30; Klaus Rosenthal, 'Myth and Symbol', *Scottish Journal of Theology* 18 (1965), pp. 411–34; Thatcher, *Ontology of Paul Tillich*, pp. 33–52.
15. Tillich, *Systematic Theology*, vol. 2, p. 114.
16. Tillich, *Systematic Theology*, vol. 2, p. 150.
17. See B. J. R. Cameron, 'The Historical Problem in Paul Tillich's Christology', *Scottish Journal of Theology* 18 (1965), pp. 257–72; *idem*, 'The Hegelian Christology of Paul Tillich', *Scottish Journal of Theology* 29 (1976), pp. 27–48.

Chapter 8: The Return to History

1. Gerhard Ebeling, *Dogmatik des christlichen Glaubens*, 3 vols. (Tübingen, 1979). See his own comments on this work in Gerhard Ebeling, 'Zu meiner *Dogmatik des christlichen Glaubens*', *Theologische Literaturzeitung* 105 (1980), pp. 721–33.
2. René Marlé, 'Foi et parole: la théologie de Gerhard Ebeling', *Recherches de sciences religieuses* 49 (1976), pp. 27–48; Wolfgang Grieve, 'Jesus und Glaube: Das Problem der Christologie Gerhard Ebelings', *Kerygma und Dogma* 22 (1976), pp. 163–80.
3. Ebeling, *Dogmatik*, vol. 2, pp. 296, 372, 395.
4. Ebeling, *Dogmatik*, vol. 2, p. 150.
5. Ebeling, *Dogmatik*, vol. 2, p. 388.
6. Ebeling, *Dogmatik*, vol. 2, pp. 210, 219–20.
7. Ebeling, *Dogmatik*, vol. 2, p. 214.
8. Ebeling, *Dogmatik*, vol. 2, p. 315.
9. James M. Robinson, *Kerygma und historische Jesus* (Zurich: Zollikon, 2nd edn, 1967), *passim*.
10. On this, see James M. Robinson, *A New Quest of the Historical Jesus* (London: SCM Press, 1959), especially pp. 48–125; Raymond Brown, 'After Bultmann, What? An Introduction to the Post-Bultmannians', *Catholic Biblical Quarterly* 26 (1964), pp. 1–30.
11. The issue demands careful study: Ernst Käsemann, 'The Problem of the Historical Jesus', in *Essays on New Testament Themes* (London: SCM Press, 1964), pp. 15–47. Note that this essay translates *Historie* as

'mere history' and *Geschichte* as 'history' – a potentially serious confusion to the unwary reader. For a study of Käsemann's theology, see David V. Way, *The Lordship of Christ: Ernst Käsemann's Interpretation of Paul's Theology* (Oxford: Clarendon Press, 1991).

12. See Ernst Käsemann, 'Blind Alleys in the Jesus of History Controversy', in *New Testament Questions of Today* (London: SCM Press, 1969), pp. 23–66.

13. Joachim Jeremias, *New Testament Theology* (London: SCM Press, 1975), vol. 1.

14. See Käsemann, 'Problem of the Historical Jesus', pp. 37–45.

15. Günther Bornkamm, *Jesus of Nazareth* (London: Hodder & Stoughton, 1960).

16. Reinhard Slenczka, *Geschichtlichkeit und Personsein Jesu Christi* (Göttingen: Vandenhoeck & Ruprecht, 1967), p. 311.

17. Wolfhart Pannenberg, 'Redemptive Event and History', in *Basic Questions in Theology* (London: SCM Press, 1970), vol. 1, pp. 15–80.

18. Pannenberg, 'Redemptive Event and History', p. 15.

19. For the hostile reaction to this notion of revelation, see Paul Althaus, 'Offenbarung als Geschichte und Glaube', *Theologische Literaturzeitung* 87 (1962), pp. 321–30; Lothar Steiger, 'Offenbarungsgeschichte und theologische Vernunft', *Zeitschrift für Theologie und Kirche* 59 (1962), pp. 88–113. For Pannenberg's response to Althaus, see Wolfhart Pannenberg, 'Einsicht und Glaube: Antwort an Paul Althaus', *Theologische Literaturzeitung* 88 (1963), pp. 81–92.

20. Ernst Käsemann, 'Die Anfänge christlicher Theologie', *Zeitschrift für Theologie und Kirche* 57 (1960), pp. 162–85; quote at p. 180. (This represents a studied reaction against Martin Kähler's famous assertion that 'mission is the mother of Christian theology'.)

21. Ulrich Wilckens, 'The Understanding of Revelation within the History of Primitive Christianity', in *Revelation as History*, ed. W. Pannenberg (New York: Macmillan, 1968*)*, pp. 55–121.

22. Dietrich Rössler, *Gesetz und Geschichte: Untersuchungen zur Theologie der jüdischen Apokalyptik und der pharisäischen Orthodoxie* (Neukirchen: Neukirchener Verlag, 1960).

23. Rössler, *Gesetz und Geschichte*, pp. 43–68.

24. For example, William R. Murdock, 'History and Revelation in Jewish Apocalypticism', *Interpretation* 21 (1967), pp. 167–87; Hans Dieter Benz, 'The Concept of Apocalyptic in the Theology of the Pannenberg Group', *Journal for Theology and the Church* 6:

Apocalypticism (New York: Herder & Herder, 1969), pp. 192–207.

25. Wolfhart Pannenberg, 'Dogmatic Theses on the Doctrine of Revelation', in *Revelation as History*, pp. 123–58.

26. Wolfhart Pannenberg, 'Insight and Faith', in *Basic Questions in Theology* (London: SCM Press, 1971), vol. 2, p. 39.

27. Wolfhart Pannenberg, 'The Revelation of God in Jesus of Nazareth', in *Theology as History*, ed. J. M. Robinson and J. B. Cobb (New York: Harper & Row, 1967), pp. 101–33; quote at pp. 126–7. For further reflection, see Iain G. Nicol, 'Facts and Meanings: Wolfhart Pannenberg's Theology of History and the Role of the Historical-Critical Method', *Religious Studies* 12 (1971), pp. 129–39.

28. Van A. Harvey, *The Historian and the Believer* (London: SCM Press, 1976), p. 32.

29. Wolfhart Pannenberg, 'Redemptive Event and History'; *idem, Jesus – God and Man* (London: SCM Press, 1968), pp. 88–106. For studies of this specific point, see Ted Peters, 'The Use of Analogy in Historical Method', *Catholic Biblical Quarterly* 35 (1973), pp. 474–82; Herbert Burhenn, 'Pannenberg's Argument for the Historicity of the Resurrection', *Journal of the American Academy of Religion* 40 (1972), pp. 368–79; Gordon E. Michalson, 'Pannenberg on the Resurrection and Historical Method', *Scottish Journal of Theology* 33 (1980), pp. 345–59.

30. Pannenberg, *Jesus – God and Man*, p. 109.

31. See Michalson, 'Pannenberg on the Resurrection'.

32. See Stanley J. Grenz, *Reason for Hope: The Systematic Theology of Wolfhart Pannenberg* (New York: Oxford University Press, 1990).

33. Pannenberg, *Jesus – God and Man*, pp. 66–73. The German title of this section reads 'The Significance of the Resurrection of Jesus in the Traditio-Historical Situation of Primitive Christianity'. For comment, see David P. Polk, *On the Way to God: An Exploration into the Theology of Wolfhart Pannenberg* (Lanham, MD: University Press of America, 1989), pp. 198–215.

34. Pannenberg, *Jesus – God and Man*, p. 69.

35. For a criticism of Pannenberg at this point, see Alister E. McGrath, 'Christology and Soteriology: A Response to Wolfhart Pannenberg's Critique of the Soteriological Approach to Christology', *Theologische Zeitschrift* 42 (1986), pp. 222–36.

36. Wolfhart Pannenberg, *Systematic Theology*, vol. 1 (Grand Rapids: Eerdmans, and Edinburgh: T. & T. Clark, 1991). At the time of writing, the English translation of the second volume, containing the

bulk of Pannenberg's Christological reflections, has not been published. References are therefore to the original German edition: Wolfhart Pannenberg, *Systematische Theologie*, vol. 2 (Göttingen: Vandenhoeck & Ruprecht, 1991). For an excellent survey of these volumes, based upon Pannenberg's lectures at Munich, see Grenz, *Reason for Hope*.

37. See the useful observations of Elizabeth Johnson, 'The Ongoing Christology of Wolfhart Pannenberg', *Horizons* 9 (1982), pp. 237–52.

38. Pannenberg, *Systematic Theology*, vol. 1, pp. 198–214.

39. Pannenberg, *Systematic Theology*, vol. 1, p. 208.

40. Pannenberg, *Systematische Theologie*, vol. 2, pp. 385–405.

41. Pannenberg, *Systematische Theologie*, vol. 2, p. 392.

42. Pannenberg, *Systematische Theology*, vol. 2, pp. 441–511.

Chapter 9: The End of the Enlightenment

1. See Dietrich Bonhoeffer, *Christology* (London: SCM Press, 1978), published in the United States as *Christ the Center* (New York: Harper & Row, 1978). For an excellent survey of Bonhoeffer's thought, see Eberhard Bethge, *Dietrich Bonhoeffer: Theologian, Christian, Contemporary* (London: Collins, 1970); John D. Godsey, *The Theology of Dietrich Bonhoeffer* (Philadelphia: Fortress Press, 1960).

2. Dietrich Bonhoeffer, *Letters and Papers from Prison* (London: Collins, 1953), pp. 104–22. Of interest here are John A. Phillips, *Christ for Us in the Theology of Dietrich Bonhoeffer* (New York: Harper & Row, 1967); British edition published as *The Form of Christ in the World* (London: Collins, 1967); John D. Godsey, 'Barth and Bonhoeffer: The Basic Difference', *Quarterly Review* 7 (1987), pp. 9–27.

3. Jürgen Moltmann, *Theology of Hope* (London: SCM Press, 1967), p. 74. For secondary texts of importance, see M. Douglas Meeks, *Origins of the Theology of Hope* (Philadelphia: Fortress Press, 1974); John J. O'Donnell, *Trinity and Temporality: The Christian Doctrine of God in the Light of Process Thought and the Theology of Hope* (Oxford: Oxford University Press, 1983), pp. 108–58.

4. Jürgen Moltmann, *The Crucified God* (London: SCM Press, 1974), p. 5.

5. See Alister E. McGrath, *Luther's Theology of the Cross* (Oxford: Blackwell, 1985), for a full analysis.

6. Moltmann, *Crucified God*, p. 212.

7. There is a substantial literature: see R. B. Edwards, 'The Pagan

Dogma of the Absolute Unchangeableness of God', *Religious Studies* 14 (1975), pp. 305–13; T. E. Pollard, 'The Impassibility of God', *Scottish Journal of Theology* 8 (1955), pp. 353–64; J. G. McLelland, *God the Anonymous: A Study in Alexandrian Philosophical Theology* (Cambridge, MA: Harvard University Press, 1976), pp. 37–40.

8. Moltmann, *Crucified God*, p. 4.

9. Moltmann, *Crucified God*, p. 192.

10. Jürgen Moltmann, *The Way of Jesus Christ: Christology in Messianic Dimensions* (London: SCM Press, 1990). For an overall review, see Richard J. Bauckham, 'Moltmann's Messianic Christology', *Scottish Journal of Theology* 44 (1991), pp. 519–31.

11. Eberhard Jüngel, *Paulus and Jesus: Eine Untersuchung zur Präzisierung der Frage nach dem Ursprung der Christologie* (Tübingen: Mohr, 1962), p. 265.

12. Jüngel, *Paulus und Jesus*, pp. 2–4.

13. Eberhard Jüngel, 'Thesen zur Grundlegung der Christologie', in *Unterwegs zur Sache: Theologsiche Bemerkungen* (Munich: Kaiser, 1972), pp. 274–95; Theses B. 2.23; 2.231; 2.32; p. 286.

14. Jüngel, *Thesen* B. 242; pp. 286–7; *cf.* B. 2.2433; p. 287.

15. Jüngel, *Thesen* B. 2.215–217; p. 285.

16. Jüngel, *Thesen* B. 2.221; p. 286.

17. Jüngel, *Thesen* A. 6.1; p. 278. See also his essay 'Das Sein Jesu Christi als Ereignis der Versöhnung Gottes mit einer gottlosen Welt: Die Hingabe der Gekreuzigten', *Evangelische Theologie* 38 (1978), pp. 510–17.

18. Eberhard Jüngel, *God as the Mystery of the World* (Edinburgh: T. & T. Clark, 1983), p. 13.

19. Jüngel, *Thesen* B. 1.45; p. 283: 'Die Ursache aller Häresien ist die Unhähigkeit (die Unlust), Gott in Jesus Christus ausreden zu lassen.'

20. Jüngel, *Thesen* B. 5.2; p. 293.

21. Jüngel, *Thesen* B. 5.21; p. 293.

22. Jüngel, *Thesen* B. 5.5; p. 294.

23. William Hamilton, 'The Death of God Theology', *Christian Scholar* 48 (1965), pp. 27–48; pp. 31, 41, 45.

24. More intrepid readers might care to decipher Rolf Ahlers, 'Hegel's Theological Atheism', *Heythrop Journal* 25 (1984), pp. 158–77.

25. Jüngel, *God as the Mystery of the World*, pp. 57–100. See also his 'Vom Tode des lebendigen Gottes: Ein Plakat', in *Unterwegs zur Sache*, pp. 105–25.

26. See his difficult essay 'Deus qualem Paulus creavit, Dei negatio: Zur Denkbarkeit Gottes bei Ludwig Feuerbach und Friedrich Nietzsche', *Nietzsche Studien* 1 (1972), pp. 286–96.

27. Jüngel, *God as the Mystery of the World*, p. 202. The German original is very difficult to render in English.

28. Walter Wink, *Transforming Bible Study* (Nashville: Abingdon, 1980, and London: SCM Press, 1981), pp. 155–6.

Index

Pannenberg, W., 187–98
Peterson, E., 132
Pietism, 17–18, 40–1
Proust, M., 125

'Quest of the historical Jesus':
   critique of classic form of,
   103–22
   new form of, 180–96
   origins of, 27–8

rationalism, 15–16, 36–8
Reimarus, H. S., 21, 27, 33–5
Religionsgeschichte, 101–3,
   172–3
Rendtorff, R., 187
revelation, notion of, 20–1,
   24, 34–5, 123–53, 187–98
Riehl, W. H., 57
Rist, J., 217
Ritschl, A. B., 82–7, 101–103,
   144
Ritschl, O., 115
Rössler, D., 187, 189–90
Romanticism, 38–40
Rosenkranz, K., 56
Rothe, R., 77
Rousseau, J.-J., 24

Sartre, J.-P., 162
Schelling, W. J. F., 77
Schlatter, A. von, 123
Schlegel, A. W., 38
Schlegel, F., 38
Schleiermacher, F. D. E.,
   36, 41–49, 62–6, 70–1, 74–5,
   82–4
Schmoller, O., 103
Schweitzer, Albert, 35, 102,
   104–8

Schweitzer, Alexander, 78
Seeberg, R., 123
Semler, J. S., 20, 90
Slenczka, R. E., 186
soteriological approach to
   Christology, 71–2, 86–7, 178,
   187–98
Spalding, J. J., 20
Spengler, O., 125
Spinoza, B., 16, 31, 36
Steinbart, G. F., 26
Strauss, D. F., 55–63, 65–6

Thiry, P. H. de, 22
Thomas Aquinas, 15, 205, 208
Thomasius, G., 78–9, 81
Tillich, P., 173–8
Tindal, M., 20–1
Toland, J., 20
Trenchard, J., 22
Troeltsch, E., 23, 102, 115–22
Tyrrell, G., 98, 100

Vahanian, G., 216
Voltaire, 24

Weiss, J., 102–5
Wesley, C., 215
Wesley, J., 17
Whitehead, A. N., 95
Wilckens, U., 187, 190
Wolff, C., 16, 36
Wordsworth, W., 39
Wrede, W., 102, 108–10
Wurm, T., 97

Xenophanes, 68

Zinzendorf, N. von, 79
Zwingli, H., 13